Understanding Everyday Communicative Interactions

Understanding Everyday Communicative Interactions is a unique text that uses a situated discourse analysis (SDA) framework to examine basic human communication and the interactions of those with communicative disorders in everyday and clinical settings.

The book introduces SDA as a theoretical and empirical approach for examining the complexities of communicative interaction. It explores how people collaborate in everyday contexts to communicate successfully and how they learn to do so. From close analysis of a pretend game played by two children and their father to an observation of a man with aphasia and his family at a football match, the present volume offers rich portraits of communicative lives and illustrates the applications of SDA. The final part of the book uses SDA methods to demonstrate how clinicians can function as communication partners even during assessments and can design rich communicative environments for therapeutic interventions.

In explaining the SDA framework and equipping readers with the tools to understand the nature of human communication, this sophisticated and engaging book will be an essential reference for students, researchers, and clinicians in communication sciences and disorders.

Julie A. Hengst is Associate Professor of Speech and Hearing Science at the University of Illinois at Urbana-Champaign. She has worked in hospitals, supervised student clinicians, and researched everyday communication in order to reshape clinical practice. She is the Co-editor of *Exploring Semiotic Remediation as Discourse Practice* (Palgrave Macmillan, 2010) and has published in varied journals.

"Everyday communication is the cornerstone of research and clinical care across a number of disciplines (e.g., communication sciences and disorders, linguistics, psychology, neuroscience). Yet, paradoxically, training in these fields largely focuses on the deconstructed and decontextualized building blocks of communication (phonetics, syntax, discourse) with little consideration of how individuals weave this knowledge together across time, place, and communicative partners in everyday interactions. Hengst's *Understanding Everyday Communicative Interactions* fills a critical gap in the multidisciplinary training of future researchers and clinicians offering a rich theoretical framework and a practical set of tools and methods for observing, analyzing, and improving everyday communication across a range of settings and populations."

— **Melissa C. Duff**, PhD, CCC-SLP, Vanderbilt University, USA

"This forward-thinking volume represents a major theoretical, methodological, and clinical leap forward for the field of CSD. The robust conceptual framework Hengst develops, situated discourse analysis, is astutely illustrated through case studies and innovative interventions that will greatly benefit clinicians, researchers, and ultimately, clients and their families."

— **Steven L. Thorne**, PhD, Portland State University, USA, & University of Groningen, Netherlands

"In this beautifully written book, Hengst brings situated discourse analysis to the field of Communication Sciences and Disorders. By recognizing communication as a distributed accomplishment, which involves not just language, but all semiotic resources, the author presents an innovative lens for understanding where communication disorders reside, their dynamics, and how one might address them. Drawing on rich and relatable examples, she makes complex theoretical concepts and intricate analyses accessible and relevant. This book is a pleasure to read, and will benefit SLPs, teachers, and others who interact with and wish to support someone identified with a communication disorder."

— **Michiko Hikida**, PhD, The Ohio State University, USA

Understanding Everyday Communicative Interactions

Introduction to Situated Discourse Analysis for Communication Sciences and Disorders

Julie A. Hengst

Routledge
Taylor & Francis Group

NEW YORK AND LONDON

First published 2020
by Routledge
52 Vanderbilt Avenue, New York, NY 10017

and by Routledge
2 Park Square, Milton Park, Abingdon, Oxon, OX14 4RN

Routledge is an imprint of the Taylor & Francis Group, an informa business

Library of Congress Cataloging-in-Publication Data
A catalog record for this book has been requested

ISBN: 978-0-367-47200-9 (hbk)
ISBN: 978-0-367-47202-3 (pbk)
ISBN: 978-1-003-03453-7 (ebk)

Typeset in Bembo
by Apex CoVantage, LLC

Contents

Preface

It is stunning to recognize the diversity of communicative interactions that fill our days and the apparent ease with which we typically manage those interactions, even when facing subtle or profound disruptions. Most of our communicative interactions seem relatively routine and are easily overlooked. Consider interactions like talking with family or roommates over breakfast; greeting bus drivers and regular riders during a daily commute; coordinating school and work assignments with others; or setting up meetings, appointments, and other dates. Some interactions—such as teaching a class, responding to an insult from an acquaintance, taking wedding vows, or presenting a proposal you are deeply invested in at work—feel more remarkable because of the preparation that goes into them, the emotional impacts of the interaction, the formality of the events, or the consequences of success or failure. These more remarkable interactions often become stories that are told and retold over years in varied settings, with varied details, and for varied purposes. This book explores rich worlds of everyday interaction through situated analysis of discourse and applies that approach to clinical, diagnostic, and research work in Communication Sciences and Disorders (CSD).

Discourse is a tricky term with varied meanings. Doing a search in Google Scholar for the phrase "a discourse on" will turn up titles of a number of books and articles from the last several centuries in philosophy, mathematics, science, and politics. The *Oxford English Dictionary* (OED: Oxford English Dictionary, 2019) traces the etymology of discourse to the Latin verb *discursus*, which meant "the action of running off in different directions, dispersal, action of running about, bustling activity, (of celestial objects) course," but it notes a shift by the fourth century CE to the sense of "conversation or discourse." The *OED* describes varied meanings in current usage, but a key point is that definitions either take discourse as a thing (e.g., "a body of statements" or "a more or less formal treatment of a subject in speech or writing") or a process (e.g., "interaction" or "the action or process of communicating thought by means of the spoken word").

Even within linguistics, discourse has varied senses, although all point to some dimensions of context. In formal linguistics, where the sentence has typically been the largest grammatical unit, discourse signals linguistic contexts above the level of the sentence (e.g., how a pronoun in one sentence points to an object stated in an earlier sentence). In sociolinguistics, discourse signals extra-linguistic context, identifying how specific linguistic forms (phonology, morphology, syntax, semantics) connect to social groups (e.g., national languages, dialects), cultural and professional registers (e.g., school discourse, informal conversation, medical jargon), and genres (e.g., narratives, scientific reports). In functional linguistics, discourse refers to ways that extra-linguistic contexts support meaning-making by integrating grammatical phenomena (e.g., verb patterns) with semantic features (e.g., mental or material processes) and pragmatic functions (e.g., managing interpersonal relations); in this view, discourse involves ways specific linguistic utterances are styled by speakers to highlight contextual dimensions like speakers, addressees, and language codes. Regardless of these differences, traditional linguistic, sociolinguistic, and functional linguistic approaches all understand discourse as something an individual produces, as the products rather than the processes of interaction. In contrast, situated discourse analysis (SDA) approaches discourse as processes of communication among people in their sociomaterial contexts.

In the 1990s, I was working at a university clinic as a speech-language pathologist supervising student clinicians. Most clinical sessions were held in small clinic rooms with adjacent spaces for people to observe either through a one-way glass or over a closed-circuit camera system. Sessions typically involved multiple people, including the client (often with a family member), the student clinician (and sometimes student observers), and the supervisor. As a supervisor, I was routinely engaged in at least five intertwined activities: doing speech-language therapy with the clients, discussing issues related to that therapy with the client and family, helping student clinicians learn how to provide therapy and assess clients' communicative abilities, managing the business of clinical work, and engaging in everyday conversation (e.g., about the weather, parking, local and world events). In this setting I was almost always managing multiple activities simultaneously: providing direct therapy to the client while modeling it for the student; talking with family members in an observation room while monitoring the session on the other side of the glass; or taking notes about my observations for later discussions with the student clinician while talking with the family about what I was observing. Despite the institutional design of such clinical spaces, I was struck by the sheer complexity of these communicative interactions—and the ease with which all of us aligned around varied activities and goals. Although much of the literature about conducting speech therapy and doing supervision described single activities accomplished one at a time during one-to-one (dyadic) interactions between clinicians and clients, my day-to-day clinical interactions mostly involved multiple participants engaged in multiple activities. These complex interactions (and their relative invisibility in the clinical literature) shaped my interests in studying SDA when I returned to school to pursue a PhD.

Across my career (as a student, clinician,[1] clinical supervisor, researcher, and faculty member), I have come to recognize that managing communicative interactions is at the core of every aspect of the field of CSD. Communication is what we assess, what we aim to impact through therapy, how we conduct both assessment and therapy tasks, and how we document our clinical work. Indeed, master clinicians need to flexibly wield their own communicative practices to meet clinical goals of their patients, clients, and students. The challenge of such mastery has given rise to the idea that clinical practice is an art that some people are just good at rather than technical expertise clinicians can study and develop (see Hengst & Duff, 2007).

The American Speech-Language-Hearing Association (ASHA) states that the overall objective of clinical services is "to optimize individuals' abilities to communicate and to swallow, thereby improving quality of life" and to do so in a manner that respects the cultural and linguistic diversity of individuals and communities (ASHA, 2016). Yet, students and clinicians rarely get a thorough introduction to theories and methods that could help them understand and analyze everyday communicative interactions, much less opportunities to apply those theories and methods to communicative disorders or to draw on them when designing clinical interventions and honing their own clinical skills. This book assumes clinicians need to become communication experts, both in what they know about communication and disorders and in intentionally wielding their own communicative practices. It addresses this glaring absence in CSD education and professional development by offering specific tools for understanding and managing the communicative interactions at the center of every aspect of our field.

Fortunately, significant theoretical and methodological attention has been devoted to everyday communicative interactions by what I refer to here as SDA in fields of study such as semiotics, sociolinguistics, conversation analysis, ethnography of communication, and cultural psychology. I first encountered this kind of work as an undergraduate linguistics major at Indiana University, Bloomington, where I studied descriptive linguistics, took classes on semiotics from Thomas Sebeok (who shaped the modern field of semiotics through his writing and editing), and worked as a research assistant for a project cataloging gestures in Gulf Arabic at the Research Center for Language and Semiotic Studies. Those experiences gave me initial frameworks to think about how language happens not in isolation, but situated within complex patterns of semiotic resources. Those frameworks shaped how I later took up my clinical work in adult neurogenic disorders.

I began working with clients with adult-acquired neurogenic communication disorders like aphasia in the mid-1980s. My patients then were typically told their recovery from brain injury would plateau when physiological healing had occurred. The message was that whatever they had recovered by 12 months after their brain injury was all they should expect to regain. After this acute stage of recovery, the chronic phase was seen as a period of stagnation, a time to learn to make do with deficits and seek at best compensatory solutions. However, like many of my clinical colleagues, I kept finding people in the chronic phase making marked progress in their ability to communicate. Although in hospital settings I rarely worked with clients more than a year post-injury, at university clinics I had numerous opportunities to work with clients far into the chronic phase. Many of my clients shared stories of the bleak prognoses they had been given (e.g., "they told me I would never talk again, and look at me now!"). It was not unusual for strangers, learning I worked in hospitals as an SLP, to launch into stories about their own recoveries or those of their friends. Continued personal and communicative growth long after a brain injury has also been detailed in a growing number of biographical and autobiographical accounts. Such stories have often been dismissed as curiosities or rare outliers—people whose communicative recoveries were far better than average or than could be predicted by the extent of the damage caused by their injuries. Instead, I have taken such stories as challenges. How are these people achieving such successes, and how might we learn from their recoveries to improve outcomes for our clients?

This book introduces SDA as a theoretical and empirical approach for examining the complexities of everyday communicative interactions. The nine chapters are organized into three parts around settings and questions important to clinical work. Part 1 draws on research literature outside of CSD to introduce basic issues and concepts of SDA in everyday settings. In this part, I use examples from data I collected in my family on a pretend game called *Cindy Magic* to illustrate specific methods used in SDA. Chapter 1 focuses on describing the complexity of everyday interactions, Chapter 2 explores the diverse ways people align in interactions to achieve communicative success, and Chapter 3 focuses on situated learning by tracing change over time. Part 2 builds on SDA approaches from Part 1 to examine everyday communicative interactions involving individuals with communication disorders. Using data I collected across several settings on adults with communication disorders, this part of the book introduces additional SDA concepts, methods, and tools that are critical for diverse communicators. Following the same pattern as Part 1, Chapter 4 focuses on communicative complexity, Chapter 5 on communicative success, and Chapter 6 on situated learning. Part 3 applies the tools of SDA to the specialized work of clinical settings to better understand how communication and learning can be promoted through therapeutic talk and activity. Chapter 7 offers a critical account of the talk typical of clinical assessment and therapy, Chapter 8 explores how SDA can enrich clinical assessment, and Chapter 9 explores ways SDA can be employed to design rich communicative environments in support of therapeutic goals. Each part begins with an introduction that offers an overview of the chapters it contains.

Central to SDA theories are ethnographic and qualitative case study methods. The methods are developed throughout the book, and each chapter includes a Note on Methods before the final summary to highlight specific methodological issues such as designing and conducting participant observations and interviews, transcribing interactional data, developing thick descriptions (Geertz, 1973; Marcus, 1998) of communicative practices, and of course developing a systematic and trustworthy approach to discourse analysis. Dyson and Genishi (2005) highlight that qualitative case studies build generalizable knowledge by detailed investigation of people in particular events, by focusing on social units, and by attending to the range (variability) of human behaviors rather than only seeking averages (whether statistical means or cultural norms). As the anthropologist Clifford Geertz (1996) noted: "No one lives in the world in general. Everybody . . . lives in some confined and limited stretch of it—'the world around here'" (p. 262). Case study methods investigate "the world around here" and the interplay between situated particularities and our abstract ideas of everyday communication, learning, and use.

Generalizing from cases really is nothing new for the field of CSD. For example, classic neurological case studies identified patterns of behavioral disruption after brain damage and led to diagnostic categorizations that continue to be central to the field. Analyzing research evidence in the literature of CSD, Hengst, Devanga, and Mosier (2015) argue that "clinical reasoning about individual cases involves a specialized form of thick description that requires an understanding of clients' (dis)abilities in relation to the activities and practices of their everyday life worlds" (p. S839). Case study methods thus offer a particularly valuable model for clinical translation to particular cases. In short, the methods in this book may originate in research, but are also central to the fundamental work of clinical assessment and intervention.

SDA is a diverse, multidisciplinary field. Building a deep and flexible understanding of its concepts and methods and a sense of how to apply them to particular settings requires immersion—reading multiple examples of SDA and noting ways that general tools are deployed and reworked or new tools are developed to understand specific communicative interactions. To give you a starting point for such immersion, each chapter offers summaries of specific research studies conducted in diverse settings and includes Suggested Readings after the summary. Reading about diverse cases that may be far from the specific clinical or school settings you plan to work in can be immensely valuable. For example, some of the key research that has informed my understanding of clinical practice and the communicative lives of people with aphasia has involved situated analysis of navigation teams on the deck of a naval ship (Hutchins, 1995), of delivering traditional insult poetry at Wolof weddings in Africa (Irvine, 1996), of narratives across the lifespan (Miller, Fung, & Koven, 2007), and of mundane home interactions between Mayan parents and their children (Rogoff, Mistry, Göncü, & Mosier, 1993). And, as I have noted, the first part of the book focuses on data from pretend play in my family, data that have deeply shaped my general understanding of communicative interactions.

Finally, I opened this preface by noting how reflections on my own clinical practices sparked my fascination with the complexity of communicative interactions, how my reading in fields like semiotics supported those reflections, and how my research in varied settings deepened my understanding of SDA. In short, actively applying SDA concepts and methods to familiar settings is critical to learning to perceive and use them in practice. Thus, each chapter concludes with Reflective Observations. Becoming more aware of and learning to better understand your own communicative practices (strengths, weaknesses, routines) is a key goal of this book. As clinicians and researchers, we need to draw not only on our expert knowledge, but also on our ability to attend to and marshal our own developing communicative skills. Communicative practices are the tools of our profession.

Overall, this book will introduce you to a range of concepts and methodological tools associated with situated theories of cognition, communication, and human development. The parallel structure of the chapters across sections is designed to build a map of the territory of SDA as it relates to the work of CSD. I recommend that you work through the book sequentially but not spend too much time struggling with a particular concept or example. The concepts and examples build across chapters, and as you work through the book you may find it helpful to return to earlier chapters to delve more deeply into particular concepts or examples. To help you navigate these concepts, Table P.1 lists key terms by chapter, with room for you to add more terms and concepts from your readings.

Finally, to help you integrate concepts across book parts and to ground your developing understanding of SDA, each chapter introduces three guiding questions. Table P.2 offers an overview of the 27 questions by part and chapter. The core questions presented in Chapter 1 focus attention on describing sociocultural activities, patterns of participation, and communicative resources of communicative interactions. Moving down the chart, those initial questions are adapted to address questions of communicative success and situated learning, and moving across the chart, the questions shift to address issues of communication disorders in the middle column and to clinical interactions in the final column. You might find it helpful to return periodically to both of these tables as you build your understanding of SDA across chapters, parts, activities, and additional readings.

Table P.1 List of SDA concepts related to complexity, success, and learning introduced in Chapters 1–9 (chapter noted by superscript) and organized by their relevance to sociocultural activities, people's patterns of participation, and communicative resources. The table leaves room for you to list additional SDA concepts you are finding particularly useful for your research and clinical thinking.

	Describing Complexity	Identifying Success	Tracing Learning
Sociocultural Activities	Everyday communicative interactions[1] Sociocultural activities[1] Goals[1] (motives) Sociomaterial spaces[1] Figured worlds[4] Social roles and identities[4] Role inhabitance[4] Power dyanmics[7]	Alignments[2] (goals, people, & resources) Functional systems[2] Communicative success & competence[2] Mobility of functional systems[5] Activity frames[8]	Situated learning[3] (learning with) Cultural practices[3] Common ground[6] Rich communicative environments[9]
People's Participation	Patterns of participation[1] Gatherings[1] Interaction orders[1] Participation frameworks & production formats[1] Positioning[4] Identity work[4] Stance (clinical stance)[7]	Distributed communication[2] Brokering[5] Communicative repertoires[5] Communication partners[8]	Peripheral & guided participation[3] Socialization[3] Repeated engagement[6] Affinity spaces[9]
Communicative Resources	Semiotic[1] (signs) Modalities[1] (sensory channels) Embodied[1] Typified social voices[1] Discourse registers[4] IRE discourse[7] (initiation-response-evaluation)[7] Adjacency pair[7] Backchannel[7]	Interactional resources[2] Indexical ground[2] Constructed dialogue[2] Interactional Discourse Resources (IDRs)[5] Building tasks[5] Bit competencies[5] Conversational repetition[5] Involvement devices[8]	Durable & emergent resources[3] Repurposing[3] (flexible use of durable resources) Recognizable resources[3] Collaborative referencing[6] Interactional correlates[9]

Table P.2 Guiding questions for situated discourse analysis (SDA), organized by part, chapter, and focus (complexity, success, learning).

	Part 1: Understanding Everyday Communicative Interactions	Part 2: Understanding Communicative Disorders in Everyday Interactions	Part 3: Understanding and Designing Clinical Interactions
Describing Complexity	_Chapter 1:_ What is going on here? What are people's patterns of participation in this sociomaterial space? What communicative resources are being used in this interaction?	_Chapter 4:_ What social identities and roles are associated with these sociocultural activities? How are people positioning themselves and others in this sociomaterial space? How are communicative resources indexing potential identities?	_Chapter 7:_ What are the sociocultural activities and social roles in clinical spaces? What are the patterns of participation by clients and clinicians in clinical spaces? What communicative resources are clients and clinicians using in their interactions?
Identifying Success	_Chapter 2:_ What is being accomplished by the functional system? How are people successfully coordinating their participation in functional systems? How are people using interactional resources to build indexical grounds that support communicative success?	_Chapter 5:_ How are accomplishments being flexibly distributed? How are people brokering one another into social roles and successful patterns of participation? How are communicative resources distributed and jointly deployed to successfully coordinate activities and meanings?	_Chapter 8:_ What is being accomplished by clinical functional systems? How can the clinician partner support the client's successful participation? How can the clinician flexibly draw on and use diverse communicative resources to support successful client-clinician interactions?
Tracing Learning	_Chapter 3:_ How are the functional systems changing over time? How are people's patterns of participation changing over time? How are durable and emergent resources changing	_Chapter 6:_ How does common ground change among participants over time as they repeatedly engage in functional systems? How do changing patterns of participation index multiple sociocultural activities and identities? How are people's recognition and use of communicative resources changing over time?	_Chapter 9:_ How can clinical activity display features of rich communicative environments while also being accountable to clinical goals? How can the concept of affinity spaces help clinicians optimize clients' participation and situated learning? How can clinical activities leverage interactional correlates to support clients' voluntary use of communicative resources?

Note

1. Given that I completed my clinical training the United States and received professional certification through ASHA, I use speech-language pathologist (SLP) as my clinical title. However, in different clinical settings and countries professional titles vary, including speech therapist and speech clinician, among others. Therefore, I use the generic terms "clinician" or "therapist" as well as the title SLP.

Acknowledgments

The process of writing and developing this book has been distributed across a lifetime of personal and professional experiences. Throughout the book, I have worked to highlight the many researchers, colleagues, students, clients, and research participants that have been critical to this project.

Much of the research discussed in this book was conducted through my Discourse Analysis Lab housed in the Department of Speech and Hearing Sciences at the University of Illinois at Urbana-Champaign. Research funding for that work was provided by the Mary Jane Neer Research Grant sponsored by the College of Applied Health Sciences, and campus funding that has supported specific projects, including a Graduate College IN3 Grant (funding the Robo-Buddies project) and several Campus Research Board Grants. Many undergraduate and graduate students have spent long hours transcribing, coding and discussing these specific studies. I would especially like to acknowledge the contributions of Larissa Mazuchelli, Martha Sherrill, Suma Devanga, Ai Leen Choo, Amie King, Erin Fabry, Hannah Schwimmer, Hillary Valentino, Maeve McCartin, and Jaime Pratzel. My long-standing and multiple research collaborations with Melissa C. Duff have been central to forming the perspectives presented in this book.

I have learned much over the years from thought-provoking discussions about theory and methods with a number of colleagues. I especially thank Peggy J. Miller, Laura DeThorne, Cynthia J. Johnson, Gloria Olness, Jacqueline Laures Gore, Steven Thorne, Keven Roozen, Jody Shipka, Andrea Olinger, Katherine Flowers, and the CHAT reading group.

A special thanks goes to colleagues who have offered insightful responses to earlier versions of this book, including the anonymous reviewers of the proposal. I am particularly grateful to Keven Roozen, Suma Devanga, Martha Sherrill, and Nora, Anna, and Paul Prior for detailed responses to multiple drafts and to Martha Gullo for assisting with the final stages of manuscript preparation.

Finally, I am deeply indebted to my family for a lifetime of support and encouragement. I especially appreciate Nora, Anna, and Paul Prior's generosity for inviting me into their many imaginative worlds and sharing my curiosity about how those worlds worked. Paul has been a life partner and lifetime colleague and has contributed not only to my thinking but to the material production of this book in innumerable ways. I dedicate this book, with love, to my granddaughter Ardea Sandkam and future generations of creative, flexible, and persistent communicators.

Part 1

Using Situated Discourse Analysis to Understand Everyday Communicative Interactions

> "[I]t will not do to begin with language, or a standard linguistic description, and look outward to social context. A crucial characteristic of the sociolinguistic approach is that it looks in toward language, as it were, from its social matrix. To begin with language, or an individual code, is to invite the limitations of the purely correlational approach, and to miss much of the organization of linguistic phenomena. Functions and contexts of use join together what structural description by itself may leave asunder."
>
> Dell Hymes (1974) (*Foundations in Sociolinguistics, p. 76*)

The approach I take throughout this book draws on a long line of research grounded in the central premise that *everyday communicative interactions* are first and foremost social interactions. In the mid-twentieth century, Dell Hymes heralded an approach to linguistics that situated language fully in the social contexts of its use. As eloquently described in the epigraph, Hymes argued the study of language use must begin with the *social matrix* of interactions and then move in to focus on particular *patterns of interaction* and specific *communicative resources* (including language). A focus on linguistic forms (e.g., syntax, phonology) or patterns of interaction (e.g., use of silence, turn-taking) can provide insights about population-level issues such as regional dialects and gendered language; however, they offer us little when we want to understand how specific interactions unfold among specific people at specific times, or how particular individuals are socialized into and develop the ability to successfully communicate in a range of everyday settings. *Situated discourse analysis* (SDA) takes up Hymes's call to focus on *processes of communication among people* as they engage in sociocultural activities within particular sociomaterial contexts.

The three chapters in Part 1 introduce theoretical and methodological traditions of SDA and explore the embodied, distributed, and dynamic nature of *everyday communicative interactions*. Chapter 1 introduces some basic concepts of SDA by focusing on three key principles for understanding *everyday communicative interactions*. Chapter 2 draws on the three principles of SDA from

Chapter 1 to define communicative success as people's meaningful align-ments within functional systems assembled in particular sociomaterial spaces. Chapter 3 turns to questions of learning and development, asking how people learn to communicate successfully in functional systems and how participa-tion in such interactions is simultaneously the way people learn. The SDA concepts introduced in each chapter of this part (see Table P.1) are illustrated with examples drawn from my research on a family pretend game. Taken together, these chapters offer a technical toolkit that will guide us in applying SDA in Part 2 to the interactional experiences of individuals with commu-nicative disorders and in Part 3 to clinical practice.

As you reflect on your own activities and everyday experiences, make these concepts and methods your own. By developing frameworks that enhance your understanding of everyday communicative interactions, you will be better able to apply them as tools in your own clinical practice. The reflective observations at the end of each chapter are designed to guide you in developing skills in observing, analyzing, and documenting everyday communication; the suggested readings will point you to research from cul-tural psychology, sociolinguistics, anthropology, and discourse studies that will help you build a useable understanding of SDA.

Chapter 1

Exploring Everyday Communicative Interactions

Everyday communicative interactions can involve a wide range of participants, timescales, and technologies. Consider these examples:

- two people engaging in a slow series of written interactions over several months via mail to plan a vacation;
- a group of friends engaging in fast, animated, face-to-face interactions over a few minutes as they settle on where to meet for dinner in the evening;
- the uneven pace of an active social media site (with posts mixing written language, videos, images, and audio) monitored across the span of a day;
- the complexity of a group meeting in real time where some participants are joining via speaker phone or video conferencing; or
- a rushed exchange with a friend during a chance encounter while shopping.

The theoretical frameworks and methods presented in this book have been applied to all these kinds of interactions by researchers. However, in this book we will focus on the study of *real-time, synchronous face-to-face interactions* among people who come into contact with one another in both fleeting and more sustained ways.

We are focusing on face-to-face interactions for two reasons. First, such interactions are often described as the basic ground for human sociality and have, thus, served as a basic model for understanding other types of interactions. Second, face-to-face interactions are the primary means of clinical work, especially in behavioral fields such as communication sciences and disorders (CSD). Unlike most texts in CSD, this book does not focus on populations as the object of study (e.g., the linguistic patterns typical of people with aphasia), on particular systems of resources (e.g., language vs. gesture), or on isolated dimensions of interaction (e.g., turn-taking, eye-contact). Instead, it focuses on communicative interaction as the object of study, approaching each interaction as an integrated whole that participants create, respond to, and make sense of. In particular, *situated discourse analysis* (SDA) examines *how* people navigate everyday communicative interactions in real time.

This chapter starts by introducing a family pretend game (*Cindy Magic*), a dataset that we will explore throughout the first three chapters to concretely ground the basic framework we will use for analysis. It then introduces three key principles for thinking about and tracing the complex dynamics of communicative interactions:

1. communicative interactions are always situated in sociocultural activities;
2. communicative interactions draw on, and are shaped by, people's patterns of participation in sociomaterial spaces; and
3. communicative resources are embodied and multimodal.

The chapter then addresses *methodology* by taking up issues of data collection and transcription for SDA. After a brief summary, the chapter ends with suggestions for engaging with these ideas through reflective observations and further readings.

The Case of *Cindy Magic*: A Make-Believe Game

My earliest research on everyday communicative interactions focused on *Cindy Magic*, a verbal make-believe game played by my husband (Paul) and our two daughters (Nora and Anna). Briefly, *Cindy Magic* was a game Nora and Paul first developed and played to pass the time on an eight-hour car trip when Paul was 35 years old and Nora was 3;11.[1] The original game focused on Cruella Magic, a good counter character who saved baby animals from the evil Cruella de Vil (a villain in Disney's animated movie *101 Dalmatians*). In its earliest version, the game involved acting out conversations between Cruella Magic (played by Nora) and the parents of lost baby animals (played by Paul). *Cindy Magic* quickly became a game Paul and Nora enjoyed playing as they ran errands or did household chores. Over years of play, the game world grew to include a whole family of Magic characters, a host of villains working with Cruella de Vil, and more complex scenarios ranging from the mundane to the fantastic.

Intrigued by the complex social and communicative demands of the game (as Paul, Nora and eventually Anna acted out multiple characters) and by the apparent ease with which they coordinated game play with family chores, I studied *Cindy Magic* for about two years. I kept a log of their play, videotaped play episodes, and conducted both individual and group interviews. Although my data collection ended two decades ago, I continue to find myself returning to *Cindy Magic* data as a touchstone in my thinking about the complexity of everyday talk and publishing analyses on my own and with colleagues (e.g., Hengst, 2015; Hengst & Miller, 1999; Prior, Hengst, Roozen, & Shipka, 2006). In the next two chapters, I will build more context for this game as we look at different episodes and consider its history, but in this first chapter we will examine moments of play to explore the processes involved in situated communicative interactions.

When I began my study of *Cindy Magic*, Nora and Paul had been play-ing regularly (often several times a week) for almost five years, and Anna had begun joining game play about a year earlier. Although I had tried to play with them, my attempts quickly led to conflicts with Nora over my character's role and potential scenarios. So, instead of playing, I became an interested audience, listening over the years to their reports of varied epi-sodes. My first video observation of their play took place in March when Paul was 39 years old, Nora was 7;11, and Anna was 3;5. To make it easier to record, they agreed to play this episode in our family living room while folding clothes. The episode lasted 22 minutes, ending when the basket of laundry was folded. Nora was playing Mary Magic, the oldest Magic sister; Paul was Elizabeth, the middle sister; and Anna was Jane, the youngest. After announcing their characters (e.g., "I'm Elizabeth"), they launched a scenario that involved N(Mary)[2] and P(Elizabeth) talking about how they were clean-ing up the house to prepare for a party they were going to have while watch-ing as A(Jane)'s kitty climbed a tree. I was standing in the dining room next to the video camera, which was set up on a tripod to record the interaction.

Transcript 1.1 shows a brief interaction early in this episode. In this tran-script each participant has a speaking line represented by their initials—i.e., P, N, A, and J stand for Paul, Nora, Anna, and Julie, respectively—and all participants are represented continuously throughout the transcript. The transcript is set up in segments that should be read much like the written staff of a musical score, with actions and talk temporally arranged and wrap-ping continuously from segment to segment; simultaneous actions are writ-ten on different lines in vertical alignment (like musical notes in a chord). Spoken language and speech-like vocalizations are written using standard

Transcript 1.1 Discovering mud on the rug, from the March episode of *Cindy Magic* (26 seconds of interaction).

P:	Does she still like milk? She's hungry!	*	Yeah
N:	*--This is good. ... Hey, is this yours?**		
A:	**		
J:			

*N pulling shirt from basket, shaking it out   **N holds up shirt
          **A having kitty drink from P's hand   *P looks at shirt

P:	that's- that looks like it might need to be ironed. Oh kitty! When she gets
N:	*--
A:	** [laughing]
J:	

*N shaking out shirt, watching P & A   **A shaking kitty in P's face
                                                            1:14:23

P:	milk she just goes so funny. *Nora, do you have mud on your shoes?
N:	* ** hm nope.
A:	**Grrrr
J:	

*N lays out shirt to fold   **A shaking kitty in P's face.   **N picks up shirt, looks down at rug
                              *P leaning over looking at/touching muddy spot

orthography, and non-speech vocalizations (e.g., laughs and coughs) are described in square brackets. Gestures and actions are marked by an asterisk (*) and described beneath the speaking lines. Speaking lines for each player are marked by the initial of their first names (e.g., P: for Paul) while their use of character voices is marked by font changes, with *Times New Roman* depicting participants speaking as themselves (e.g., Paul speaking as Paul) and *Comic Sans MS* depicting character voices (e.g., Paul speaking as Cruella de Vil).

This transcript begins with P(Elizabeth) asking A(Jane) if her kitty likes milk. A(Jane) responds by having the kitty drink milk out of a (pretend) dish held by P(Elizabeth). At the same time, N(Mary) is working on folding a shirt which she then holds up while asking P(Elizabeth): "Hey, is this yours?" Paul seems to slip out of his character role to respond in his own voice, saying that it was his shirt and it probably needed ironing. A(Jane) initiated more play by wiggling the kitty in Paul's face, and he responds by speaking again as P(Elizabeth) says: "Oh kitty! When she gets milk she just goes so funny!" Paul then discovers some mud on the rug and shifts out of character voice to ask Nora if she has mud on her shoes. At this point game play and laundry folding stop as Paul organizes cleaning up the rug.

Figure 1.1 shows two images from the video. The first one is at the beginning of the interaction in Transcript 1.1 where P(Elizabeth) and A(Jane) are

(a)

Figure 1.1 Two screen-captures from the March episode of *Cindy Magic*. a) A(Jane) giving kitty some milk while P(Elizabeth) asks, "Does she still like milk?" b) Paul discovers mud on the rug and asks, "Nora, do you have mud on your shoes?"

Source: Prior et al., 2006.

(b)

Figure 1.1 (Continued)

feeding the kitty, with P(Elizabeth) saying: "Does she still like milk?" Paul is turned toward Anna and her kitty, holding his hand out, while Anna is looking down and putting the kitty's mouth in his hand as though it is drinking milk from a dish. Nora meanwhile is reaching into the laundry basket. The second image is at the point when Paul discovered the muddy spot on the rug and is asking: "Nora, do you have mud on your shoes?" Paul is in the foreground leaning over to inspect the muddy spot on the rug, Nora is in the back of the image folding a shirt and looking down toward the muddy spot, and Anna is on the right side holding her toy cat and watching.

Sociocultural Activities

Echoing Hymes's (1974) argument for beginning with the social matrix, the first principle of SDA we will focus on is that everyday communicative interactions are always situated in sociocultural activities. Thus, the first task of SDA is to ask the question: *What is going on here?* From my experiences leading a discourse analysis lab with other faculty, graduate students, and undergraduates, I anticipate you might at first find recognizing and naming sociocultural activities to be challenging. As skilled social actors, we tacitly recognize and navigate the many sociocultural activities of our everyday lives, but rarely need to name them in any systematic way or trace the complex ways they are accomplished.

Although marked by highly salient or durable configurations of features (including rituals/routines, special clothing, physical alignments of people, patterns of talk, and specific social roles), sociocultural activities are best identified in terms of the goals or objectives people are working to accomplish. For example, eating dinner at home after work and eating dinner on stage during a play may involve many similar features (e.g., tables, chairs, plates, silverware, food, patterns of dinner table talk). However, when we consider the different goals and objectives participants bring to these two settings, we recognize they are two quite different sociocultural activities. Close inspection of what is going on makes plain the many differences in how actions and talk unfold (how the food appears; how lighting is managed, the presence of a memorized script for the talk in the play, but not the home dinner; and so on.). In crafting a psychological theory of activity, Leontyev (1981) noted that surface similarities between moments of interaction often make it difficult to discern what goals are motivating an activity. For example, two students may be reading a book for their final exam; however, when they learn the exam has been cancelled, one student stops reading the book whereas the other continues. At that point, Leontyev argues we can see the students' reading was tied to different activities with different motives—perhaps the one who kept reading had been more engaged in gaining knowledge while the other was more focused on passing the exam.

Cultures and communities organize interactions around a wide variety of highly recognizable and easily named activities—a wedding, a card game, a shopping trip, a class meeting, a dinner, a date, a chemistry experiment, a baseball game, and so on. Within social groups, such highly recognizable activities have long histories, broadly understood goals, and recognizable social roles and patterns of participation. As long as people align around the anticipated goals, such activities remain recognizable even with extreme variations in how they are accomplished. Other activities are less easily bounded and named but are just as influential in organizing social interactions. Some sociocultural activities operate over extended time frames and are layered into many interactions. Consider such familiar dispersed activities as being a friend, managing your reputation in your family, or building up a professional identity. Although the goals may be clear (e.g., enhancing my reputation), the features are diffuse and integrated with other activities (e.g., taking an exam). Other activities are routine, but emerge fleetingly and often unpredictably, such as being alert to dangers or disruptions (e.g., localizing an unexpected noise) or managing self-care in public (e.g., sneezing and blowing your nose).

It is important to stress that interactions always involve multiple sociocultural activities people are managing simultaneously or moving rapidly among. Communicative interactions reflect people's shifting engagement with different activities (e.g., a teacher briefly interrupting her lecture to respond "Bless you" to a student who just sneezed). In short, SDA begins with the recognition that human activities are always socioculturally situated and that communicative interactions are situated within various goal-directed activities. Let's turn back now to *Cindy Magic* and analyze some of the sociocultural activities participants were engaging with during these interactions.

Activities of Cindy Magic

We begin our analysis of the communicative interactions in these data by positing potential answers to the question: ***What is going on here?*** Broadly, we can identify three readily named sociocultural activities that shaped these interactions: a) playing a familiar make-believe game known to this family as *Cindy Magic*; b) completing the familiar family chore of folding clean clothes; and c) making a video-recording of the three people playing *Cindy Magic* for a research project. Before game play began, the participants worked together to set up for all three activities. Julie set up and tested the recording equipment with some help from Paul, Nora, and Anna; Paul brought a basket of clean clothes to the living room; and Anna hung around in the living room playing with a toy cat. Once the physical space was set up, the four of us coordinated getting things started—Julie starting the recording; Paul, Nora, and Anna announced their character roles for *Cindy Magic*; and Paul and Nora selected clothing items from the basket.

This episode of *Cindy Magic* also highlights local and fleeting activities the participants were managing. For example, managing the mud on the rug was an emergent activity (not part of the planned activities), though broadly related to another routine family task (taking care of the house). Vacuuming a muddy spot on the rug was by no means a typical occurrence in the repeated activities of folding laundry or playing *Cindy Magic*. Integrating activities and objects into game play was routine. For example, it was common to reinterpret the family chore (folding laundry) within the game world (cleaning up for the party). Less typical was the use of props to create local activities, such as playing with and feeding A(Jane)'s (toy) kitty. In a diffuse but active way, the sociocultural management of long-term identities and relationships was also layered into these interactions. For example, Paul and I were being partners, parents, and academics; Nora and Anna were being daughters and sisters. The communicative interactions I recorded can be interpreted as supporting and being shaped by the goals of all these activities, often simultaneously. In the next two sections of this chapter we will explore how we made those interpretations.

Patterns of Participation in Sociomaterial Spaces

The second core principle of SDA is that everyday communicative interactions draw on, and are shaped by, people's patterns of participation in in sociomaterial spaces. Thus, SDA asks: ***What are people's patterns of participation in*** *this sociomaterial space?* Drawing on the work of sociologists such as Erving Goffman (1961, 1981) and Aaron Cicourel (1964, 1992), we can begin by defining *sociomaterial spaces* as physical spaces (e.g., an office, a park, a bus) where two or more people are gathered. In such spaces, a *gathering* refers to all the people who are *physically co-present*, whether or not they seem to be engaging in the same activities.

We routinely interpret the *what's going on here* of sociomaterial spaces by attending to the ways people are physically coordinating their postures, actions, movements, eye gaze, and so on. Goffman referred to the highly recognizable patterns of interaction among people participating in specific activities as *interaction orders*. For example, we recognize when groups of people in public spaces are waiting in lines to buy tickets for a movie versus chatting with one another in small groups as part of a larger family picnic in a public park. Indeed, cities and buildings are designed to support *interaction orders* typical of specific sociocultural activities. Take, for example, the formal stage and audience seating built into a theater that support various types of performances, or the temporary stages and roped off seating areas erected in city parks for outdoor summer concerts. Drawing on these familiar interaction orders, street musicians arrange themselves in ways that invite people to pause and listen as an audience to their playing (and perhaps drop money in their open music cases).

Moving in from the social matrix toward language, Goffman (1981) identified *participation frameworks* around "talk," that is, how people align to specific utterances in a communicative interaction. In a gathering, some people will align as *ratified participants*—as recognized partners in the interaction. Others may minimize their attention to the interaction by looking away and/or actively engaging in another activity or conversation, thus positioning themselves as unratified *overhearers* of the talk. This social distancing from the talk might be marked by greater physical distance between speakers and overhearers, by facing toward or away from a speaker, or by the speakers projecting the volume of their talk, perhaps speaking quietly, making the words clear only to their immediate circle of ratified listeners, or loudly, recognizing that others can easily overhear. Other participants may feign disinterest by not overtly attending to the talk but actively *eavesdropping* on the ratified conversational partners. Of course, participants in a gathering do not only attend to talk; they will also monitor sights (e.g., gestures, facial expressions, and movements) and sounds (e.g., forks and spoons clicking on plates as people eat; hammers pounding in a mechanic's shop).

Speakers routinely design their utterances and actions in ways that reflect the gathering, both acknowledging and shaping people's roles in conversations. Two people may talk in somewhat coded terms about a friend because they know others can overhear the conversation. In this way, sociomaterial spaces form a landscape of possibilities that shape people's patterns of participation. Likewise, when I join the end of a line at a theatre, I'm signaling my intention to buy a ticket and to follow one cultural routine for doing so (e.g., waiting my turn). When I look up and smile at the people in front of me talking about the bad weather, I shift my role from an overhearer to a ratified participant in their conversation, which shapes it as a casual (not-private) conversation. Goffman (1981) identified the ways speakers take different stances to their own talk, what he called the utterance's *production format*. For example, a speaker can voice another's words (*animating* words *authored* by another person, sometimes speaking *figuratively* as that person) or say something that represents another's interests or commitments (*principalship*, such as when employees speak for the company not themselves or a lawyer represents a client's interests in a negotiation). Participation frameworks and production formats help us describe the complex ways people participate in interactions: signaling and proposing who gets to talk, to whom talk is directed, how talk is taken up, and what relationships people may have to specific utterances and actions. In this way, every utterance is understood as a distributed process of production influenced by, and staged for, multiple people.

People's *patterns of participation* also signal (or index) various histories of the people involved. For example, you may interpret two people walking together as paired intentionally (e.g., a couple on a planned date) or incidentally (e.g., strangers talking about bus schedules as they approach a bus stop). Face-to-face interactions are not as neatly bounded as they may appear. Indeed, mundane interactions are routinely parts of longer chains of interactions occurring over days, weeks, and even lifetimes. In his research on medical residents and physicians doing patient rounds in a hospital, Cicourel (1992) noted the physicians not only directed interaction in ways that reflected institutional and professional histories (e.g., calling on a pathology resident to interpret and explain the lab results), but that students and physicians would routinely arrive at the bed of a patient and immediately continue conversations and activities from the previous day's rounds with that patient. Thus, he found moments of interaction in these rounds only made sense in the context of the ongoing and repeated participation of the medical team over days.

Patterns of Participation in Cindy Magic

We can begin to outline patterns of participation during *Cindy Magic* by describing the sociomaterial space of these interactions. This episode took place indoors, on the main floor of the family home. Four people were co-present throughout the episode, with three (Paul, Nora, Anna) gathered around the laundry basket in the living room (see Figure 1.1), and one (Julie) off to the side by the video camera. The activities could be read in part from the interactional alignments of the participants to this physical context. Folding clothes around the laundry basket put Paul, Nora, and Anna in close conversational distance to one another, affording their playing *Cindy Magic*. In contrast, Julie stayed in the adjacent room (about 10 feet away).

The close proximity of the three, their collaborative actions around folding clothes, and their talk framed them as ratified participants in both the family chore and game play, while the distance helped frame Julie as a (ratified) overhearer/observer who was not participating in the chore or play.

Paul, Nora, and Anna spoke and gestured to manage the family chore, but also discursively layered their characters and *Cindy Magic* with their family identities. After P(Elizabeth) asked about A(Jane)'s kitty (ratifying her contribution to the game play), A(Jane) took up P(Elizabeth)'s offer to pretend that his hand was a dish of milk and began dipping the toy cat's nose into his hand as if it were lapping up the milk. A(Jane) and P(Elizabeth) faced one another and jointly looked at the kitty, while N(Elizabeth) was turned away, able to overhear the interaction as she folded clothes. Sometimes diffuse family identities and activities superseded game play, as when Paul broke game frame to ask Nora if she had mud on her shoes and began parentally directing clean up.

Even in these brief moments of play, we can see the complexity of managing multiple stances and participating in multiple activities. For example, as a participant observer, I was an audience to the game, in a soft supervisory role to the family chore, and in a management role to the research. Aligning with my role as researcher-observer, the three players actively *disattended* to me and the camera during the game play (not talking to or looking at me). However, during the disruption in play to clean up the mud, Nora came over to look more closely at the camera and ask questions about the taping.

Communicative Resources in Use

The third core principle of SDA is that communicative resources are embodied and multimodal. Communicative interactions involve specific people in specific sociomaterial spaces (not abstract or idealized actions of populations), and people attend to diverse communicative resources in these spaces (not just language or talk). Thus, SDA asks broadly: *What communicative resources are being used in this interaction?*

In face-to-face interactions, people attend to diverse communicative resources across multiple sensory *modalities*, including:

- *visual modalities*, paying attention to gaze, gestures, facial expressions, embodied actions, and information in the environment that is referenced and gestured to;
- *aural modalities*, paying attention to multiple vocal characteristics (e.g., prosody, loudness, speed, fluency, non-speech sounds), other embodied sounds (e.g., foot-stamping, hand clapping, fingers tapping on a table), and environmental sounds (e.g., a car horn blaring, music, a bird singing);
- *tactile modalities*, paying attention to human touch (e.g., a handshake, a hug, a hand briefly touching the back of the other's hand) as well as to the feel of objects in the environment (e.g., the softness of a wool scarf,

the texture of a document, the heat of food on a plate, the vibrations of loud music);

- *olfactory modalities*, paying attention to the embodied and added odors of others (e.g., smells of sweat, garlic on the breath, perfumes and soaps) and the odors of the environment (e.g., smells of food cooking, something burning, freshly cut flowers on a table); and
- *proprioceptive modalities*, paying attention to our own bodily positions, balance, movements and patterns of acceleration.

In the field of *semiotics*, what we are calling communicative resources are referred to as *signs*—anything that stands for something else, like the written letters d-o-g might stand for a specific animal.

Highlighting the way face-to-face interaction always involves multiple channels (each tied to a particular array of sensory modalities), Thomas Sebeok (2001) noted that, as embodied phenomena, a *sign source is coupled by a channel to a destination*, all of which are dependent on the material characteristics of given moments of interaction. Likewise, Asif Agha (2007) noted that what is often called *language-in-use* actually refers to situations in which "an array of signs is being performed and construed by interactants, of which language is but a fragment . . . of a *multi-channel sign configuration*" (p. 6, emphasis added). Some communicative resources are highly recognizable and codified (e.g., language, semaphore, Morse code, hand signals used in baseball games), whereas others are less codified (e.g., facial expressions, laughter, how close you position yourself to another person in a conversation). However, no communicative resources ever arise in isolation: they are always parts of complex multimodal orchestrations.

One dimension of multimodal orchestration is physical location, that is, where and when communicative resources are deployed. To capture how a sign's meaning relates to location in sociomaterial spaces, linguistic anthropologists Ron and Suzie Scollon (Scollon & Scollon, 2003) introduced the term *geosemiotics*. They were particularly interested in written forms of language used on the various signs posted on streets and buildings. For example, they note that when a stop sign is lying flat in the bed of a pick-up truck it does not mean the same thing it would when posted at an intersection. In both instances, the object is highly recognizable as a stop sign (octagon shape, bright red background, bold white capital letters spelling the word STOP). Although the visual and linguistic codes and material objects are identical, the activities the stop signs align with and orchestrate are different. A car approaching the stop sign on the back of the pick-up truck should not stop, whereas a car approaching the sign at the intersection should. Thus, location is critical to understanding the stop sign as an active legal directive. The location of spoken words in everyday communicative interactions also informs their meanings: the same words uttered by the same people in different places take on different meanings and provoke different reactions.

In everyday communicative interactions, the timing (temporal location) of words and other signs also matters. For example, conversational analysis (CA), a specific sociological theory of how to analyze talk, has focused on how conversational interactions among ratified participants are organized *sequentially* around interactional turns-at-talk. CA examines how participants negotiate whose turn it is to talk and the complex signals people orchestrate as they sustain or switch speaking roles (Schegloff, 1996). For example, a speaker may use a preliminary comment (e.g., "Hey, did you hear about the party on the corner last night?") to signal the intention of taking multiple speaking turns to tell a story or may ask a question to someone (e.g., "So, what did you do after you left class?") as a means of encouraging the addressee to take the next speaking turn. CA researchers have also documented how people deploy arrays of signs to signal turn boundaries. In casual conversations, speakers often signal the potential for a turn transition (a change in speakers) through a combination of phrase final intonation, a pragmatic/semantic endpoint to a topic, the completion of a syntactic unit, and patterns of gaze (Ford & Thompson, 1996; Goodwin, 1981). In everyday interactions, turn taking is routinely synchronized with other activities. For example, during a friendly game of catch, the pitcher may signal when she is ready to throw the ball with a combination of actions and words (e.g., exaggerated arm movements toward, and eye contact with, the intended catcher while saying "Are you ready?").

Communicative resources also function in and take meaning from social locations, from our sense of who is speaking and what sociocultural voices the speaker is enacting. At one moment I may be speaking as a professor, at another as a parent, and at the next as my friend whose voice I am animating as a part of a story I'm telling. One key dimension of sociocultural voice is *typified social voices* associated with social identities (Prior, 2001). Enacting a social voice constructs the person as a member of a socially recognizable category or group. Enacting the voice may be a way the person claims social identities, rights, and responsibilities, or may be an animated performance that discursively conjures the *figure* of another person, whether to voice people in a narrative or another participant in the interaction by acting/ speaking as them. Typified social voices are signaled by blends of typical content, addressees, and forms of language, but also by typical paralinguistic cues, embodied stances and actions, and so on. Gesture, posture, and facial expressions all contribute to the performance of recognizable social voices. The stand-up routines of comedians are often rich illustrations of how these resources work together to *perform* identities in interactions. Social voices may be well established or situationally improvised, maintained over long stretches of discourse or deployed fleetingly, claimed as one's own identity or *styled* as another, and signaled strongly by aligning multiple resources or circumspectly with only a single resource.

Situating Communicative Resources in Cindy Magic

Transcript 1.1 and the images in Figure 1.1 display the richly embodied and multimodal resources woven together in these interactions. All four of us were watching and listening to one another, coordinating movements and actions, and managing our own bodies in these spaces. A striking feature of *Cindy Magic* was the flexible way players enacted and responded to different character voices. Paul marked different characters mostly through changes in pitch, rate and voice quality—using a higher lilting voice for Elizabeth and a deeper, raspier voice for Cruella de Vil. In contrast, Nora used a louder and more commanding voice when speaking as Mary, the oldest Magic sister, but did little to adjust her voice quality or pitch. In this transcript, Anna laughed with Paul and made growling noises as the kitty. Although not shown in this transcript, when she spoke as Jane, there was very little change in her voice. To further explore the use of communicative resources, we can compare the two utterances depicted on the images in Figure 1.1.

In the first image, Paul and Anna face each other—Anna standing up and holding her toy kitten, Paul kneeling with his right hand cupped under the kitten's head, and both looking down at his hand/the kitten. Paul, speaking in his Elizabeth voice, asks A(Jane) a question: "Does she still like milk?" A(Jane) seemed to respond to P(Elizabeth)'s question by moving the kitty's nose up and down into Paul's cupped hand (mimicking lapping up milk). P(Elizabeth) responds to this physical act: "She's hungry!" Understanding this utterance involves hearing it in the context of the previous question, but also in the embodied space of the living room, where the environment includes a stuffed toy kitten that is being animated as a live kitty and where milk has been imagined into the environment through a combination of Paul's verbal question, Anna's actions holding the cat, and Paul's coordination of his cupped hand with Anna's actions.

In the second image, Paul is leaning on the couch over the basket to look at the rug, Nora is standing up folding a shirt and also looking down at the rug, and Anna is walking towards them. Although not visible in this image, Paul is also touching the rug to figure out what the spot is while addressing Nora (not Mary) using his own voice: "Nora, do you have mud on your shoes?" Interestingly, Paul did not verbally contextualize this question. Nora seemed to understand his question by his embodied attention to the muddy spot on the rug (something Nora and Anna could both see if they looked there) and his change in voice. Given the ongoing activities of folding clothes and playing *Cindy Magic*, Paul's question is out of place, but cast within the discovery of mud and Paul's parental role in household cleaning, this question makes sense—and Nora took it up that way (looking at the soles of her shoes to check for mud). Anna displays attentive uncertainty at the shift, watching closely and then echoing Nora's embodied action by lifting her own foot up and twisting it to make the sole of her shoes visible. These two brief examples highlight the complex ways even the most mundane utterances are situated in and emerge from a multichannel array of signs in sociomaterial spaces.

Note on Methods: Selecting, Collecting, and Transcribing Interactional Data

Whether you are researching communicative interactions or developing a rich account of your client's communicative practices, you will need to make decisions about selecting, collecting, and analyzing interactional data. The questions or interests that drive your inquiry, along with the working relationships you have with your participants, will guide your decisions (Miller, Hengst, & Wang, 2003). For example, I decided to record my family playing *Cindy Magic* because their game play was complex (e.g., multiple people of different ages enacting multiple characters and complicated game scenarios while simultaneously accomplishing chores), which reminded me of the multiple activities I managed as a supervisor with graduate students and clients (as I described in the preface). My insider status in our family provided me frequent access, making it easier for me to observe episodes of play, interview participants, and trace changes in game play over the two years of data collection. Given my interests and access, I then made core decisions about how to collect and analyze data. Throughout the book we will return repeatedly to these issues, but here we begin to address decisions about how to record interactional data and transcribe it for analysis.

Obtaining quality video recordings of interactions is a critical component of most SDA. In their book *Video in Qualitative Research*, Heath, Hindmarsh, and Luff (2003) emphasize the importance of planning ahead and working closely with participants to ensure quality recordings. You will need to make decisions about who will manage the recording equipment, how many and what types of cameras and microphones you will use, where the recording equipment will be placed, and whether equipment will be in fixed locations or mobile. For example, to record Nora, Anna, and Paul playing *Cindy Magic*, I used one video camera (with a built-in microphone) and an additional audio recorder with an external omnidirectional (tabletop) microphone. I positioned the equipment in fixed locations—the camera on a tripod about 20 feet from the participants and the external microphone of the audio recorder about 4–6 feet away. I kept both running without interruption throughout the session. The video frame captured all three participants throughout game play (but not when they left the room), and the audio recorder allowed me to get good quality audio (sounds and voices) even when participants were off camera. As I will note in future chapters, supplementary data (e.g., still photos of the material space and artifacts, researchers' notes about what is not captured on camera, conversations with participants) collected at the time of the recording were also critical for understanding and interpreting data captured by video.

Decisions about how to transcribe video data and what communicative resources to focus on depend on the researcher's theoretical lens, the research questions being addressed, and whether the transcript is being used primarily for analysis or to display data in research presentations and publications (Leander & Prior, 2004; Ochs, 1979). Given the complexity and variability in how people manage everyday communicative interaction, the guiding rule in my research lab is *nothing gets thrown out*. So, my preliminary analysis of video data routinely includes preparing a complete transcript of the full recording. I developed my transcription system (see Transcript 1.1) around SDA principles. First, to focus on the gathering of people involved in the interaction, the transcript includes a continuous "speaking" line for each person (e.g., Nora, Paul, Anna, Julie) regardless of how they were involved and whether or not they were speaking. Second, to display the temporal unfolding of the interaction the transcript is organized much like the staff of a musical score that wraps around continuously with time. Third, to focus on diverse communicative resources, the transcript is loosely organized by semiotic channels. Speaking lines depict spoken language (written in standard orthography), prosodic features (denoted by punctuation marks and font styles), voice or register changes (denoted by font styles and bracketed descriptions), and other vocalizations such as laughter or tongue clicks (described in brackets). Visible gestures and actions are temporally located with an asterisk (*) in a person's speaking line and described in a note below all speaking lines.

In contrast, many transcription systems are organized by speaking turns, anchoring gestures and timing (including pauses) to spoken language. People in the gathering are only represented on the transcript when they are speaking. For example, the transcription system developed for CA was designed to highlight the temporal organization of talk around speaking turns (Sacks, Schegloff, & Jefferson, 1974). A turn-by-turn transcript of the first few speaking turns in Transcript 1.1 might look like this:

P: Does she still like milk? (2) She's hungry!
N: This is good. (. . .) Hey, is this yours?
P: Yeah that's- that looks like it might need to be ironed.

Comparing this turn-by-turn transcript with Transcript 1.1 illustrates how significant such theoretical decisions are.

Summary: Situated Discourse Analysis Tools

This chapter has introduced SDA as a theoretically and empirically grounded approach to the study of everyday communicative interactions. SDA recognizes that all communicative interactions are real-time, embodied events situated in specific sociomaterial spaces and sociocultural histories. People (whether participants or researchers) interpret what is going on through the ways moments of interactions are situated across those dimensions. This chapter has discussed how analysis of communicative interactions must begin with the social matrix by identifying the multiple goal-directed activities people seem to be engaging in, by tracing how people are participating in such activities, and finally by examining the diverse multimodal communicative resources that are indexing people's activities, ways of participating, and meanings. Three critical questions will help guide our understanding and use of SDA:

- *What is going on here?*
- *What are people's patterns of participation in this sociomaterial space?*
- *What communicative resources are being used in this interaction?*

Taken together, these three questions offer a heuristic that focuses us on the unfolding complexities of everyday communicative interaction situated in social matrices.

SDA research often offers striking illustrations of complex multimodal orchestration of communicative resources as people manage their participation in interactions and engage in sociocultural activities with often diverse goals. For example, Goodwin and Alim (2010) analyze conflict talk among a group of 5th grade girls who had known each other since kindergarten, tracing the skillful ways the girls enacted sociocultural voices and values by fusing language, gestures, and other semiotics. Specifically, they analyzed how some girls built and tore down identities by orchestrating a multimodal array of signs: "clueless Valley Girl" talk ("Like-totally"), "Ghetto Girl" gestures (teeth suck, eye roll, and neck roll), and insults associated with socio-economic class ("At least I don't get my shoes at Payless"). It is striking how successfully these girls blended communicative resources in embodied performances of sociocultural voices to simultaneously create social solidarity among an insider group and ostracize one girl as an outsider.

It is axiomatic in SDA that the interpretive work of researchers and clinicians in understanding what is going on in interactions is very much like the work participants and clients engage in as they manage communicative interactions, a point we will explore more in Chapter 2. However, SDA also brings a specialized toolkit to that interpretive work including: increased attention (e.g., repeatedly watching a video of a short conversation aided by a careful transcription representing the talk and gestures of participants), systematic and critical engagement (e.g., working to understand a range of possible interpretations of interactions), and theoretical framing (e.g., grounding interpretations in theoretical concepts).

Reflective Observations

1. *Observing and transcribing everyday communicative interactions.*

   a. *Select an activity that interests you and that you want to understand better:* Think about activities you are familiar with in your everyday life. This could include ones you are directly involved in (e.g., practices for sports teams, music lessons, club meetings) or ones where you function more as an interested observer (like *Cindy Magic* for me). The activity should be one that involves several people, that happens frequently, that you have easy access to, and that you feel comfortable asking the people involved for their permission to record and analyze.

b. *Recording interactions:* Make arrangements to video-record about 30 minutes of interaction (this may be done in one or more observations). If you are an observer (like my role with *Cindy Magic*), you can manage the camera and quietly observe from the sidelines, but if you are part of the interaction, you will need to set up the camera on a tripod or elicit the help of another person to make the video.

c. *Transcribing video data:* First, watch through the video paying attention to what activities people are engaged in, how their patterns of participation within activities shift across the interactions, and what communicative resources are being used to manage alignments. Then, using the *Cindy Magic* transcript (Transcript 1.1) as a model select about two to three minutes of your data to transcribe in detail.

2. ***Analyzing the complexities of everyday communicative interactions.*** Write up a brief analysis of your observation of the interaction by providing preliminary responses to the three questions outlined in this chapter.

a. *What's going on here?* Identify the multiple sociocultural activities people are engaged in and how the sociomaterial space and communicative practices shape the activities. Be sure to note when activities seem to shift.

b. *What are people's patterns of participation in this sociomaterial space?* Trace people's patterns of participation within the gathering and with the various activities, describing the interaction orders and participation frameworks that emerge.

c. *What communicative resources are being used in this interaction?* Catalogue the communicative resources that are evident in your video, paying attention to the range of semiotic channels and how participants are deploying social voices. How many different communicative resources (e.g., semiotic modalities and channels, social voices, linguistic codes) were you able to capture or display in your transcript?

3. ***Comparing interactions.*** Despite the obvious similarities across interactions (e.g., people use similar words, interact around similar activities), a core assumption of SDA is that each interaction is unique as individuals are managing varied goals and conditions of specific interactions. To explore this assumption, compare the preliminary analysis of your interactional data with analyses completed by others (either published

data, or analyses from other members of your class or research group). Discuss what is unique to each interaction.

Suggested Readings

To become more familiar with how SDA can contribute to our understanding of everyday communicative interactions, it is useful to read a wide range of analyses by different researchers. In addition to the articles referenced throughout this chapter, here are three readings that provide fascinating situated analyses of very different everyday interactions. Taken together, these three readings highlight that communication is always much more than language use.

a. "Musical spaces" (Haviland, 2011). In this chapter, John Haviland presents situated analyses of interactions among members of three different musical groups (a string quartet; a jazz combo; and a musical trio).
b. "Laborious intersubjectivity: Attentional struggle and embodied communication in an auto-shop" (Streeck, 2008). In this chapter, Jürgen Streeck presents a situated analysis of an interaction between people in an auto-mechanic shop, focusing especially on the diverse resources and obstacles the participants are managing.
c. "Learning to serve: The language and literacy of food service workers" (Mirabelli, 2004). In this chapter, Tony Mirabelli presents an analysis of interactions between waiters/waitresses and their customers.

Notes

1. I am using the convention of reporting children's ages in years and months separated by a semi-colon (e.g., 3;11 means 3 years 11 months). Ages for adults are given in years only.
2. Using the initial of a participant's first name followed by a character name in parentheses, indicates they are speaking for that character, e.g., N(Mary) = Nora speaking as Mary.

Chapter 2

Defining Success in Everyday Communicative Interactions

In Chapter 1 we began examining the diverse, complex, and dynamic nature of everyday communicative interactions. In this chapter, we turn to how to identify *communicative success*, an issue that is often central to clinical practice. In *situated discourse analysis* (SDA) *communicative success* is best identified by tracing peoples' ongoing patterns of *alignment*. However, common ideas about communicative success focus on transmitting meanings through a shared linguistic code. One dominant model involves what has been called the *conduit metaphor* (Reddy, 1979; Lakoff & Johnson, 1980). The conduit metaphor appears in many everyday expressions as well as being reflected in linguistic theories, such as the common image of the speech chain (Denes & Pinson, 1993). It assumes words carry meanings: speakers encode meaning into language and transmit the coded language to listeners through some medium, and listeners receive it and then decode meanings. This model accounts for communicative success in terms of speaker and listener sharing the same linguistic code. This account is literally the way machines communicate. However, it is not the way humans make meaning and orchestrate activity. People don't download fixed linguistic programs and then run them in interactions. Instead, people learn from specific diverse experiences in their lives and are constantly updating their knowledge, which means people at best have partially overlapping knowledge and strategies for aligning with others.

For example, consider this statement: "She bought six already!" As someone who is comfortable using English, you are all probably confident that "she" refers to a girl or woman, but you don't know who "she" might be. You probably infer that "six" references purchasable items (e.g., foods items, school supplies, or raffle tickets) and "bought" indicates the transaction was completed. Focusing on the exclamation mark, you probably sense this utterance was said with some surprise, but it won't be clear what was surprising about it, maybe that she (not he?) bought them (not made them?) or that six was a lot (or too few?). You may guess that the speaker is describing something he/she had witnessed (or at least knew about) from the past, but it won't be clear if that past was immediate or distant. It is also not clear what this sentence hopes to achieve: is it just gossip or does it have immediate implications (e.g., so you should buy them quickly before they run out or you don't need to buy any since you will get some of the six)?

The words offer clues to make meaning, but the meaning depends on situated context and purpose. Among a group of four friends walking into a theatre to watch a play, when one says, "Should we buy programs?," and another tilts his head at Beth and says, "She bought six already!," the meaning and implications seem so clear that we are tempted to imagine the words do carry the meaning. However, key work involves both short and long term history (the immediate question but also earlier planning), the place (geosemiotics again), and the gestures, yet with all that we still aren't sure why Beth's purchase was surprising. This example illustrates the stark communicative limits of words on their own.

Recognizing those limits, SDA begins first by focusing on what *sociocultural activities* are active within a particular interaction, tracing *patterns of participation* displayed by the people involved, and identifying the *diverse range of communicative resources* available in this sociomaterial space. Simple encoding-transmission-decoding models cannot account for *communicative success*. In spite of the speed and ease that seems to characterize many interactions, it is safe to assume that all communicative interactions involve some degree of miscommunication. The miscommunication might be hidden (e.g., discussing the Vietnam War, we don't realize that we have very different understandings of that history). It might be a fleeting miscommunication participants seem to ignore (e.g., when my daughter, Nora, responds even though I address her by her sister's name). It might be a more disruptive miscommunication people need to actively work through (e.g., a group working to clarify confusion over day/date/time for a meeting). Some miscommunications lead to sustained breakdowns (e.g., a married couple realizing they were not on the same page when they discussed their roles as married partners) or even to public disasters, like the professional miscommunication that led to the *Challenger* space shuttle exploding on launch (for an analysis see Herndl, Fennell, & Miller, 1991).

Building on the basic concepts of SDA introduced in the first chapter, we approach *communicative success* as an issue of *alignment*, alignments around meanings, goals, people, resources, spaces, and activities. Recognizing that the work of alignment is always negotiated in real time, we begin by introducing *functional systems* as a distributed unit of analysis for the study of communicative interactions, tying measures of communicative success to the activities and goals of the functional system. Turning then to people's patterns of participation, we examine *distributed communication* as a way of anchoring notions of communicative competence in the distributed alignments of functional systems, not the isolated skills of individuals. Finally, thinking about resources, we focus on *interactional resources* as recognizable configurations that establish and align *indexical grounds* as frames-of-reference people orient to as they work to interpret communicative resources, make sense of communicative interactions, and orchestrate activity. We begin this chapter with another interaction from *Cindy Magic* that will be used to illustrate points throughout the chapter and again conclude with a Note on Methods.

The Case of *Cindy Magic*: Creating the Vampire Bats

We continue here with interactions from the March episode of *Cindy Magic*. At the end of Figure 1.1, Paul had paused game play and clothes folding to clean up the mud he discovered on the living room rug. After vacuuming the rug and taking off muddy shoes, Paul, Nora and Anna resume playing. P(Elizabeth) suggests that the loud noise reminds him(her) of Cruella de Vil, and the Magic sisters quickly agree that the loud noise had not been the vacuum cleaner after all, but was Cruella de Vil stirring up trouble in their back yard. The first image in Figure 2.1 shows the Magic sisters focused on the living room rug where the mud was just vacuumed, but now they have imaginatively refigured it as looking down (as if from the second floor

(a)

Figure 2.1 Two screen-captures from the March episode of *Cindy Magic.* a) The Magic sisters discover Cruella de Vil in their backyard while P(Elizabeth) asks, "What's she doing in our backyard?" b) Two Magic sisters pointing to Cruella de Vil while N(Mary) asks P(bat), "Can you go and suck up blood?"

Source: Prior et al., 2006.

(b)

Figure 2.1 (Continued)

of their house) at the Magics' backyard and P(Elizabeth) asks: "What's she doing in our backyard?"

The Magic sisters had been discussing what they should do to fight Cruella de Vil. P(Elizabeth) suggested calling routine allies: "Maybe we should call the robot?" and "How about the cheetahs?" At the beginning of the interaction in Transcript 2.1, N(Mary) is rejecting both of these suggestions, saying: "Cause the robot is already with her, don't you see him?" and "The cheetahs are in their cage." P(Elizabeth) then appeals to A(Jane) for ideas, "What do you think, Jane? What should we do?" Looking down at the backyard, A(Jane) proposes a new ally (one never before used in the game): "We call .1. the bats." N(Mary) enthusiastically supports and expands this idea, "The vampire bats, good idea," going on to tell P(Elizabeth) that she and Jane know eighteen vampire bats. A(Jane) begins calling the bats. Then Nora tells Paul: "Dad, you be the vampire bats," and Anna watches as Paul and Nora discuss how he will act out a vampire bat.

The game moves forward when A(Jane) reaches out to P(bat)'s chest and swings her arm around to point at the space on the rug projected as the 'backyard' as if directing him to fly down and get Cruella de Vil. As shown in the second image in Figure 2.1, N(Mary) echoes A(Jane)'s gesture while giving the bats instruction "Get Cruella de Vil, can you go and suck up blood?" P(bat) confirms the target by saying "Cruella de Vil," calls the other bats to join him, and acts out flying down to the backyard.

Transcript 2.1   Calling the Vampire Bats, from the March episode of *Cindy Magic* (55 seconds of interaction).

P: What do you think, Jane. What should we do?
N: The cheetahs are in their cage. ..2..
A: Yeah
J:

P: You call the bats?
N: The vampire bats, good
A: ..2.. We call .1. bats   Yeah, then you can .1. (him in) X
J:

P: Vampire bats? I didn't even know we knew any.
N: idea!   (Yeah) we do, don't
A: Yeah.
J:

P: You guys know vampire bats?   Okay, well
N: we Jane?   Eighteen of them.
A: Yeah, XX.   (Hey) VAMPIRE
J:

P: call them, lets see what happens.
N: Vampires?   Dad, you be the vampire bats
A: BATS?   Vam bats   Vampire?
J:

P: I'm gonna be the vampire bats? I don't know how to be a vampire bat.
N: Go like *[squeaky
A:
J:
                                                                *N flapping arms

---

P: na na na na [sucking noise] what to eat?
N: noises]   **(Get) Cruella de Vil.
A: *
J:
              *A touches P's chest, then swings arm down
              to point at floor, as if showing him where to fly
                                              **N mimics A, touches P's chest
                                              then swings arm to point at floor

---

P: Cruella de Vil ... come on everybody **
N: Can you go and suck up blood?   *
A:
J:
                    *N nods head enthusiastically   **P diving hands to touch rug

Functional Systems: A Complex and Dynamic Unit of Analysis

As discussed in Chapter 1, the question *What is going on here?* focuses our attention on sociocultural activity. However, for analysis of specific interactions, it is important not to rely only on our sense of generically named activities or places. For example, although I may be sitting in a classroom as my instructor lectures about the functions of different laryngeal muscles,

I may also be whispering with my neighbor about our plans to study for a different class that evening before we go out for dinner. Moments later, I might use my phone to connect to a library website to reserve study rooms and then make reservations at a restaurant. Indeed, as we noted in Chapter 1, it is quite routine for a number of things to be going on in any stretch of interaction and for people in a gathering to be engaged in multiple activities, whether divergent or tightly aligned. If we rely only on generic assumptions about what's going on in classrooms (e.g., teachers lecturing, students listening and taking notes), we will miss the multiple, diverse, and layered activities people are successfully managing. Thus, to focus on the success of interactions, the first question we will ask is: ***What is being accomplished by the functional system?*** As a unit of analysis *functional systems* offer us a way to think about how activities are assembled, aligned, and accomplished in the sociomaterial spaces of specific interactions.

Hutchins (1995) introduced the notion of functional systems, defining them as ongoing assemblages of people and environmental resources (natural and human-made) orchestrated in real-time to achieve goals. In terms of our framework from Chapter 1, functional systems are sites where *sociocultural activities* are enacted. However, functional systems are dynamic assemblages that have the potential to rapidly respond to and reorganize around changing needs and goals. In fact, Hutchins argues that the power of human cognition lies precisely in our abilities to create environments and artifacts and then flexibly (re)organize them around specific goals by assembling those resources into functional systems. Functional systems should be understood then not as static contexts within which activity happens, but as the processes of assembling sociomaterial spaces, resources, and people to accomplish activities.

While Hutchins analyzed functional systems to track the distributed nature of cognition, we focus in this chapter on the distributed nature of communicative success. As Clark (1992) argued, communicative interactions are fundamentally collaborative accomplishments. Like shaking hands or paddling a two-person canoe, communicative success depends on how people align to collaborate in activity. Several characteristics of functional systems are particularly important. First, functional systems as a whole have properties different from those of any one person or artifact involved in them, so they help us attend to the collaborative nature of communication. Second, the success of functional systems in achieving goals depends on how various elements across levels are aligned. For example, as a team of people work together on a task, their success will depend on alignments among the functional neural networks within individual brains (e.g., Luria, 1963; Nguyen, Vanderwal, & Hasson, 2019), the communicative interactions of people engaged in collaborative referencing about objects and actions in the sociomaterial space (e.g., Clark, 1992), and use of cultural tools to accomplish goals (e.g., Hutchins, 1995). Third, the success of any team's work involves ongoing realignments as the functional system responds flexibly to changing conditions and the unanticipated. If one person's attention wanders, another person may step in. If one tool breaks, people figure out work-arounds. If people anticipate challenges in future interactions, they plan ahead to have needed tools and people available.

This dynamic perspective holds for analyses of functional systems across long time scales as well as for the moment-by-moment emergence of everyday interactions. We should never assume that a given environment predetermines the activities and interactions that occur there (e.g., in a classroom learning is happening; in a store shopping is happening). SDA recognizes multiple activities are always possible in, and are quite typical of, everyday sociomaterial environments. To analyze success then, it is not enough to note individual and momentary contributions. Instead, we need to trace the way situated functional systems are being assembled and reassembled as people dynamically pursue multiple and shifting goals, align resources, and realize *distributed accomplishments*.

Functional Systems and Cindy Magic

By a variety of metrics, we were successful in aligning within this functional system to accomplish all three planned activities during this observation. I conducted a research observation as Paul, Nora and Anna worked together to complete the family chore and play a full episode of *Cindy Magic*. Of these three planned activities, the family chore and research activity were relatively easy to document in part because they were associated with very specific goals. Together, Paul, Nora, and Anna folded all 54 items of clothing in the basket and stacked them in piles to be put away. As the researcher, I maintained an observer stance while Paul, Nora, and Anna disattended to me during play. The camera worked, which yielded a successful recording for later analysis, and ultimately these data led not only to the seminar papers I originally envisioned, but also to a number of publications (e.g., the analysis of the "mud on the rug" episode in Prior et al., 2006).

It was more complicated to identify metrics for what would make an episode of *Cindy Magic* successful. As an observer, I thought it was successful because everyone participated, the scenarios that came up during game play seemed to have been resolved, and all three players wanted to play again during a planned errand after the clothes were folded. In later separate interviews, Paul, Nora and Anna all agreed that that this was a relatively successful episode of *Cindy Magic*, in part because it was relatively long (giving them time to develop interesting scenarios and explore solutions), all three players contributed ideas to the game, and disagreements were worked out within the game and never brought game play to a complete standstill. Nora indicated that she defined *Cindy Magic* episodes as successful when the players identified problems to solve (like discovering that Cruella de Vil was in the Magic sisters' backyard), and then worked together to solve them (like calling on the vampire bats to help them).

As noted earlier, the success of functional systems requires flexibility. In this episode, flexibility was displayed through responses to disruptions and novelty. Finding and dealing with the mud on the carpet (shown in Figure 1.1., Transcript 1.1) was one such disruption. How the functional system would respond to that disruption was not a given. I could have chosen to pause the camera during the vacuuming but didn't. There was some tacit negotiation over whether cleaning up the mud would be done in the *Cindy Magic* or family frame, but the shifts from game to family then back to game were accomplished quite smoothly overall. Another disruption in the game arose (just before Transcript 2.1), this time within the game frame. N(Mary) rejected calling on routine allies (cheetahs and robots), saying they were not able to help. This disruption led to P(Elizabeth) asking A(Jane) who they should call on and A(Jane) proposing a new ally, bats, which N(Mary) then elaborated into vampire bats. This new ally led to a brief interaction between Nora and Paul (outside of game frame) about who should play the vampire bats and how to enact them. In short, even during this relatively routine and short episode, the functional system had to be assembled and reassembled as Paul, Nora, Anna dynamically pursued, negotiated, and accomplished multiple, shifting, and situationally emergent goals.

Distributed Communication in Functional Systems

The notion of functional systems offers a way to think about how a mix of activities is being accomplished in a situated sociomaterial space. Success in some part of the activity (like folding the clothes during the *Cindy Magic* episode just discussed) routinely involves active coordination among participants. We turn our attention next to *distributed communication* to analyze *how* people successfully coordinate their participation in functional systems. The notion of distributed communication (Hengst, 2015) extends Hutchins'(1995) account of distributed cognition to communication. Here we ask: ***How are people successfully coordinating their participation in functional systems?***

Consider, for example, the activity of two people baking a cake. The two people communicate around selecting a recipe, assembling the ingredients and tools needed, and coordinating the processes of mixing and baking. The activity depends partly on the biological memory of each individual (their history of baking, talking, and coordination), but is also interactively distributed with texts (as they read recipes and labels on food products), with specialized tools (like a kitchen timer and measuring cups), and across people (as one asks the other questions and relies on the other's memory for different steps in the process). Perhaps for example, one person reads the recipe while the other mixes the ingredients, one asks the other to grease the pan or pre-heat the oven to 350 degrees, or one works on the cake while the other shares stories from a recent trip. The challenge for researchers is to trace the fine-grained ways that communication is distributed in such functional systems.

This core assumption—that human activity is always distributed—holds even though our routine ways of describing success usually hide its distributed nature. For example, in baseball, a pitcher's success if often assessed by their win-loss record. A pitcher with a 20–5 win-loss record in one year is considered a star (and that is indeed impressive performance). However, a pitcher cannot win a game alone; it takes a team to win (and another team to lose). Pitching success is also measured by how many earned runs (not due to errors) the other team gets, the Earned Run Average (ERA). One of the lowest (i.e., best) ERA records in history was credited to Bob Gibson. Pitching for the 1968 St. Louis Cardinals, Gibson gave up an average of just 1.12 runs a game, yet his win-loss record that year was 21–9. He lost 9 games because the 1968 Cardinal team was relatively weak offensively and defensively. People also have a tendency to attribute the success (or failure) of a communicative interaction to the performance of one individual who stands out (usually the speaker), but success or failure is always a matter of *distributed communication* in functional systems.

Distribution points not only to the immediate contributions of people and resources assembled in the functional system, but also to the work achieved across time. In baking, if I mixed the batter last night, then we have less to do and coordinate now. Likewise, if we talked through our baking plans last night, then we can jump straight into baking instead of spending time deciding here-and-now what kind of cake to bake or what ingredients each person will contribute. If I see you and immediately ask: "Do you have the chocolate?" and you respond by smiling and pulling a bar of pure unsweetened chocolate out of your bag, that is clear evidence of how we are distributing communication and action over time. You can also trace this kind of distribution in formal communicative events. For example, you might see me giving a formal presentation. I might be speaking extemporaneously, or I might have spent hours crafting my remarks on my own or have worked intensely over days with a group to compose and practice the presentation. You cannot directly see such prefabricated work in my presentation, but it typically has a major impact on what happens in the here-and-now.

Communicative success does not require perfect mutual understanding (something that likely never happens), but instead needs to be understood as partial and dynamic. *Good enough understandings* are routinely sufficient to achieve the alignments needed around meanings, roles, and accomplishing goals. Participating in anticipated ways (a mark of distribution over time) may make interaction and coordination more familiar and success relatively easier. However, misunderstandings, breakdowns in coordination and other unanticipated moments are routine and often easily tolerated in functional systems. If such disruptions are recognized, they may be quickly resolved, or only resolved over time. Successful participation in functional systems then depends not only on what people bring to the interaction, but also on the flexibility to make and remake alignments, to persist in the face of challenges, and to build new practices, identities, and artifacts as we move ahead. Communication is central to this routine work of making things work.

Traditionally, *communicative competence* has been a key term for thinking about communicative success. Much like the records of baseball pitchers, communicative competence has often been attributed to an individual; however, for success in an interaction, my history of language experiences needs to be aligned with the histories of other people, texts, and tools in the interaction and we need to align well together in the immediate interaction. In short, communicative competence is always a matter of distributed communication and the situated alignments among those interacting.

Distributed Communication and Cindy Magic

We can only make sense of the communicative interactions during *Cindy Magic* by attending to people's broader patterns of alignment around functional systems working to get things done (e.g., playing a game episode, finishing the folding clothes chore). For example, the emergence of "vampire bats" in *Cindy Magic* was a highly marked example of distributed communication. It displayed very clearly how particular meanings are situated in and emerge from both immediate interactions and distributed alignments over time. The interaction in Transcript 2.1 shows about a minute of play where the Magic sisters work together to outmaneuver Cruella de Vil, who has (suddenly) appeared in their backyard. The scenario begins with the first image in Figure 2.1 when P(Elizabeth) says: "What's she doing in our backyard?," referring to Cruella de Vil. N(Mary) and A(Jane) are huddling with him(her) looking down at the rug—enacting the three Magic sisters studying what she is doing in their backyard. In interviews, Paul reported that fighting Cruella de Vil was a familiar, oft-repeated scenario, so he quickly suggested routine solutions from past games by calling on familiar allies, robots and cheetahs.

However, Nora unexpectedly rejects these familiar allies (e.g., at the beginning of Transcript 2.1, when N(Mary) says: "The cheetahs are in their cage.") and does not offer alternatives. As the interaction unfolds, P(Elizabeth) seeks A(Jane)'s help, A(Jane) suggests the new ally (bats), and N(Mary) enthusiastically supports A(Jane)'s idea, acting as if bats were routine allies and quickly elaborating on the suggestion (vampire bats). In a fast series of interactions, the three decide (in and out of game frame) how to enact vampire bats and then deploy them in the game to achieve routine results (successfully defeating Cruella de Vil). This novel ally emerges successfully through the immediate distributed communication that aligns the players in this episode, but also through the long-term distributed work of the players (e.g., their history of creating and playing routine game scenarios) and the many cultural resources, practices, and identities assembled (e.g., use of English words and syntax, general ways of playing pretend games, and family identities).

Interactional Resources and Indexical Grounds

Communicative success depends critically on the interactional work of figuring out how language and other signs are situated in and *index* (i.e., point to, refer to) specific worlds, people, and activities of social spaces. We saw in the "She bought six of them!" example that, to make sense of this utterance, you need to imagine scenes where the reported event occurs (what she was doing, where the action happened) and the contexts of the report (the relationship of the speaker to the utterance, what the speaker was trying to achieve). We begin to explore now the ways communicative resources not only index objects and people, but also help in building both the indexed scenes and the interactional contexts. Linguists (e.g., Hanks, 1990, 1996) have described the scenes and interactional contexts as *indexical grounds.* The key question for us then is: ***How are people using interactional resources to build indexical grounds that support communicative success?***

Communicative success requires establishing and attending to the various indexical grounds that situate specific communicative resources (e.g., words, gesture, glances). Hanks (1990) described *indexical grounds* as central to referencing. The immediate sociomaterial space, including the co-present gathering of people, offers a default ground for *indexicality.* People routinely anchor communication by indexing people, things, and events in the immediate space of the interaction. People gesture to or look at people or objects to establish joint attention as well as using explicit verbal deictics (e.g., this, that, here, there, I, you, she, it, now, then). Although the immediate sociomaterial spaces always remain relevant, people also routinely refigure these spaces with imaginary indexical grounds. For example, as a speaker tells a story about a recent trip to Colorado, she may look over her shoulder and point up to the mountains whose peaks she is describing, as if she were in Colorado (even though there is just blue sky over her shoulder as she tells the story in Illinois). We also saw this kind of imaginary indexical ground in *Cindy Magic.* When Paul, Nora and Anna finished cleaning the mud off the rug, they resumed playing the Magic sisters and reimagined the rug as a window into the backyard where Cruella de Vil was lurking. They then spoke about, pointed to, and acted figuratively (P(bat) flying there to attack de Vil) in that scene.

Managing indexical grounds is constant work for people in all interactions, so the communicative resources people use to signal, build, and shift indexical grounds are particularly important for understanding how people communicate successfully. We focus here on two common *interactional resources* that signal who's talking: *modes of address* that index social identities and *reported speech*, where people speak as/for someone else.

Modes of address are a common communicative resource for conjuring particular indexical grounds, particularly in immediate sociomaterial spaces. Think about how you address people in your everyday interactions—you may call some family members by their first names, use special nick-names (or pet-names) to mark close ties (e.g., sweetie, honey), or use family relations alone (e.g., mom, dad) or in combination with other names (e.g., Auntie Anna; Grandma Mabel). We often switch modes of address to call forth different sociocultural activities and highlight different social positionings. For example, doctoral students and colleagues who call me by my first name (Julie) during research meetings will often refer to me by my title (Dr. Hengst) when they guest lecture in my large undergraduate classes. Likewise, before a city council meeting, members may use first names as they greet one another, but moments later may address one another by institutional roles (Ms. Mayor, Mr. Chairman, Councilperson Haddad). The sociomaterial space and gathering across these moments may *look* the same, but the switch from first names to titles both proposes and indexes a change in the sociocultural activity and indexical grounds: it encourages members and audiences to align to moments of interaction as a government meeting of officials.

Reported speech involves the diverse resources people use as they speak for or as someone else. In reported speech, the indexical grounds shift as the words I utter no longer index me in the here-and-now, but someone else (or me elsewhere). We can easily recognize highly marked cases where actors play a role on stage, comedians perform impersonations of others, and children speak as characters in make-believe play (as illustrated in transcripts from *Cindy Magic*). However, in everyday interactions people are so remarkably agile in speaking for others and following when others do the same that we often do not even notice it.

An interesting example of this agility can be seen Deborah Tannen's (2007) analysis of a conversation between a group of mothers over lunch. The mothers were talking about how, when their children reached a certain age, the parents could choose not to participate with them in activities. Look at the three lines of Tannen's transcript (2007, p. 113) featuring one mother, Daisey:

> Daisey: Yeah, that's when I start to say . . .
> "Well . . . I don't think I'll go in the water this time.
> Why don't you kids go on the Ferris wheel. I'll wave to you."

Daisey offers three utterances in sequence. In the second, she says: "I don't think I'll go in the water this time." With no transition, she then says: "Why don't you kids go on the Ferris wheel, I'll wave to you." The first utterance is indexically grounded in the here-and-now lunch conversation. It is clear that the indexical grounds for the next two utterances are not (e.g., that the "you" she will wave to is not one of the other mothers at the table). What is fascinating is how economically three distinct indexical grounds are managed here. The second conjures up Daisey speaking to one or more of her children by some (unspecified) swimming site (a pool, river, lake). The third then seamlessly conjures up a different indexical ground, an amusement park. We can be pretty sure the other mothers followed these fast, sparse jumps and didn't imagine that there was a Ferris wheel in the water or that Daisey had shifted to recommending that they (the other mothers at the table) go on a Ferris wheel.

We can see another striking example of this agility in speaking as/for others in a SDA of solid-state physicists in a laboratory meetings at a US university (Ochs, Gonzales, & Jacoby, 1994). As members of the team talked about their work, they routinely referenced themselves as agents (e.g., "when I added this . . .") as well as referencing the physical characteristics of their objects of study as agents (e.g., "it then searched for . . ."). However, the physicists also used blended forms where they used first person pronouns to speak *as* their objects of study. An example of this is displayed by Ron, the principal investigator, in the following transcript. (Note: This transcript uses CA conventions discussed in Chapter 1, with square brackets and doubled parentheses indicating the relative timing of actions, gestures and talk, and it stipulates for this interaction that "a" and "b" indicate two specific areas on a graph Ron points to on the whiteboard.)

Ron: Well you also said [(the) same thing must happen <u>h</u>ere.
                               [((moves to board, points to b))
         [When [I come down [I'm in [the domain state.
         [((points to a))   [[
                  [((moves finger to b)) [
                               [((moves finger to a))
                                  [((moves finger to b))
Miguel: Yeah
                                              (Ochs et al., 1994, p. 343)

The "domain state" refers to an area Ron is pointing to in the graph as he moves his finger between two areas of the graph (a and b in the transcript). The domain state is a condition where atomic spins in specialized magnetic materials (diluted antiferromagnets) are partially ordered, a phase transition between conditions (temperature and magnetic field strength) in which the atomic spins are disordered and ones in which they exhibit stable, long-term order. The properties of such magnetic materials have potentially exciting applications in electronics.

What is interesting from a communicative perspective is that Ron's utterance, "when I come down, I'm in the domain state," conjures up an indexical ground where the conditions of temperature and magnetic state are imagined as a physical space and where "I" refers not to Ron (the PI in the lab group), but to Ron as a diluted antiferromagnet. Ron is *speaking as* the phenomena, which Ochs, Gonzalez and Jacoby noted was a common occurrence as the physicists repeatedly *spoke as* physical phenomena (using "I' and "we") across multiple meetings. Ochs et al. (1994) suggest these utterances enabled the "physicists to routinely manifest an extreme form of subjectivity by stepping into the universe of physical processes to take the perspective of physical constructs (i.e., to symbolically live their experiences) . . . [l]ike actors playing characters or reporters quoting others." (p. 349). Using the conventions of *Cindy Magic*, we might say that, when R(diluted antiferromagnet) says "When I am down . . .," he is also shifting indexical grounds from the here-and-now of the lab meeting to the theoretically imagined world of magnets experiencing changing physical conditions. These complex ways of speaking as and for others led Tannen (2007) to argue that—instead of referring to such utterances as linguistic forms for quotation (reported speech)—we should recognize them as instances of *constructed dialogue* and, I would add, as interactional resources for constructing indexical grounds.

Interactional Resources and Cindy Magic

In Chapter 1 we highlighted ways that Paul, Nora, and Anna routinely shifted between speaking and acting as themselves and speaking and acting as different characters. Within these interactions, social voices were also a powerful resource for creating and signaling the indexical grounds of *Cindy Magic*. Indeed, as they resumed speaking in character voices after the clean-up, the rug was refigured as the Magics' backyard, their social relationships were refigured as the three Magic sisters with N(Mary) the oldest (instead of Paul), and the family chore was reframed as cleaning up in preparation for a party the Magic sisters were hosting (instead of putting away Nora, Anna, Paul and Julie's clean laundry).

Modes of address served as a prominent interactional resource to manage the indexical grounds around *Cindy Magic*. When Nora, Anna, and Paul addressed one another by their character names (e.g., Mary, Jane, and Elizabeth), they were signaling that the *Cindy Magic* world was the relevant indexical ground for making sense of what they were saying. Likewise, when Paul switched to using their family names (Nora, Anna) he was shifting from the world of *Cindy Magic* to their family identities and the sociomaterial space of the living room (e.g., the mud on the rug). Addressing each other with the names of the Magic sisters, as opposed to using Paul, Nora, Anna, or Dad, was often the most striking indication that they were even playing a make-believe game.

An analysis of speaking turns during this 22-minute episode identified 236 speaking turns that were addressed to a specific individual, with 76

(32 percent) of those turns directly addressing a recipient by name (e.g., "Nora, do you have mud on your shoes?" "What do you think, Jane?"). As shown in Table 2.1 Paul and Nora accounted for almost all of this direct address, most of which addressed a character. Paul used direct address over three times as often as Nora, and Anna did not produce direct address to signal alignment to the game. Of 34 utterances directed to specific individuals, Anna used direct address only two times, both addressed to Paul (e.g., "Daddy), not a character. Nora, on the other hand, used direct address much as Paul did (with 88 percent of direct address to characters compared to 79 percent for Paul). Although there were marked differences in *production* of modes of address, all three participants, including Anna, routinely responded appropriately to the name they were addressed by, aligning successfully around either the game or the family.

It was also fascinating to analyze the complex ways that *speaking and acting as* characters (constructed dialogue) were used in *Cindy Magic* by all three players. For example, at one point, when Paul asked Anna to not fold the towels on the floor, she did not respond at all (not even looking at him). Nora then said, "Say Jane." Paul then repeated his request, this time addressed to A(Jane): "Jane . . ." However, A(Jane) next rejected Paul's request by imaginatively reporting (in a calm, matter-of-fact manner) "my mom told me to do it this way." Invoking the indexical grounds of a directive from the absent "Cindy Magic" as authority over middle sister P(Elizabeth) was effective in fending off the request, and N(Mary) confirmed A(Jane)'s representation. In Transcript 2.1, we see another interesting example of *speaking/acting as* practices. Nora uses direct address ("Dad") to shift out of game frame and they have a side-conversation about how to play the new ally, vampire bats. Nora suggests to Paul both a bat voice: "Go like * [squeaky noises]" and an embodied way to act out vampire bats [*flapping arms]. The combination of gestural and vocal resources reinforces the point made in Chapter 1 about social voices: that voicing others routinely blends language, content, ways of speaking (e.g., paralinguistics), facial expressions, embodied stances, and ways of gesturing/acting.

Table 2.1 Number of turns each speaker (Paul, Nora, Anna) directed to another person during the 22-minute episode, the number of those turns that included a direct address (DA) form, and the number of DA turns that referenced either CM characters or family.

Speaker	# turns addressed to specific person	Use of Direct Address (DA)		
		# turns using DA	DA to CM Character	DA to Family
Paul	129	57	45 (79%)	12 (21%)
Nora	73	17	15 (88%)	2 (12%)
Anna	34	2	0 (0%)	2 (100%)
Totals	**236**	**76**	**60**	**16**

Note on Methods: Keeping Field Notes and Conducting Interviews

Participant observation is an approach to data collection developed by anthropologists and widely used in qualitative methods (see Miller et al., 2003). The term highlights that observers are always participants in observations and that decisions about how to interpret observational data depend on the nature of that participation. Participation involves not only the observer's immediate role during an observation, but also their longer-term participation around the activity and with the people. For example, although I remained a silent off-camera observer during the *Cindy Magic* episode reported here, as a family member my long-term participation in the *Cindy Magic* game and with these participants was quite engaged and complex. I drew on that long-term participation to understand and interpret this particular play episode. As noted in the last chapter, it is axiomatic that the interpretive work of observers in understanding what is going on is very much like the interpretive work of participants in interactions being observed; however, ethnographic methods have also emphasized the importance of taking a more critical, open, and systematic stance to interpretation. Thus, researchers keep *field notes* to systematically record their evolving interpretation of interactional data, revisit and elaborate on those interpretations over time, and seek multiple perspectives relevant to the interactional data by conducting *interviews* with participants.

Ethnographic *field notes* are designed to capture both details about the study and the researcher's evolving perspectives. Researchers may use field notes to document logistical and factual information (e.g., dates/times of contact with participants; schedules of planned data collection activities), to capture their on-the-fly reflections and questions about the data, and to draft emerging interpretations. As I suggested in Chapter 1, field notes allow researchers to document details from observations that are not captured by video recording, including descriptions of the broader sociomaterial space, how/when participants arrived, a sense of participants' moods and stances, and the researcher's perspective on the manner of their own participation and their post-observation impressions. Finally, researchers also use field notes to keep a record of unexpected opportunities, such as unplanned interactions with participants (e.g., informal or incidental interviews and observations). In my study of *Cindy Magic*, I kept a spiral notebook with hand-written chronological entries about the study. Since unplanned conversations about *Cindy Magic* were common in our family, I would often take notes on scraps of paper and later transfer them to my field notebook. Between data collection sessions, I would periodically review my notes and make new entries on my emerging understandings and questions.

As noted in this chapter, SDA recognizes that communication involves partial and varied understandings of what is going on and that people's experiences of communicative success change during an interaction as well as over longer times (as people reflect on what happened). Ethnographic research has developed ways of interviewing people to elicit their situated interpretations. Interviews with individual participants or small groups are typically *semi-structured*, which means the researcher plans some specific topics or questions but does not stick strictly to a script, allowing for an interview that builds off of participants' responses and invites participants to raise unexpected topics or ask questions. Early in a study, interviews can be useful ways for researchers to gain understanding about the site and negotiate plans for observations and data collection (e.g., deciding together with participants what activities, participants, and places would be best for the research). Another rich way of building dialogue, *stimulated elicitation interviewing*, asks participants to view and discuss already collected data. For example, after a video observation, the researcher might prepare some segments of the video, play them for one or more participants, and ask them to discuss particular points or to stop the tape anytime they notice something interesting. Although asking general questions in semi-structured interviews can produce interesting responses, I have found that stimulated elicitation interviews often result in participants offering precise, richly detailed observations.

In studying *Cindy Magic*, I conducted a series of semi-structured interviews with Paul, Nora, and Anna; stimulated elicitation interviews with each of them from the videotapes; and an informal group interview with all three where I asked them to talk together about what made the game fun (thus capturing their responses to one another as they engaged in these reflections). Interviews can provide critical insights into interactions. For example, in one episode, Nora had initiated making the cheetahs invisible. I wondered how Anna, then a bit over 4 years old, understood invisibility. So, in an interview I asked Anna to tell me about invisible cheetahs, she replied by covering her eyes and said, "you can't see me." Although she aligned smoothly with the activity in the game, her reply in the interview suggests her sense of what it meant to be "invisible" was different from Paul's and Nora's.

Clinicians routinely keep case notes about their work with individual clients. However, in my experience, clinical case notes are focused on routine clinical data (e.g., what assessments have been or should be done, names of client's family members, what treatments were done, professional referrals the client requested) and offer limited space for promoting interpretive work by clinicians or clients. SDA invites us to rethink clinical case notes to consider how to make them sites of inquiry that support case-based clinical inquiry to inform interpretations of diagnostic measures, to learn about the communicative needs of clients in everyday sociomaterial spaces, and to tailor interventions to those needs.

Chapter Summary: The Communicative Competence of Functional Systems

This chapter has explored ways to recognize and understand how interactional alignments determine communicative success (understood as good enough, not perfect agreement). First, we identified *functional systems* as a situated unit of analysis designed to examine the real-time, dynamic work of assembling shifting mixes of sociocultural activities. Second, we identified *distributed communication* as the situated ways people creatively align and coordinate participation and flexibly re-organize around the unanticipated. Distributed communication means that communicative success is always distributed and thus must be seen as the distributed accomplishment of the functional system, not of any individual speaker. Finally, turning to resources, we focused on *interactional resources* that establish, sustain, and shift *indexical grounds*. To focus on questions of success, we modified our questions from Chapter 1 about activity, participation, and resources to ask:

- *What is being accomplished by the functional system?*
- *How are people successfully coordinating their participation in functional systems?*
- *How are people using interactional resources to build indexical grounds that support communicative success?*

With these questions, SDA starts from the assumption that judgments of communicative success must always be couched in terms of the goals of people in specific interactions—i.e., of success for something as defined by someone. Given that people routinely manage and orient to multiple activities, both anticipated and unanticipated, SDA also recognizes that analysis of success must be complex (not simple), distributed (across people and tools, not attributable to any individual), and a matter of degree (with some successes in any interaction and different perspectives on success by different participants).

SDA details the distributed and collaborative work, sometimes quite extended across time and sociomaterial spaces, that people engage in to achieve successful interactions. For example, in an article exploring the diverse semiotic resources people use to represent others (Prior et al., 2006), we highlighted the kind of embodied rehearsals that are regularly a part of everyday interactions. In that article, Kevin Roozen analyzed interactions among members of a college sketch comedy group, *Potted Meat*. Observing the group's rehearsals as well as their public performances, Roozen analyzed the development and performance of a skit called "That's what little dreams are made of." In it, a member of the group, Lindsey, repurposed a poem she had written in high school in response to an assignment to use vocabulary of the week in a Valentine's Day card. Lindsey had written a sad poem that featured a bee dying after stinging a child. She decided to use that poem as the basis for a sketch about grade school children asked to use advanced vocabulary words in a play for their parents. Initially, stanzas of the poem were broken out for multiple speakers (Child 1; Child 2, etc.). In rehearsals, the Meats distributed roles, worked to give the kids personalities (e.g., very sweet child seeking approval), and added stage directions. After deciding they would perform as children acting out the sun's rays, wind blowing, trees, and flowers, the rehearsals often centered on figuring out *how* to embody, for example, a child representing the rays of the sun. Like Paul and Nora discussing how Paul should play vampire bats, the Meats would try out and discuss different ways to voice and embody each child. Finally, the rehearsals led to a public performance of the sketch. Whether in the fleeting interactions of *Cindy Magic* analyzed in this chapter or the longer chain of interactions from Potted Meat rehearsals to their performance, people were developing specific arrays of semiotic resources to become recognizable as being a vampire bat or a schoolgirl acting as flower.

In communicative interactions, people routinely construct, follow, and change indexical grounds as activities shift and as imagined indexical grounds are layered into sociomaterial spaces. The communicative resources that signal such shifts and build indexical grounds represent the basic machinery of communicative interaction and are key to communicative success. When considering the relationship between Nora's recommendations to Paul on how to voice and act out a vampire bat and the conversations among the Potted Meat group about how to enact particular kids in the skit acting as trees, birds, or rays of sunshine, a key question is how people learn to participate in such complex activities and manage these communicative resources. We turn to that question in Chapter 3.

Reflective Observations

1. *Extending your sample analysis*. Review the video data and transcript you made for Chapter 1 to begin to trace *how* people were successful in communicating:

    a. What functional systems are evident in your data and what is being accomplished?

    b. How is the distributed communicative competence of the functional system different from the skills/abilities of any one person or tool?

    c. What interactional resources are people using to establish the relevant indexical grounds (e.g., what are people pointing to with gestures and words)?

2. *Marking social identities*. Think about people you know well in your everyday life and keep a log of the modes of address you use when talking with them, or when talking about them to others. Now, do the same thing for strangers. Compare your analyses and discuss how varied social identities impacted your indexical work.

3. *Assembling and coordinating functional systems*. Think about something you are particularly skillful at doing *and* are willing to teach to someone else. It could be using tools for a specific hobby (e.g., using binoculars for bird watching; doing a long-tail cast-on for knitting), a life skill

(e.g., reading a city bus schedule, using google maps), or a practical activity (e.g., putting together a new piece of furniture, fixing a sink). Arrange for at least two people to join you in this task (i.e., people willing to learn the skill or assist in the activity). Record your interaction in some way (e.g., video or audio recording with still photos and field notes). Review the recordings and consider these questions: How successful do you think your interaction was? How did you set up the sociomaterial space and use it? How did you use interactional resources to manage indexical grounds? How did each person participate in the activity?

Suggested Readings

SDA offers detailed insights into how people can be successful in communicating and managing everyday activities. Reading multiple examples from varied settings will help you hone your attention to the complexity, dynamics, and resources for communicative success. Here are three texts (in addition to those cited throughout this chapter) that offer insightful situated discourse analyses of ways people communicate successfully. As you read, use the guiding questions in this chapter to understand the interactions each describes.

1. "Language in context and language as context: The Samoan respect vocabulary" (Duranti, 1992). In this chapter, Alessandro Duranti details respect vocabulary in Samoan, analyzing how its use in everyday interactions doesn't just index status or relationships, but actually proposes and, if successful, activates certain identities, rights and responsibilities, highlighting the dynamic ways social roles are constructed by participants within specific interactions.
2. "Interactive frames and knowledge schemas: Examples from a medical examination/interview" (Tannen & Wallat, 1987). In this article, Deborah Tannen and Cynthia Wallat draw on Goffman's concept of participation frameworks to analyze the complex ways a physician in a medical consultation manages multiple frames in simultaneously interacting with a child-patient and the child's mother.
3. "Seeing as situated activity: Formulating planes" (Goodwin & Goodwin, 1996). In this chapter, Charles and Marjorie Goodwin analyze communicative interactions in an airport operations room where airline employees monitor and coordinate ground crews managing planes. The analysis highlights the surprising ways the professionals in this setting coordinate their attention and interpretations as they build and then deconstruct a particular indexical ground from a visual display of a jet bridge.

Chapter 3

Situated Learning and Everyday Communicative Interactions

In the first two chapters, we have begun exploring the marvelously complex and dynamic texture of everyday communicative interactions. In this chapter, we shift from questions of what is going on and how communication can be successful to questions of learning. In its broadest sense, learning involves how behavior changes over time in response to experience. However, learning is often conceptualized as novices (often children) gaining knowledge and skills from experts (often adults) through some kind of intentional instruction. That general representation of learning is codified in school curricula, promoted in how-to books and websites, and conveyed through common ways we talk about teaching and studying. Much like the example of baseball statistics (where a team's success playing against other teams is collapsed into a pitcher's win-loss record), this way of talking about learning collapses complex histories of participation in functional systems into a simple matter of transmitting isolated skills from one person to another.

In contrast, *situated discourse analysis* (SDA) recognizes learning as always situated. The core premise is that people *learn how* to participate in communicative interactions *by* participating in communicative interactions: learning is, therefore, a dimension, or consequence, of every interaction. Learning may lead to positive changes we value (e.g., getting better at telling stories), may result in changes that are negative (e.g., learned helplessness, learned prejudice), or may function mainly to reinforce and sustain existing practices, which is still change as is acknowledged in the maxim *use it or lose it.* Situated learning then is distributed as all participants (adults/experts and children/novices) in any give interaction are learning through their engagement in functional systems. SDA understands people's engagement in communicative interactions and communicative environments as the fundamental *mechanism* of learning, not simply a *medium* for transmitting knowledge and skills.

The challenge for researchers and clinicians alike is to identify *what* learning is happening and at what level. To do so, we need to attend to complex patters of change over time. Thinking about teams and other specialized groups designed to perform specific activities is useful here. For example, as an orchestra practices, you can trace multiple points of learning. Individual players are maintaining and enhancing their skills with their instruments. They may also be learning to read the written music, to enact a specific emergent interpretation of the music under the conductor's direction, and to coordinate the strengths, limits, and goals of the orchestra. They are learning to perform *this* music *with* the others in the group. Learning is not individual and isolated; it is *learning with—with* their instruments, *with* a specific piece of music, *with* the other players and the conductor in the orchestra, *with* the acoustics of the spaces they play in, and ultimately *with* the audiences they play for.

As in the example of the orchestra, this chapter focuses on learning as optimization, as positive (or desired) changes in persons and in functional systems of activity. We will explore ways of analyzing the processes and outcomes of *situated learning*. After introducing another episode of *Cindy Magic*, we first ask how functional systems (like the orchestra) are changing over time. Then, we consider how people's *shifting patterns of participation* within and across functional systems serve as a key marker of learning. Finally, we explore the value of differentiating *durable* (more predictable) from *emergent* (more improvised) communicative resources.

The Case of *Cindy Magic*: Enacting Invisible Cheetahs

When I designed the two-year study of *Cindy Magic*, I was very interested in tracing situated learning—that is, how the game world was evolving, how the players patterns of participation were shifting, and how their use communicative resources stabilized or expanded. I recorded four observations of Paul, Nora, and Anna playing *Cindy Magic*, two in the car when they were running errands, and two folding clothes in our living room. The two living room observations were recorded seven months apart, the first in March and the second in October. Chapters 1 and 2 focused on excerpts from the earlier (March) recording; in this chapter, I introduce an excerpt from the later (October) recording, analyze what happened in it, and compare it with the March observation. In October everyone was seven months older: Nora was 8;5, Anna was 4;0, and Paul was 40. The October episode lasted about 10 minutes (about half the length of the March episode). The images in Figure 3.1 show two screen captures of Paul, Nora and Anna gathered in the living room folding clothes and playing *Cindy Magic*. Again I was positioned off camera in the adjacent room.

The first image in Figure 3.1 shows A(Jane) down on one knee as she starts a dialogue with the cheetahs where she will take on both character roles. She then jumps up and runs to the cheetahs (behind Paul), addressing them in a space toward the window, and finally turns around, pauses, and starts an embodied performance of a cheetah attacking P(CdV), pulling on Paul's left arm while she growls. The second image comes a bit later in the interaction. P(CdV) has just complained about the cheetahs attaching her. N(Mary) confronts P(CdV)'s complaint with a long turn first speaking as herself ("they're invisible"), then speaking for the pants: "How can you tell it's cheetahs. I'm

(a)

(b)

Figure 3.1 Two screen-captures from the October episode of *Cindy Magic*. a) A (Jane) calls the cheetahs "Cheetahs, come here quick!" and A(Cheetah) quickly answers "Why?" b) After N(Mary) asks P (Cruella de Vil) "how do you know it's cheetahs? You can't see anything" then A(cheetah) takes Paul's head in her hands and, looking intently says, "See:: I'm a cheetah."

Julie the pants. I'm Julie the pants. How d'you know it's cheetahs, you can't see anything." Anna responds to Nora's turn by grasping the side of Paul's head and moving nose to nose with Paul. Then, speaking as a cheetah directly to Cruella de Vil, she immediately refashions Nora's "You can't see anything," saying "See:: I'm a cheetah!" P(CdV) responds: "I can see you."

Transcript 3.1 shows the interactions around these images. Shortly before this excerpt begins, N(Mary) had initiated a scenario familiar to Paul and

Transcript 3.1 "See:: I'm a cheetah!" from the October episode of *Cindy Magic* (approximately 1 minute of interaction).

P:	uhhh I'm
N:	XXXXX These pants* don't like Cruella deVil .1. These pants are-
A:	No it wasn't. It was- **
J:	
	*N shakes pants a lot ** A looks at N

P:	going to go get my hunters .1. and get to the bottom of this
N:	
A:	Cheetahs come here quick! Why?
J:	

P:	
N:	(XXXXXX XXXXXXXXXXXXXXXXXX)
A:	C- *Caus- Cause the hunters are coming in our house an- an- and* the .1. and Cruella
de	
J:	
	*A runs to cheetahs *P looks at A over his shoulder

P:	.... 4 .... Are you a
N:	(XXXXXX XXXXXXXXXXXXXXXXX)
A:	Vil is in our house. Okay, come get. Okay I will. Grrrr grrr **
J:	
	* N leans in toward P ** A tugging at P's arm

P:	Cheetah? Who am I? Do it again ..2.. Anna could you fold it up on
N:	
A:	Yeah Cruella de Vil*
J:	
	* A folding towel again

P:	the couch? Come on hunters
N:	Make the Cheetahs invisible. Make the cheetah invisible They're
A:	
J:	

P:	Ah no*not cheetahs ahhh **
N:	invisible. How can you tell it's cheetahs I'm Julie the pants. I'm Julie
A:	
J:	
	* A tugging at P again ** N wiggling pants a lot while folding them

P:	I can see you
N:	the pants how d'you know it's cheetahs you can't see anything
A:	*See:: I'm a cheetah.
J:	
	* A leans in face-to-face with P

Nora where the Magic sisters become invisible to confuse Cruella de Vil, and P(Elizabeth) handed out "invisible pills." At the top of the transcript, N(Mary) is acting out being invisible by making the pants (she is folding) dance around as if on their own, saying: "These pants don't like Cruella de Vil." Acting out a slightly confused Cruella de Vil (who can only see pants dancing and talking), P(CdV) interrupts N(Mary) saying: "Uhh I'm going to go get my hunters. .1. And get to the bottom of this." Then, Anna starts calling their allies (the cheetahs) to combat Cruella de Vil. When Anna plays (and plays out) both sides of an interaction between A(Jane) and A(cheetahs), Paul loses the thread of the scenario, breaking out of character to confer with Anna about what their roles are. He asks, "Are you a cheetah?" and "Who am I?" Still acting out the cheetah, but with less physical intensity (lightly pulling on Paul's arm), Anna answers "yeah" to the first question, then turns away to resume folding a towel on the floor, answering the second question "Cruella de Vil." Paul then says to Anna: "Do it again." Anna does not respond. After a moment, Paul again addresses Anna, asking her to fold the towel (which is already folded) up on the couch. Anna carries the towel to the couch while N(Mary) resumes the invisibility scenario calling for them to make the cheetahs invisible too. At this point, A(cheetah) begins grabbing onto P(CdV)'s arm and P (CdV) complains of the cheetah's attack, leading N (Julie the pants) to ask P (CdV) how she knows it's cheetahs. A(cheetah) then takes Paul's head in her hands, looks him in the eye and says "See:: I'm a cheetah."

Situating Learning in Functional Systems

In Chapter 2 we introduced functional systems as a basic unit of analysis for the study of everyday communicative interactions. Although functional systems are highly dynamic (continually assembled and reassembled around people's needs and goals), societies have many names for highly recognizable and routine functional systems: sports teams, orchestras, families, line crews with power companies, military units, and so on. These highly marked cases help us see that we routinely focus on the learning and accomplishments of functional systems. Teams are ranked by win/loss records across seasons regardless of which players were on the field for each game. Teams can improve their performance not only by improving individual skills but also by improving how players work together, and not only by flexibly using available tools, but also by redesigning existing tools or inventing new ones. Thus, we begin to explore situated learning by asking: *How are functional systems changing over time?*

Researchers taking up situated learning (e.g., Scollon, 2001; Lemke, 2000; Vygotsky, 1987) have argued that it is critical to trace how the moment-by-moment unfolding of specific interactions is linked to the patterns of change across broader timescales. In his research on how sailors on the bridge of a

US Navy ship used tools to repeatedly compute the ship's position, Hutchins (1995) traced changes across three timescales:

- the moment-to-moment changes in the immediate interactions (how the goals for functional systems get accomplished and how people communicate to coordinate those accomplishments);
- the consequences of that activity for the development of the people involved (how individuals get better at what they are doing, but also get better at working with specific, or specific kinds, of other people); and
- the consequences of the immediate activity for changes in sociocultural practices and specialized tools.

Hutchins's (1995) analysis traced the way the ship's location was calculated in the moment-to-moment activity of a team of sailors working with an array of sociocultural tools.

However, to understand how this functional system could successfully calculate the ship's current location, Hutchins had to trace the longer histories embedded in the sailors' navigational tools (e.g., maps and charts produced and annotated in preceding decades, years, months, weeks, days, hours, and minutes) and *cultural practices* (repeated cultural ways of doing things that spread across functional systems over time). Because the specialized and varied abilities of individuals filling different roles on the bridge navigation team were important, Hutchins also considered their (ontogenetic) development.

His analysis also highlighted the need for flexibilities within functional systems. For example, as he observed the team navigating into port one day, the ship experienced a dangerous and unexpected loss of power. The loss not only disrupted their access to navigational tools and routine means of communication, but also severely limited the ship's maneuverability. The bridge team had to make rapid changes in their functional system to maintain control of the ship. They changed goals, abandoning the aim of sailing into port and redirecting the ship to anchor offshore. They also shifted the ways they communicated, did calculations, and worked together. When imagined only in terms of change in an individual, learning is reduced to only the middle facet of Hutchins's three trajectories. However, from the perspective of distributed communication, all three of these trajectories must be integrated to trace situated learning.

Functional Systems and the Changing World of Cindy Magic

We will start our analysis of changes in *Cindy Magic* by tracing changes in the play world created by Paul, Nora, and later Anna. In the October episode, Paul, Nora, and Anna were drawing on histories of play and details of the *Cindy Magic* world that had developed over five and a half years. Looking at the emergence of *Cindy Magic* over years of play in this family is valuable in understanding the mix of activities around game play. As they repeatedly played together, the repertoire of scenarios accumulated, players developed a feel for both the game world and how it integrated into everyday spaces and activities (like folding clothes in the living room), and certain actions became routine. Drawing on interviews, research notes, and observations of play, I was able to trace both changes in the *Cindy Magic* world the players were creating as well as changes in the routine patterns of play.

As noted in Chapter 1, *Cindy Magic* grew from Nora's fascination with Disney's animated *101 Dalmatians* movie, and her concern for the puppies Cruella de Vil had kidnapped. On a long highway car trip, Nora (then aged 3;11) began imagining and talking about a good counter-character who would save baby animals from Cruella de Vil. She named that character Cruella Magic. Nora and Paul began acting out scenarios where Cruella Magic (played by Nora) would find and save lost or stolen baby animals. Paul would play the part of an animal parent who would call Cruella Magic (Nora) by phone or knock on her door (actually, the driver's side window) to ask about their lost babies with alliterative names: "Hello, this is Holly Hippopotamus. I've lost my children: Henry, Heather, Homer, and Hannah. Do you have them?" Cruella Magic (Nora) would always have rescued the animal children and would return them to the parent, who would express her relief and gratitude. After a brief pause, the next animal parent would arrive and ask about her missing children. The make-believe world of these first episodes was limited in scope, with only two main characters and highly repetitive scenarios of reuniting animal children with their parents.

Across months and years of play, the world of *Cindy Magic* expanded. Nora and Paul added new members to the Magic family and the world and its scenarios became more elaborated, complex, and connected. Nora and Paul acted out both mundane activities (e.g., Mary and Elizabeth chatting about their days while preparing a dinner—a scenario typically not played in the kitchen) and extended fantastic plots (e.g., the Magic sisters using satellites and robots to discover and fend off Cruella de Vil's planned attack or kidnaping). Similar scenarios were played out over and over (much like household routines of real families). As in the first car trip, playing the game to pass the time continued to be a motive, but spaces and activities expanded to include running errands around town and household chores (e.g., cleaning house, folding clothes, doing dishes). As part of that pattern, game play often paused during breaks (e.g., a stop at a gas station, shopping in a store) or an episode was brought to a just-in-time conclusion as the other activity ended. In other words, the background activity of the family chore was instrumental in regulating the foreground activity of game play, that is, when and how each episode of *Cindy Magic* would unfold.

As the world of *Cindy Magic* grew, new characters and players came (and sometimes left), each leaving their mark on the game world. Nora shifted her usual role from Cruella Magic to *Cindy Magic* (Cruella Magic's sister) and eventually Mary Magic, Cindy's oldest daughter. Paul started routinely playing Elizabeth Magic (Mary's younger sister) as well as acting out Cruella de Vil and her growing number of evil henchmen. During the brief time I joined in (about a year into playing), Nora and Paul had already settled into a routine of playing primarily as Mary and Elizabeth Magic. I entered as Aunt Penelope, and quickly became Great Aunt Penelope, the oldest living member of the Magic family. However, I could never get the hang of the game, and Nora was often frustrated with, and directive of, my participation (in ways she wasn't with Paul)—she didn't trust me to play right. I stopped playing, but Great Aunt Penelope lived on—often referred to as an off-stage presence during game play.

Although Anna had been present for many episodes of game play since she was born, the functional system and game world went through marked alterations when Anna began playing around 2;6 years (much younger than Nora when Nora and Paul first began playing). Anna had to be socialized into motivations of playing (e.g., to pass the time while completing a chore), to the Magic family relationships and personalities, and to a repertoire of scenarios (many of which were oriented to Nora, then 6 years old). Anna shifted the game to faster, more routinized interactions (more like the ones Nora initially engaged in). For Anna, finding and dealing quickly (and often loudly) with Cruella de Vil was one of the most engaging parts of *Cindy Magic*.

My research on the game took place as *Cindy Magic* was about to become rarer. Nora was getting older and Nora and Anna sought different kinds of fun in the game, often struggling to realize their goals (which made game play harder). However, as a research study *Cindy Magic* continues to be discussed two decades later, and it has been a focus of several articles and chapters (Hengst, 2015; Hengst & Miller, 1999; Prior et al., 2006). And, of course, the game owes particular debts to the story of *101 Dalmatians* and the animated and live action Disney movies depicting that world. *Cindy Magic* then offers a glimpse of how moment-to-moment interactions in very local spaces shape human lives that move across temporal scales as practices and resources persist over decades and across wider spaces.

Situated Learning as Shifting Patterns of Participation

Situated learning can be traced through changes in how people participate in functional systems over time. Lave and Wenger (1991) introduced the term *legitimate peripheral participation* to describe the way patterns of participation shift as people become more familiar with particular sociocultural activities, engage more fully and deeply with them, and come to be recognized by others as full participants in those practices. Defining learning as changes in participation, they observed newcomers to a practice typically participate in limited, peripheral ways, but as they continue to engage with the practice, their participation may expand and the practices themselves are altered by their ways of engaging in them. So, a central question for situated learning is: *How are peoples' patterns of participation changing over time?*

Lave and Wenger's account of *legitimate peripheral participation* focuses attention on the implicit as well as explicit ways novices are apprenticed into becoming fuller participants. One example they drew on came from Carole Cain's research on how alcoholics learn to tell a personal narrative of being an alcoholic through participating in Alcoholics Anonymous (AA) meetings (Cain, 1991). If you have never been to a meeting, you may have seen TV shows or movies that depict the recognizable moves in these narrative acts (e.g., a person walking to the front of a room in a church or community center and opening by saying, "Hi, I'm [first name], and I'm an alcoholic."). Cain documented a wide range of features that describe how people learn to participate in the AA narrative of being an alcoholic (e.g., that it is a disease that has no cure) and at the same time come to engage in a range of practices of recovery as they work to develop an identity as a non-drinking alcoholic. By hearing and reading AA stories and engaging in formal and informal interactions at AA meetings, people implicitly learn to tell this story, to take on the identities of living in recovery, and to change their social practices.

Research on situated learning has highlighted how children's participation in sociocultural activities is organized in very different ways across different cultural communities. Barbara Rogoff and her colleagues (Rogoff, 1990, 2003; Rogoff et al., 1993) have studied the ways mothers guide children to attend to, participate in, and converse with others during everyday communicative interactions. Rogoff describes situated learning as *guided participation*, emphasizing that "instead of viewing children as separate entities that become capable of social involvement, we may consider children as being inherently engaged in the social world from before birth" (1990, p. 22). Of course, adults organize children's participation in social interactions in diverse (often subtle and unmarked) cultural ways. For example, carrying a baby facing toward the mother focuses an infant's attention on the mother-child dyad, whereas carrying the baby facing out focuses the infant on multiple participants in activities. Guided participation is the means of *socialization*, which refers both to how children and other newcomers learn specific cultural practices and also how their uptakes of those practices continually produce and change those practices.

In comparative research across cultural contexts, Rogoff and her colleagues analyzed how mothers responded to their young children's requests for attention during group interactions. They found that when mothers in a Salt Lake City community in the US were interacting with adults, they would disattend to their children, but then would interrupt their interactions with adults to respond to their child's request. The Salt Lake City mothers marked these shifts from adult-focused to child-focused interactions with strong signals across multiple semiotic channels (particularly talk and gaze). In contrast, mothers in a Mayan community in Guatemala typically managed child–adult interactions simultaneously, without displaying sharp shifts of interactional focus. They divided semiotic resources, subtly sustaining some ongoing channels of contact (e.g., touch) with a child while directing other channels (e.g., talk) to an adult. The channels varied. For example, a mother might be talking to an adult while keeping a hand on a child and then turn slightly to talk to the child while handing something to the adult.

Rogoff and her colleagues showed how these different cultural approaches to guided participation shaped how children were *socialized to learn* to participate in new activities. These early practices with toddlers resonated with broader sociocultural activities of learning. For example, the middle-class US parents were guiding children into sociocultural practices that emphasize formal didactic learning in social spaces often sharply separated from daily life (much like US schools), whereas Guatemalan parents were guiding children to participate across their lifespan in sociocultural activities of everyday social spaces, what she and her colleagues have termed *Learning by Observing and Pitching-In* (LOPI) (Rogoff, 2003).[1]

Changing Patterns of Participation in Cindy Magic

Across the two years of my research, changes in Anna's participation were the most striking—both as captured in my analysis of their interactions and reported by Nora and Paul in interviews. To illustrate shifting patterns of participation in *Cindy Magic*, I focus here on the changes in Anna's participation from the March to October episodes (seven months apart in the life of a 3-year-old). In both episodes, Anna was a ratified, active, and effective participant: she engaged in the three main sociocultural activities (game play, folding clothes, and the research project) and maintained interactive alignments with others during points of transition into and out of game play (e.g., starting, ending, pausing play). Measures of productivity (e.g., number of clothing items folded; number of words spoken) indicate that Anna participated less than Nora and Paul did in both episodes; however, quantitative and qualitative changes in Anna's patterns of participation with folding clothes and playing *Cindy Magic* highlight changes in both the functional system and her participation.

The folding clothes activity was organized as a 3-step process: 1) selecting an item from the basket, 2) folding it, and 3) stacking it in the correct pile. I analyzed Nora, Anna, and Paul's ongoing participation by noting who completed which steps for each item of clothing. The 3-step process could be completed independently by one person or distributed across two or three people. Of the 54 clothing items in the March episode only 35 were folded independently (15 by Paul and 20 by Nora). Anna helped fold 19 items (15 jointly folded by Anna and Paul; 4 by Anna, Paul, and Nora) with Paul actively scaffolding her participation. For example, Paul would select and hand items to Anna with verbal directions for selection (e.g., "Let's do this big one together"), folding (e.g., "you take that corner") and stacking (e.g., "Are you done with that one Jane?"). Accompanying talk about the folding was rare with independently folded items and mostly limited to announcing overall progress (e.g., putting down a folded item, Paul said "Okay, now we got all the towels done"). In October, the three participants folded a total of 33 items, all done independently (21 by Paul, 11 by Nora, and 1 by Anna). In part due to the lack of distributed folding, there was very little talk about the folding process. Across these two observations then, Anna shifted from only jointly folding clothing items with verbal scaffolding and embodied support from Paul and Nora in March to folding one item independently in October. More subtly, the functional system also changed (e.g., from co-folding and intense verbal guidance in March to largely independent and non-verbal coordination in October).

During the October episode Anna also displayed fuller, more complex participation in *Cindy Magic*. Recall that this make-believe play was primarily managed through in-game dialogue, that is, by participants speaking as different characters. Indeed, a striking feature of these interactions was how densely verbal they were (evident in the lack of silence in the transcripts) and how agilely participants shifted speaking roles. Thus, as a broad measure of participation within and across sessions, we can look at both number of words and number of different character voices produced by Paul, Nora, and Anna. Table 3.1 shows the word counts for each speaker for excerpts from the episodes in March (Transcripts 1.1, 2.1) and October (Transcript 3.1).

Taking these samples as representative of their relative talk time, we can see that overall Anna used fewer words than either Paul or Nora during both the March and October scenarios. However, in October both Anna and Nora showed an increase in the percentage of words spoken and Paul showed a decrease when compared to the earlier (March) scenario.

Table 3.2 displays the character and personal voices used in the March and October episodes. Each column represents a participant and each row represents a voice that figured an identity (self or character). The use of character voices varied somewhat based on the scenarios being played during game episodes. The table shows it was fairly common for the same character to be voiced by more than one participant. For example, in the March episode, Paul and Nora both voiced a cheetah (which might or might not be

Table 3.1 Number (and percentage) of words spoken in excerpts from March (see Transcripts 1.1, 2.1) and October (see Transcript 3.1) *Cindy Magic* episodes.

Participant	Words (%) in March	Words (%) in October
Paul	99 (53%)	46 (35%)
Nora	58 (31%)	49 (38%)
Anna	29 (16%)	35 (27%)
Totals	**186**	**130**

Table 3.2 Voices used by Paul, Nora, Anna, and Julie in the March and October episodes of *Cindy Magic*. (Participants' ages at the time of the observations are included after the names. Parentheses around a voice indicate a *keying* as described in the text.)

March Episode (22 minutes)

Paul (39)	Nora (7;11)	Anna (3;5)	Julie (39)
self	self	self	self
Elizabeth	—	—	—
—	Mary	—	—
—	—	Jane	—
—	kitty	kitty	—
(bat) bat	(bat)	—	—
Cruella de Vil	—	Cruella de Vil	—
cheetah	*cheetah*	—	—

October Episode (11 minutes)

Paul (40)	Nora (8;6)	Anna (4;0)	Julie (40)
self	self	self	self
Elizabeth	—	—	—
—	Mary	—	—
—	Jane	Jane	—
Cruella de Vil	—	Cruella de Vil	—
cheetah	cheetah	cheetah	—
robot	robot	robot	—
door	—	—	—
hunters	—	—	—
—	—	door locks	—
—	(Micky the towel)	(Mickey the towel)	—
—	(Julie the shirt)	—	—
—	(Nighty the nightgown)	—	—
—	(Greenie the pants)	—	—
—	—	Aunt Cruella Magic	—
—	teacher	—	—
—	—	student	—

the same cheetah), and Paul and Anna both voiced Cruella de Vil. A voice with parentheses indicates the voice was framed as what Goffman called a *key*, such as an actor rehearsing or playing a role on stage. For example, in the March episode, Paul and Nora used a *rehearsal key* in a side conversation to confer about how to act out and voice a vampire bat before Paul played a bat in the game. In the October episode, Nora used a *pretense key* to act out voices for different clothing items (Mickey the towel, Julie the shirt, etc.) when N(Mary) was invisible and pretending to speak for clothes she was flapping in the air in order to confuse and taunt Cruella de Vil (who in the game world could only see the dancing clothes). During the 22 minutes of the March episode, the four of us used 11 different voices, including each of us speaking as ourselves. Paul and Nora each used 5 different voices and Anna 4 different voices. During the 11 minutes of the October episode, the four of us used 20 different voices with Nora using 10 different voices, Anna using 9, and Paul using 7 (Hengst & Prior, 1998; Prior, 2001).

Although Anna used multiple voices in both episodes, her repertoire of voices seems to have expanded. Not only did Anna use twice as many character voices in October in half the time, a really marked change, but she also shifted her use of different voices to create her own multi-turn dialogues between characters (as was seen in Transcript 3.1). Across these two episodes, using a keyed voice (e.g., rehearsing how to speak and act as a bat) was rare, and mainly done by Paul and Nora. However, in October, Anna did quietly repeat Nora's "Mickey the towel," seemingly to try out Nora's animated pronunciation (which involved a retroflexed /l/ sound, possibly imitating a Scottish accent from an audiotaped Disney story she listened to). Overall, Anna's participation in *Cindy Magic* play expanded from March to October as she displayed a deeper understanding of the game world and its communicative options. Interestingly, game play became more challenging for Paul and Nora as Anna participated more fully, as was seen in Paul losing the thread and asking Anna outside of the game frame what their characters were—"Are you a cheetah?" and "Who am I?" (see Transcript 3.1).

Durable and Emergent Communicative Resources

We recognize communicative resources of all kinds (e.g., a glance, a word, a gesture, a voice) as *potentially* meaningful (i.e., that they are, or could be meant to, communicate something) even if we struggle with (or are baffled by) their meaning. *Recognizable resources* are key for understanding what is going on and for coordinating interaction, that is, for *meaning-making* in communication. For example, in multilingual environments, we recognize when people are using language even if we don't know what language they are using. We may also recognize the familiar sounds, rhythms, and gestures of a specific language (e.g., Italian) even if we don't understand that language. Likewise, we often recognize people are speaking in English (or our native language) even when we can't make out what they are saying because of competing sounds (e.g., at a party, on a busy street). We may recognize a *register* like medical discourse (even when we don't understand its specialized terminology), a *genre* like a plenary talk in linguistics (even when we cannot understand the specific points), or a type of *utterance* like reported speech (even when we don't get the meaning of that report). It is important to realize that even partial understanding of highly recognizable (durable) resources supports communicative success and may be evidence of learning. Communicative success and learning also require making sense of resources that emerge in an interaction (including emergent repurposing of durable resources). In terms of the questions of learning in this chapter then, we are asking: ***How are durable and emergent resources changing over time?***

Briefly, *durable resources* are ones that are repeated and recognizable across interactions over time and across sociomaterial spaces. Durable resources form the bases for our named categories of communicative resources (e.g., words, gestures, turns) and routines (e.g., greeting a friend, answering a teacher's question in class). As both researchers and participants in communicative interactions, we tend to be aware of the durable resources in interactions and often focus on them in our observations (e.g., extensive attention to speaking turns). Durable resources are also most easily represented through textual conventions (e.g., standard spelling, punctuation conventions for marking a questioning intonation) and lend themselves most easily to measurement (e.g., word counts). *Emergent resources* are ones that are most uniquely and specifically situated within an interaction. Emergent resources include novel resources that participants did not anticipate or plan for (e.g., learning new words, developing nicknames for friends), as well as the novel ways that familiar resources are *repurposed* to meet the needs of specific participants within specific functional systems. Emergent resources are likely to be difficult to observe and interpret as they often involve fleeting adjustments of resources grounded in the unfolding conditions of an interaction.

Attending to emergent resources in interactions is critical for tracing situated learning. Emergent resources often highlight where there are flexibilities in functional systems, as new resources emerge in, and durable resources are repurposed for, immediate goals. Indeed, at the level of cultural change, every durable resource began as an emergent response to some situated interaction. For example, when Paul and Nora first began to play a game where Cruella Magic returned lost baby animals to their parents, there was no routine set of moves to rely on, yet they emergently built a recognizable pattern of interaction. Through repetition, it eventually became a durable routine in a small circle (though still with novel elements and situated emergence). In short, recognizability in an interaction is always built through a combination of durable and emergent resources.

Ron Scollon (2001) offers a valuable study of how such combinations develop over time in his research on *handing* as a family of practices. During weekly visits over a year, Scollon collected 1-hour observations of his wife's young cousin Brenda (from 1;0 to 2;0 years old) as she talked and played with her mother and other family members. His SDA looks at the ways family members handed things to Brenda and Brenda handed things to others, including how handing was often accompanied by, or coordinated through, linguistic and other communicative resources. As Brenda repeatedly engaged with increasingly varied and complex instances of handing, her motor and communicative repertoire grew. Scollon pointed to the way these kind of relatively simple practices continue to change as people participate in more complex sociocultural activities. Consider buying a cup of coffee from a barista, handing out leaflets on a public street, completing political rituals around the transfer of power (e.g., handing over a flag to transfer territorial control), or doing forensic police work (e.g., handing physical evidence to be bagged for analysis in a crime lab). Combining physical actions, contextual goals, and required or possible accompanying talk and gesture, handing develops into a family of practices that appear in many functional systems. Scollon's analysis highlights the way repeated engagement in everyday interactions using durable and emergent resources builds such families of practices.

Durable resources often involve multimodal arrays of communicative resources (discussed in Chapters 1 and 2) that together signal something more than the sum of the individual elements. For example, a typified social voice may be enacted through aligned combinations of linguistic, paralinguistic, nonverbal, and discursive resources. In terms of situated learning, children come to communicatively enact and display recognizable personal identities and social roles. Goffman (1981) noted the overlooked importance of the fact that children and others—dolls, toy robots and animals (like Anna's toy kitty in Figure 1.1 and Transcript 1.1)—are routinely spoken and acted for by others:

"even as the child learns to speak, it learns to speak for, learns to speak in the name of figures that will never be, or at least aren't yet, the self. George Herbert Mead notwithstanding, the child does not merely refer to itself through a name for itself that others had first chosen; it learns just as early to embed the statements and mannerisms of a zoo-full of beings in its own verbal behavior."

(p. 159)

When Goffman mentions mannerisms as well as statements, he is recognizing that children do not simply learn to speak for/as a zoo-full of beings, but also to stand, yell, and move for/as those beings; to project virtual indexical grounds populated with a zoo-full of beings over the everyday world; and, not incidentally, to re-equip and repopulate the zoo. Indeed, many of the data examples presented in the book so far, including Nora, Paul, and Anna creating vampire bats (Transcript 2.1) and the Potted Meat comedy group performing as young children acting as trees and sun rays (see the summary for Chapter 2), highlight the rich ways that everyday interactions support ongoing development of durable and emergent social voices.

Durable and Emergent Resources in Cindy Magic

Turning back to *Cindy Magic*, the question is how durable and emergent resources are changing over time. Comparing the March and October episodes, we have already noted qualitative changes in ways Anna used communicative resources to enact character voices, built dialogue to develop scenarios, and recognized and resolved potential misunderstandings with others. A particularly striking example of these changes can be seen in a long interactional turn where Anna animates both Jane and the cheetahs. I re-present that stretch (from Transcript 3.1) here as a turn-by-turn transcript to highlight how Anna enacted and shifted these character roles:

A(Jane):   Cheetahs come here quick! [A(Jane) calls out loudly, looking up toward the window by the chair]

A(cheetah): Why?

A(Jane):   C- Caus-** Cause the hunters are coming in our house an-an- and the .1. and Cruella Vil is in our house. [** A(Jane) stands up and walks to the window to address the cheetahs; her back is to Paul]

A(cheetah): Okay

A(Jane):   Come. Get.

A(cheetah): Okay, I will.** Grrr grr. [** A(Jane) turns around at "okay, I will' and then leans back and pauses looking down at the floor before looking up, growling, and embodying the cheetah attacking P(Cruella de Vil)].

In this long turn, Anna bounded her shifting embodiment of Jane and the Cheetahs with physical pauses and realignments of her body and gaze (e.g., standing and directing her statements to the window, which was presumably where the cheetahs were huddled). To mark changes in character voices, she used mode of address, typical interactional sequences, and paralinguistic resources (e.g., "Cheetahs, come here quick! Why?"). The recognizable multimodal array of resources that marked her use of voices combined with the temporal placement of her turns point to her changing participation in *Cindy Magic*.

Anna's fast, multi-character interaction is in sharp contrast to her use of resources in the March episode (compare Figures 1.1 and 2.1 to Figure 3.1). In March, Anna used a relatively limited repertoire of voices (Jane calling the "vampire bats") and gestures (pointing for P(bat) to fly down to attack Cruella de Vil), a gesture that N(Elizabeth) verbally translated and seamlessly folded into the interaction. Her use of resources was less recognizable (e.g., filler words, mispronunciations) and less differentiated (e.g., whether she spoke as Jane or as Anna, she sounded and looked the same). She used her toy cat as a prop, animating it to drink milk and playfully attack P(Elizabeth). However, the kitty voice she used was limited to animal-type sound effects (e.g., growling). In Figure 3.1, Anna's multi-part dialogue is so fast that Paul loses track. When she jumps over and starts grabbing and shaking his arm while growling, Paul looks at her puzzled and asks, "Are you a cheetah?" Apparently, he missed her whole dialogic performance.

In my interviews with Paul and Nora, they both commented on how the world of *Cindy Magic* and patterns of game play had changed when Anna joined the game. For years, *Cindy Magic* had been a two-person game that Paul and Nora played mostly in the car. Given that sociomaterial space (e.g., seat belts, limited movement, Paul's need to watch the road), *Cindy Magic* initially depended primarily on verbal resources for dialogues between characters and made limited use of sound effects or physical actions (e.g., knocking on the car window, pointing to imagined spaces, picking up imaginary phones, and handing over imagined baby animals). However, by the time of my study, they had adapted to playing with three players and had shifted toward playing during household chores (such as folding clothes). With a less physically confined space, they could engage in whole body enactments of *Cindy Magic* characters and their actions: Anna particularly began to do so. In the March episode, Anna relied heavily on gestures and postures to communicate her participation in the folding and the game. In the October episode, she was much more physically active in playing *Cindy Magic* (and relatively unengaged in the chore—folding only one item of clothing).

Cindy Magic was also becoming a durable resource that could be repurposed to negotiate interactions other than game play around family chores. In conversations, the name "Cindy" became a generative metaphor for imaged people, ideas, and scenarios. For example, during the research we got a new puppy, a Shetland sheepdog we named Dewey. Dewey would often startle and bark when she noticed her reflection in a black upright piano in the living room. We started calling Dewey's reflection "Cindy Puppy" (e.g., "Dewey, it's okay, that's just Cindy puppy!") As described in Hengst and Miller (1999), *Cindy Magic* could not only be used as a resource to help chores and errands go more smoothly and to pass the time during boring activities, it also became a resource that could mark something as a chore. During a family vacation when Nora was older (11 years), she was resisting Paul's suggestion that they paddle their two-person kayak across a lake on a windy afternoon. Negotiating with him, Nora said she would do it only if they could play *Cindy Magic*. With this request, Nora was essentially recasting Paul's fun activity (kayaking across the lake) into a family chore.

Note on Methods: Situated Learning and Thick Description

To study learning requires sampling relevant behaviors longitudinally across weeks, months, years, even decades. As I have noted, SDA draws on a wide array of ethnographic methods. Ethnographic research typically involves repeated and detailed data collection, so it should be understood as providing both situated and longitudinal data. Indeed, well-done ethnographic studies not only involve collecting the multiple observations of interactions (e.g., video recordings) needed to trace change, but also collecting multiple perspectives on those interactions (e.g., interviews, field notes) and relevant background details (e.g., diaries, archives) needed to interpret how *learning* is relevant to everyday communicative interactions. The challenge is to make decisions about *how* a series of observations can provide evidence of learning—*What counts as the "same" data? What changes should we be attending to?* These are questions, of course, that are central to both SDA research and clinical practice (which we will focus on in Parts 2 and 3 of the book).

Situated learning highlights that even when we are primarily interested in tracing learning for a specific individual, our answers to these questions must be couched in a *learning with* framework. Thus, our comparison of observations should always begin by describing the functional system (e.g., team, family, clinician-client pair). For example, the functional systems for the two episodes of *Cindy Magic* analyzed here were quite similar; they included the same people, enacting many of the same roles, accomplishing many of the same goals (i.e., game play, folding clothes, video recording), situated broadly within the same sociomaterial space (i.e., family living room). I could then focus my analysis on tracing changes across observations in the ways the players participated in accomplishing the goals and the communicative resources they used. When there is marked variation across observations in the functional system, in who is participating, what goals they are working to accomplish, and the sociomaterial spaces, then our interpretative challenge is to differentiate situated variation from marked and desired learning.

To interpret the changes in the October *Cindy Magic* episode as signs of marked and meaningful change in the play or the players (rather than just situational differences), I relied on a mixture of evidence across all data sources. I was particularly interested in understanding if the changes I noted in the October episode were new and how the players understood them. For example, to understand if Anna's use of more and different character voices was a sign of her learning, I completed a close analysis of the use of character voices by all players across both episodes (see Table 3.2), I interviewed the players to better understand how routinely each of them used different voices, and I reviewed my research notes to see where I had made notes about the introduction, use, and development of character voices across the two years of the study.

The need for such situated understandings of sociocultural activities led the anthropologist, Clifford Geertz (1973), to argue that ethnographic research requires *thick descriptions*. He noted how important it is to distinguish a blink of the eye (e.g., managing dryness) from a wink (e.g., a marked communicative resource) and then, if it is a wink, to figure out how it was used interactionally (e.g., signaling a joke). The validity of SDA analysis depends on collecting meaningful data and engaging in multiple passes through that data to develop thick descriptions of interactions (i.e., capable of distinguishing winks from blinks). To do this, you need to watch video tapes repeatedly (freezing frames and using slow-motion options), transcribe carefully and systematically, and interact with others to articulate and challenge emerging transcriptions, codes (categories), and interpretations.

Summary: Situated Learning Through Engagement in Functional Systems

No one denies experience is key to learning. Even linguists who believe all humans share a universal grammar recognize that a child growing up hearing Chinese will likely become able to participate routinely in interactions in Chinese whereas a child growing up hearing English will likely develop competencies with English. Recent work in neuroplasticity (e.g., Costandi, 2016) and epigenetics (e.g., Sweatt, 2019) underscores the powerful effects experience has on a wide array of biological structures and functions of individual bodies. Learning then is much more than a collection of isolated possessions (or skills); experience changes who we are as biological organisms and as sociocultural beings.

Typical representations of learning (often centered as I noted in the introduction of this chapter around schooling) present it as something children and youth do in instructional settings. However, learning through experience is constant across contexts and throughout the lifespan. Situated learning is an inevitable consequence of participation in everyday functional systems. Tracing it involves paying close attention to who is doing what in what ways within functional systems, and SDA offers rich tools designed to support such close attention. Finally, situated learning highlights the importance of tracing people's developing repertoires of durable communicative resources along with their developing flexibilities to manage the emergent. In this chapter, we asked three questions to focus on learning:

- *How are functional systems changing over time?*
- *How are peoples' patterns of participation changing over time?*
- *How are durable and emergent resources changing over time?*

Although we have focused on these three different questions, it is important to stress that they point to different analytical lenses (like the different perspectives offered by a telescope and a microscope), not different objects of study (like the difference between studying the molecular structure of rocks and the processes of DNA transcription).

In Chapter 2, I discussed Elinor Ochs and her colleagues' (Ochs et al., 1994) research on interactions in a physics lab. Around the same time, Ochs, Taylor, Rudolph, and Smith (1992) were also using SDA to understand interactions around family dinner tables in homes. Focusing on storytelling among family members, they found dinner table talk routinely featured joint attempts to make sense of daily events, to come to conclusions about how to value them, and to reach or review decisions. Their analysis identified surprisingly strong parallels (in communicative resources and interactional practices) between family dinner table talk (where theories about what happened and why in the lives of family members were told, questioned, critiqued, and revised) and physics lab interactions (where theories about what happened and why to certain physical phenomena were presented, questioned, critiqued, and revised). Concluding that "there is at least the potential that children sitting around a dinner table listening to and collaborating in such storytelling theory-building are being socialized into the rudiments of scholarly discourse" (p. 68), they also observed that sharing opinions and debating perspectives is risky social work which benefits from social spaces where people are familiar with and trust one another.

Understanding learning as situated highlights the power of repeated engagements in richly distributed and dynamic functional systems rather than the exact repetitions typical of many pedagogical and clinical practices. In the three chapters in Part 2, we will begin to consider how to apply SDA and situated learning perspectives to communicative interactions that include one or more individuals with a communicative disorder.

Reflective Observations

1. *Recording a second observation of a familiar activity.*

   a. *Recording a second observation:* For this activity you will need to make arrangements to complete a second video-recording of the activity you focused on in your reflective observation for Chapter 1. You do not need to structure the activity in any specific way, just plan on recording 30 minutes of the activity at this later date. Again, if you are an observer you can manage the camera and quietly observe and take notes from the sidelines, but if you are part of the interaction, you will need to use a tripod or elicit help of another person to make the video.

   b. *Transcribing video data:* Watch the video paying attention to any changes (or differences) in the functional system, patterns of participation, and use of durable and emergent communicative resources. Then select about 2–3 minutes of your data to transcribe in detail.

2. *Analyzing changes across communicative interactions.*

   a. You will need to pull together and review all the data you have on this activity, including the two video recordings, any interviews, researcher logs, and your own personal reflections.

   b. Write up a brief analysis of the changes that are evident across sessions, focusing specifically on your two transcripts. Use the guiding questions from this chapter to organize your preliminary analysis:

      i. *How are functional systems changing over time?*
      ii. *How are peoples' patterns of participation changing over time?*
      iii. *How are durable and emergent resources changing over time?*

c. Compare your preliminary situated analysis of change with analyses completed by others (either published data, or analyses from other members of your class or research group). Discuss what is unique across data sets.

3. *Reflecting on your everyday learning experiences*. A core assumption of SDA is that learning is a ubiquitous dimension of all interactions. For this reflection, identify an activity or social role that is relatively new for you—perhaps you have recently moved, or become an officer in an organization, or adopted a new hobby. Over the next week, keep a log about your engagement with this new social role, your changing patterns of participation, and the developing repertoire of resources. Pay special attention to how, when, and with whom you communicate as you learn more about this new role.

Suggested Readings

There are many ways for researchers and clinicians to support and document situated learning. Reading a diverse range of research studies will help you become more familiar with this rich evidence base and more comfortable with the wide range of metrics to trace changes. Here are three highly illuminating articles (in addition to the articles cited throughout this chapter) that provide empirical analyses of people repeatedly engaging with everyday communicative activities and illustrate the diverse ways researchers document change.

1. "'I see what you are saying:' Action as cognition in fMRI brain mapping practice" (Alač & Hutchins, 2004). Morana Alač and Edwin Hutchins focus on adult learning with their micro-analysis of interactions as an experienced researcher guides a research assistant in reading fMRI images.
2. "Young children's emotional attachment to stories" (Alexander, Miller, & Hengst, 2002). Kristin Alexander, Peggy Miller, and Julie A. Hengst combine interviews with a short-term longitudinal diary study to study how 32 preschoolers displayed engagement with and emotional attachment to different stories. They argue that story attachments support children's developing understandings of social roles and relationships.
3. "Reexamining the verbal environments of children from different socioeconomic backgrounds" (Sperry, Sperry, & Miller, 2018). Douglas Sperry, Linda Sperry, and Peggy Miller completed a SDA of longitudinal ethnographic data from five American communities to re-examine the claim (Hart & Risley, 1995) that poor children display language deficits because they hear (on average) 30 million fewer words than middle-class children. Their situated analysis of children's language exposure challenges the claimed word-gap between poor and middle-class home environments and points to key methodological decisions that likely account for the radically different findings.

Note

1. More details about research related to LOPI practices around the world are available on the Learning by Observing and Pitching-In (LOPI) website supported by the UCSC Foundation Chair in Psychology and the National Science Foundation (under Grant No.0837898) https://learningbyobservingandpitchingin.sites.ucsc.edu/overview/.

Part 2

Understanding Communication Disorders in Everyday Interactions

How much I appreciate your talking. To me, that is. That may seem like a funny thing to be grateful for, but now that I'm not able to talk, neither can some of my family and friends. At least not to me. Now only a nurse, t v, tape and radio are able and available to me. Some people simply disappear. Others make a kind, but embarrassed visit, leaving as soon as possible. Some people pop in for a few minutes; but even though they show love to me, they also have trouble talking to someone who can't talk in return.

(*Note typed by Larry, a husband and father with ALS, to his wife*)

Part 1 introduced *situated discourse analysis* (SDA) as an approach to examining the complex ways everyday communicative interactions are situated in social spaces. In Part 2 we turn to how SDA can help us understand everyday interactions that include people with communication disorders.

In the epigraph, Larry poignantly captures the impact *his disorder* had on *others' abilities* to communicate with him. A year or so before he typed this note, Larry had been diagnosed with amyotrophic lateral sclerosis, better known as ALS.[1] ALS is a progressive disease that causes degeneration of the neurons controlling voluntary movements throughout the body, leading to weakness and paralysis. As his disease progressed, Larry lost his ability to move including to speak and eat orally. His ways of communicating with others also changed: he learned, for example, to augment his speech through the use of augmentative and alternative communication (AAC) devices. At the time he typed the note, Larry was almost fully paralyzed. We had set him up with a computerized AAC system that allowed him to use a head switch to access letters and stored phrases one at a time. He often used his alone time to type out messages to friends and family he knew would be visiting him later. Although Larry was the person with ALS and an acquired inability to speak, he was struck by how many of his friends and family had "trouble talking to someone who can't talk in return." Building on the concept of *distributed communication* introduced in Part 1, Larry's comments and the analyses in Part 2 highlight that communication disorders are also distributed. In his note, Larry thanks his wife for learning along with him.

As he was one of the many patients I worked with as part of an outpatient neurology clinic's ALS team, I had gotten to know Larry and his wife well that year. After his death, she printed out a copy of this note to share with me—hoping it would be helpful in training future SLPs.

Clinical research fields (e.g., CSD, neuropsychology, special education) have defined *communication disorders* broadly as disruptions in an individual's physical ability to speak, understand, read, write, and/or interact with others in familiar ways. Linked to a variety of causes (e.g., genetic, environmental, physical traumas, disease), communication disorders can arise at any point in a person's life. Clinicians diagnose communication disorders behaviorally, differentiating disorders by behavioral and medical profiles and by time of onset (e.g., *developmental disorders* in childhood, or *acquired disorders* in adults). For example, Larry's communication diagnosis was *dysarthria*, a disruption in his ability to control and use the muscles needed to produce speech, caused in his case by ALS. In contrast, *aphasia* is an adult-acquired communication disorder caused by brain damage (e.g., stroke) and marked by a disruption in an individual's ability to use language (with relatively preserved speech, hearing, and cognition). Similar communication disorders can also arise in childhood, disrupting the development of individual skills and abilities. For example, dysarthria is a common characteristic of cerebral palsy caused by brain damage at or around birth. Difficulty developing speech and language skills also often co-occurs with genetic profiles such as Down syndrome. Because communication disorders are behaviorally defined, they can be diagnosed in the absence of a clear understanding of the etiology. Indeed, the etiologies of some disorders (e.g., *childhood apraxia of speech, developmental language disorder)* have not been clearly identified.

Whereas much of the research in CSD has focused on identifying clinical behavioral profiles (or behavioral phenotypes) of individuals, SDA focuses on how communication disruptions and disorders along with communicative abilities and success are distributed across the functional systems of everyday interactions. In SDA terms, participants' particular abilities are recast as dimensions of sociomaterial spaces that include the individual. These dimensions then range from a participant's biological characteristics to the social categories and values that position diverse communicators.

Although Part 2 focuses on how people with communication disorders engage in everyday communicative interactions, we will continue to apply the SDA approaches to data collection and analysis explored in Part 1 for studying any everyday interaction. Part 2 also introduces new concepts that build on those frameworks. Chapter 4 introduces *figured worlds* as a way to analyze how sociocultural activities in sociomaterial spaces anticipate certain social roles, how people's *social roles* in particular interactions are shaped by and reflected in their patterns of participation, and how *discourse registers* are tied to social identities. Chapter 5 highlights the *mobility of functional systems* as people traverse everyday sociomaterial spaces, *broker* one another's social roles in communicative interactions, and bring different communicative repertoires or *bit competences* to functional systems. Chapter 6 returns to questions of situated learning. It highlights ways individuals with communication disorders and their routine communication partners are learning together through *repeated engagement* in everyday interactions to accomplish goals, align around *common ground*, and build repertories of *interactional discourse resources*. The concepts in each chapter are illustrated with examples drawn from my ethnographic research on everyday communicative interactions involving adults with communication disorders. Again, each chapter ends with reflective observations and suggested readings.

Note

1. ALS is often known as Lou Gehrig's disease, named after a famous baseball player in the US struck by the disease in the late 1930s.

Chapter 4

Situating Communication Disorders in Everyday Communicative Interactions

In Chapter 4 we continue to analyze communicative interactions by locating them first within their *social matrix*, as Hymes (1974) recommended in the epigraph that introduced Part 1. Throughout Part 1, I illustrated theories and methods of *situated discourse analysis* (SDA) through examples from my early research on *Cindy Magic*, a make-believe game that grew out of my family life. In this chapter, I turn to research that grew out of my clinical work, focusing particularly on people managing *aphasia*. I chose to do my first research into communication disorders on individuals with aphasia for several reasons. First, much of my clinical experience had focused on diagnosing and treating individuals with aphasia. Second, a hallmark of aphasia is that, in spite of disruptions in use of linguistic forms, individuals are often skilled and creative communicators who retain their abilities to socially engage with others and successfully manage communicative breakdowns. Nevertheless, little research had explored *how* communication could be successful in spite of aphasia, so I designed my research to explore that question. Third, because I had worked with many clients' families, I was also interested in how other people (family, friends, co-workers) as well as those with aphasia reorganized their lives and communicative patterns in the less researched, chronic phases of aphasia.

This chapter introduces *figured worlds*, a concept that further elaborates key features of sociocultural activities introduced in Chapter 1. Attention to figured worlds highlights how social roles and identities are associated with different activities, how figured worlds can link together varied functional systems, and how people's positioning in sociomaterial spaces shapes their identities. Exploring figured worlds also highlights the diverse communicative resources (verbal and nonverbal) participants use to align within and around activities. We begin here to explore the routine and strategic ways people re-orchestrate such resources in response to communication disorders. In contrast to research focusing on patterns of disruptions at the level of the individual (e.g., stuttering, aphasia, dysarthria), my research was designed to understand how communication is distributed among participants in an interaction. To illustrate these concepts, this chapters draws on data from my early studies of individuals with aphasia and their routine communication partners (Hengst, 2001, 2003).

The Case of Steve: On the Sidelines

To study the everyday communicative practices of people with aphasia, I designed an ethnographic study to observe communication partners interacting with one another in three different settings (Hengst, 2001). I recruited eight participants who had aphasia due to stroke, all of whom were in the chronic phase of recovery and living in their own homes, and I asked each of them to invite a familiar communication partner to join them in the study. All eight participant-pairs agreed to four rounds of data collection; each round included one video-recorded observation in each of three contexts:

1.   a community observation of the pair engaged in a routine activity of their choice (e.g., shopping, baking cookies);
2.   a clinic-based session where the pairs completed six trials of a collaborative referencing game; and
3.   a semi-structured interview where the pair responded to video clips from their community observation and clinic-based sessions and discussed their communication outside the study.

In Chapter 6 we will look at data from the referencing game. Here we focus on data from a community observation with Steve[1] and Kerry, a young husband-wife pair, and from related interviews.

Steve was the second participant I recruited for the study. He selected his wife, Kerry, as his study partner. When the research began, Steve was 33 years old and four and a half years post-stroke. Steve had nearly completed his final medical residency when he had a large left-hemisphere stroke involving most of the parietal lobe and superior portions of the temporal lobe. He continued to have partial paralysis in his left leg and arm and chronic moderate-severe *conduction aphasia* which is defined by the Boston Diagnostic Aphasia Examination (BDAE, Goodglass & Kaplan, 1983) as fluently produced connected speech, relatively good auditory comprehension, and poor phrase repetition. Steve had adapted to his hemiparesis by developing left-handed skills and using a cane and foot brace to support his walking. I knew Steve and Kerry well because I had been working with them clinically for over three years, supporting a community-based treatment plan for Steve that included job trials and vocational retraining. For the third community observation, I joined Steve, Kerry, and their daughter, Cassie, on the sidelines of a football game at their hometown high school whose sports medicine clinic he had long volunteered with.

Early in the game (about eight minutes into the first quarter) the home team recovered a fumble at the opposite end of the field from us, and a player on the away team was injured. Steve immediately headed down the sideline to find out what was happening. The excerpt in Transcript 4.1 begins with Steve walking back to us to report what he learned about the injured player.

Transcript 4.1 Excerpt of interactions on the sidelines. Key: S = Steve; Kerry; C = Cassie; J = Julie; A = announcer. Note that the larger gathering (e.g., players, officials, audience) is not represented in the transcript.

S:	*(It's looking bad. First thing) ... they think he broke his tibia.
K:	
C:	(can we) sit down
J:	oh:: we don't-
(A):	STEPHENS THE BALL CARRIER A
	*S walking down sideline toward J

S:	... I think- personally I think (he) probably broke his tibia. *
K:	He broke his leg?
C:	Momma, I wanna sit do:wn with you::.
J:	
(A):	PICKUP OF ONE THAT'LL BE SECOND DOWN AND NINE
	*S nodding, looks to field

S:	** Yeah*
K:	Ouch! *Here. Okay
C:	
J:	He looked like he was in...a lot of pain, when he was coming out.
(A):	
	*K hands snow cone to C **S looking at J *S nods

S:	**Yeah.
K:	...3...take one bite at a time.
C:	
J:	Was that Dr. Lxxxxx down there you were talking to? So
(A):	
	**nodding

S:	* Yeah.**....4....or at least like a
K:	
C:	
J:	they have their own doctors that went off with him?
(A):	
	*S looks at J; **S nodding vigorously

S:	*trainer (like that or something) **Yeah.
K:	I'll hang on to it hon, til it gets (lower down)
C:	
J:	Their trainer? ... somebody? Are they taking him back home
(A):	
	*S looks at J **S nodding, looks to field

S:	*Huh? I assume probably ...ER (for the) Cxxxx Hospital.
K:	
C:	
J:	now or- Where will they take him?
(A):	ROBERT'S THE BALL CARRIER FOR CENTRAL HIGH
	*S leans ear to J

As he got close to us, Steve started speaking, announcing that they thought the player had broken "his tibia" and confirming his agreement with the assessment: "I think personally I think he probably broke his tibia." Kerry and I express concern and ask questions. Cassie meanwhile is focused on sitting down and eating a snow cone. Kerry splits her attention between helping Cassie manage her snow cone and talking with Steve and me about the injured player. The game announcer is not close to us, but his voice is very clear amidst our interactions. The transcript here represents the interaction in our focused conversational space. It is important to recognize that there is a much larger gathering here. Many people can see our interactions at the edge of the field and sometimes others are nearby enough to be overhearers and to be overheard as well.

Figured Worlds and Sociocultural Activities

Dorothy Holland and her colleagues (Holland, Lachicotte Jr., Skinner, & Cain, 1998) introduced the concept of *figured worlds* to call attention to how sociocultural activities are populated with a range of imagined *figures*—the *whos* of sociocultural activities—and the particular social roles, identities, values, and relationships associated with them. Figured worlds offer frameworks that shape our interpretations of others' actions and guide or limit our own patterns of participation. The first question we will ask here then is: ***What social identities and roles are associated with these sociocultural activities?***

Figured worlds conjure up whole scenes (sociomaterial spaces populated with particular figures, in particular places, enacting specific sociocultural activities). Just as any interaction involves juggling multiple sociocultural activities, multiple figured worlds are always co-present in interactions. For example, the figured worlds around school are populated with students, teachers, parents, office staff, principals, and so on. These worlds encompass multiple sociocultural activities, including lessons in classrooms, recreation on playground, various team practices and events (often away from the school), lunch and hallway conversations, and much more. In short, figured worlds provide a sketch about who belongs in a sociomaterial space, who (if anyone) should be in charge, who should carry out tasks and contribute to various goals, and how people should act, talk, and otherwise orient to these worlds.

When thinking about these figures, it is useful to distinguish social roles, role inhabitance, and identities. *Social roles* are situationally linked to sociocultural activities, so "teacher" is a recognizable and anticipated social role in schools. Of course, there are many teachers in a school and how individuals inhabit that role varies, so *role inhabitance* (Silverstein & Urban, 1996) points to the specific ways that individuals enact their roles in interactions and to the ways those roles are shaped by a person's *social identities*—the longer term, cross-contextual senses of self that people claim and enact and that are ascribed to them by others. Of course, the social roles a person assumes shape the longer-term building of identities (and indeed social roles like teacher or salesperson can become central to a person's identities across sociomaterial spaces), just as those identities shape a person's role inhabitance. In this sense, figured worlds are central to how people position themselves and are positioned amidst everyday functional systems (issues we will explore later in this chapter).

Just as the sociomaterial spaces of everyday interactions always weave together multiple activities, people also inhabit multiple identities that are variously enacted in functional systems. Figured worlds are *as-if worlds* that people draw on whether they are engaging in routine cultural activities (e.g., being a teacher in the classroom) or flights of imaginative fancy (e.g., being a vampire bat attacking Cruella de Vil). Being a teacher and being a vampire bat both call on people to act *as-if*, and such performances can be turned off as well as on. For example, at the end of class, I may shift from being teacher to chatting with students about current events, and in *Cindy Magic*, discovering the mud on the rug led the players to shift out of play. We can think then of figured worlds as frameworks, or starting points, for populating sociocultural activities, that is *who* should act and say what, and *who* gets the credit for the accomplishments of the functional system.

Whether imaginary worlds like *Cindy Magic* or routine cultural worlds like school, figured worlds evoke *indexical grounds* that situate communicative interactions by drawing on recognizable, but often unstated frameworks that support people interacting in *anticipated as-if ways*. Recall a wedding you attended or one you watched in a movie. Your recall must invoke scenes around the wedding where people act out certain social identities and roles. A typical wedding might evoke a variety of figures: the couple being married, someone (religious or civil) leading the ceremony, caterers, friends and family, musicians, photographers and so on. The figured world of a wedding is not limited to the ceremony: it links a dispersed chain of events and activities (e.g., shopping for special clothing and rings, rehearsals, parties for the couple, a reception afterward). Figured worlds also offer frameworks that people can work against to contest typical social roles and identities. For example, my older colleagues tell me that in the 1960's they contested conventions of marriage in the US by writing their own wedding vows, or altering traditional depictions of relationships (e.g., replacing "man and wife" with "husband and wife"). More recently, before same-sex marriages became legal in the US and were approved by their religious denomination, some ministers conducted same-sex marriage ceremonies. Figured worlds are not static and fixed.

The notion of figured worlds can help us recognize the often striking *identity work* people with communication disorders must engage in whether the disorders are developmental or acquired. Physical traumas, such as strokes, that lead to adult-acquired communication disorders, such as aphasia, are life- and identity-altering events. As patients survive the trauma and physically heal, the communication disorder disrupts their established ways of being in the world as well as their abilities and rights to inhabit sociomaterial spaces and take on social roles. Next we will look at the continuities and discontinuities in Steve's figured worlds after his stroke.

Multiple Figured Worlds and Multiple Social Roles—Steve's Case

In interviews with Steve and his family, all agreed that Steve's life revolved around the worlds of medicine, sports, education, and family. As is typical, the social roles Steve inhabited in these worlds shifted and were woven together across his life. Attention to figured worlds helps us see how Steve's identities shifted after his stroke, displaying a complex blend of continuities and discontinuities.

In his descriptions of himself and his life, Steve anchored his personal identities in the *world of medicine*. Born with a congenital heart condition, Steve's first few years were spent as a *heart patient* receiving specialized medical care. After a successful heart surgery at age 5, he became what his father called a *typical healthy kid*, and his identity as patient faded until he no longer needed annual check-ups with his cardiologist. In high school Steve set his sights on becoming a *medical doctor* and threw himself into his studies to achieve that goal. His family reported that Steve had always been an avid reader and a *strong student* who knew how to work hard. Steve admitted he never liked English classes, literature, or writing—science and math were his passions. Steve was almost finished with his residency and about to become a fully certified doctor at the time of his stroke.

Steve also anchored his personal identities in the *world of sports*. From the time he was little, he loved playing sports—especially baseball. He won a full scholarship to college as a starting pitcher. In addition to his status as a successful *amateur player*, he was an *avid fan* who collected baseball cards and kept up with statistics about the best players and teams. He also played all kinds of sports for fun—from summer softball leagues to bowling. He loved working out, building his skills, and socializing with friends, family, and colleagues around friendly games of all kinds. Kerry reported that Steve never really cared about winning, he just loved playing with friends and challenging himself to do his best. Steve also blended his interests in sports and medicine, volunteering with a high school sports medicine clinic that supported teams at his community high school.

The stroke disrupted Steve's positioning as a medical *doctor* and catapulted him back into the status of a *patient* with a serious, life-threatening condition. Steve knew how to train and study, and he threw himself into his rehabilitation programs, even attending an adult education center to develop work skills (e.g., using email, one-handed typing, using a speaker phone) and auditing a class at the university. Although Steve stopped playing sports, he worked out with a personal trainer and continued to be an avid sports fan. His sister recalled that one of the earliest things she and Steve talked about after his stroke was his baseball card collection. His mother-in-law reported that whenever Steve came to her house, he would always ask for the newspaper to read the sports page. Sprinkled throughout communication logs I asked Steve to keep were entries about sports teams and players: "How 'bout those Bulls! They won 86–85 and won the NBA Championship. 6 trophies in 8 years." Steve continued to be the go-to *sports expert* among his family and friends.

In many ways, Steve's position in his family and community remained the most stable for him. Despite his stroke he was still positioned as a son,

son-in-law, brother, and husband, and developed his new role as father (Cassie was born several months after his stroke). Extended family members called or visited Steve daily and worked to support Steve and Kerry as a couple. Kerry's mom lived with them for six months, and her dad and brothers routinely helped with major household repairs. However, Steve found it difficult to navigate the group conversations and commotion of large family gatherings. Family members adjusted to Steve's need to take breaks and find a quiet space to sit and relax. Steve connected well with people socially and worked to maintain old friendships and develop new ones. Early in his recovery, when he had very poor communication skills and lots of frustration with his condition, people still remember him mostly as someone with a smile on his face, always ready to greet people.

Based especially on the severity of his residual aphasia, Steve's therapists were convinced he would never work as a physician. Although Steve did not resist being a patient, he strongly resisted being *no-longer-a-doctor*. I began working with Steve after he was discharged from the outpatient rehab program, almost a year into his recovery. He and Kerry were seeking a therapist who could support a novel community-based program organized by the neuropsychologist. During our preliminary meeting, Steve's first question for me was about his goal to return to work as a physician—"If you tell me I can't, then I'm leaving!" He accepted unpaid work trials, took up volunteer positions, and was thrilled with the opportunity to complete paid work trials at two area clinics. For Steve, the distinction between work and school was the paycheck, and he wanted to be gainfully employed. When he was discharged from formal speech therapy and vocational rehabilitation over six years after his stroke, Steve was working 20 hours a week in four different paid positions: a medical library, a medical research center, and two medical clinics. He still had the diagnosis of mild-moderate conduction aphasia and a Social Security designation of 100 percent disabled, and he was not allowed to practice medicine.

Steve's social relationships with people at work, however, allowed him to reclaim some of his social roles as a physician after his stroke, gaining him some access to medical settings, activities, and spaces. Figure 4.1 and Transcript 4.1 offer a glimpse into the blending of Steve's figured worlds. Steve continued to sit in on the sports medicine clinic for his hometown high school football team, which brought him to the sidelines of the game. However, he could not act as a doctor for the team, and Kerry and Cassie routinely joined him on the sidelines for support and assistance, all three then enacting their roles as family members. On the sidelines, Steve and Kerry also took up the role of football fans, cheering on the home team. On the evening in Figure 4.1, I also joined them on the sidelines, recording interactions for research. We will turn next to exploring how figured worlds and social roles get enacted as people participate in functional systems.

Figure 4.1 Steve, Kerry and their daughter, Cassie, watching their hometown high school football game from the sidelines. Steve had long been involved in a sports medicine clinic with the team.

Positioning People in Sociomaterial Spaces

Figured worlds evoke the figures who populate sociomaterial spaces and assume social roles associated with specific sociocultural activities; however, the specific rights and responsibilities of individuals must be interactively enacted in particular functional systems. Thus, everyday interactions are sites of *identity work*, where people actively position themselves and others in ways that claim and project specific social roles and identities that give their words and actions specific meanings and that contribute to accomplishing specific goals. *Positioning* then is deeply tied to issues of power, access, respect, and privilege within functional systems. The question to ask then is: **How are people positioning themselves and others in this sociomaterial space?**

Much identity work in interactions is backgrounded, and people's positionings are typically tacit. For example, if we think of a classroom, we routinely recognize people's roles by how they navigate and inhabit the space. As I walk into a room to teach a class for the first time with a new group of students, I inhabit the social role of teacher by how I position myself—by walking to the front of the room, introducing myself, and telling people what to do. My age, dress, actions (e.g., connecting my computer to the projector panel), nonverbal stance (standing in front of the class and gazing at people with raised eyebrows), paralinguistics (e.g., speaking loudly to the room), and language forms (greetings and directives) all contribute to my enacting (performing) my positioning as teacher and evoking an atmosphere (which might be friendly and relaxed, or tense and demanding) that indexes what type of teacher role I might inhabit. Acting as a teacher positions others as students, and others routinely take on student roles by, for example, sitting down and facing forward, quieting down when I speak, and following my directives about classroom activities. However, people can interactionally contest my positioning by, for example, ignoring me and my directives while carrying on with interactions they were engaged in (an uptake I regularly experienced as a novice English language teacher in a private middle school in Saudi Arabia). Understanding everyday communicative interactions always involves understanding what identities are being invoked, indexed, taken up, contested, and re-formed through specific interactions.

The imagined potentials of figured worlds make them malleable, which is part of the way we can create specific indexical grounds in social spaces. *Figured worlds* become ways not only to take on or contest existing identities, but also to envision new identities by imaging new *as-if* worlds—developing "new social competencies and newly imagined communities" (Holland et al., 1998, p. 272). For example, I have often retold a story I heard from a professor who retired after a stroke left him with chronic anomic aphasia, which the BDAE (Goodglass & Kaplan, 1983) describes as a profile that includes fluently produced connected speech, good comprehension, good phrase repetition, and severe *anomia* (difficulty producing content words during assessment tasks and conversational interactions, something similar to tip-of-the-tongue phenomena). One day at a cafeteria, he found the spoon bin empty. However, when he approached an employee to ask for a "spoon," his mind went blank. He described the silence as overwhelming as the cafeteria employee stood waiting for him to speak. At a loss, he pointed to the empty bins, made gestures as if he was eating, and said "I'm looking for, oh, in English what do you call it, you have a word for it. . . ." The woman quickly filled in the missing word, "Oh, spoon" and got him what he needed. Wanting to avoid being positioned as an adult who could not find the word for spoon (evoking figured worlds of disability), the retired professor used nonverbal and verbal resources (along with the environment) in this fleeting interaction to invoke a figured world that positioned him more positively, as a non-native speaker simply searching for a word in English.

When I share this story with students and other clinical audiences, they are sometimes taken aback—reading this invocation of an *as-if* world as deceptive. Of course, people can and do position themselves for fraudulent reasons—con-artists pass themselves off as experts when they are not and there are laws against such practices. However, a key power of communication lies in ways we can shape and reshape our identities—identities are not fixed. Think of the first time you inhabited some new role. When you first step into a clinic room to do therapy, that role may be unfamiliar and uncomfortable to inhabit, but it is important (and not deceptive) to position yourself as a clinician. In everyday interactions, people inhabit, and are positioned by others in, quite diverse roles that are rarely (if ever) perfect fits.

Chapter 1 introduced the notion of geosemiotics (how locations contribute to the meaning of language and other signs) and made the point that interaction orders can be built into the architecture of our environments (e.g., the way a theatre supports a platform event interaction order). Built spaces are also designed around figured worlds, that is, with certain kinds of people and social roles in mind. For example, 50 years ago, disability rights advocates had to dramatize that the physical design of public spaces (e.g., courtrooms, classrooms, offices) made entry to these buildings easy only for people who could traverse stairs, thus effectively excluding members of the public who used wheelchairs (Shapiro, 1993). The geosemiotics of built spaces are often socially designed to filter certain categories of people. For example, public spaces have routinely been designed to exclude people based on gender (e.g., men's only clubs, gender-specific public restrooms), on attire (e.g., dress codes in schools, restaurants), or on race (e.g., Whites-only drinking fountains in the Jim Crow south). Government regulations and laws can also categorize people in ways that limit or enable their participation in different activities. For example, the US Federal Housing Administration's (1938) *Underwriting Manual* to guide implementation of Title II of the *National Housing Act* included recommended covenants for evaluating loans for new subdivisions. Under the category of "protection from adverse influences," one recommended covenant for subdivisions read: "Prohibition of the occupancy of properties except by the race for which they are intended" (Federal Housing Administration, 1938, para. 980(3g)). Likewise, before Public Law 94–142 was passed in the US,[2] children with developmental disorders were routinely blocked from attending public schools.

Acquired disorders such as aphasia significantly disrupt the ways people are positioned and participate in sociomaterial spaces. Acquired disorders routinely disrupt people's social identities and access to sociomaterial spaces, immersing them in unfamiliar figured worlds (worlds of disability, of medicine and rehabilitation, of government social programs) and challenging them to inhabit new roles and reimagine new identities and social roles. We turn next to how the stroke and aphasia reshaped Steve's participation in figured worlds, how he was positioned by others, and how he worked to reposition himself as an active participant in privileged spaces.

Re-Positioning Steve in Figured Worlds

Steve's everyday interactions on the sidelines of the high school game (see Figure 4.1 and Transcript 4.1) highlight the importance of accessing sociomaterial spaces for shaping social identities. Figure 4.2 is a diagram of the football field, a built space designed to support particular figured worlds. The *geosemiotic* space of a football stadium projects specific roles associated with

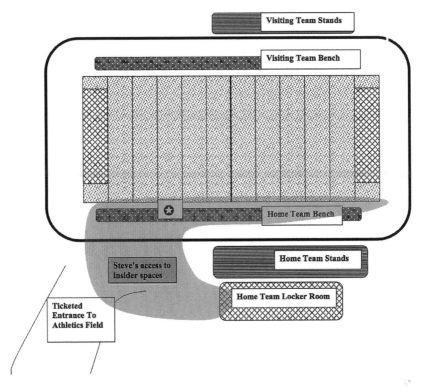

Figure 4.2 Diagram of the football field; the shaded area shows Steve's "insider" spaces, moving from the locker room to the sidelines. That the football field itself is not in that shaded area displays Steve's positioning as an "outsider," no longer a doctor.

various sociocultural activities. The grass field is typically reserved for official participants: players, referees, coaches, cheerleaders, the marching band, and medical personnel if there is an injury. Along each sideline is a chalked off space for the home team and another one for the visiting team. At the edge of the field are stands for spectators, one designated for the home team and the other for the visitors. At the top of the stands is a booth for the announcer and media. Behind the stands are locker rooms (again, one for the home team and one for the visitors). Entrance to all of these spaces is formally and informally regulated. Spectators are admitted close to game time by buying tickets and directed to sit in the stands; players and coaches arrive early to warm up, suit up in the locker room, and enter the field just before kick-off. The shaded area on the map of Figure 4.2 (from the home locker room around the stands to the sidelines) display Steve's relatively privileged access to the insider spaces of the home team. The star in Figure 4.2 shows where we were positioned on the sidelines in the image in Figure 4.1. Standing on the sidelines with Kerry and Cassie (and in this case me) positioned Steve paradoxically as both an insider and outsider.

High school football games are family and community events, and people in Steve's small community rallied around their high school team. Attending games was a family activity for Steve as well. Kerry and Cassie often joined him as they did this evening. I observed a nighttime home game early in the season, arriving at Steve and Kerry's house at seven in the evening, as prearranged. Steve had already left for the game. As an honorary (past) member of the sports medicine project, Steve always arrived early to meet with the coaching staff and players in the locker room and support pregame preparations. Kerry, Cassie, and I were to meet him at the stadium just before kick-off. We drove to the high school in Kerry's car. We paid our three dollars for adult tickets, and I fit Kerry with a microphone while we waited for Steve. He came out of the locker room by himself, using his cane and walking slowly across the ramp to where we were waiting. I fit him with his microphone just as the visiting team ran out on the field.

Being on the sidelines gave Steve lots of opportunities to interact with people and to stay involved with what was happening with and around the team, among his medical colleagues, and across the community. People greeted Steve and Kerry as they passed by us, and some stopped to visit, exchanging stories of the high school teams. Steve moved around seeking out other people to talk with. A neighbor saw Steve and came over to visit; they asked about each other's jobs and children. Shortly after the game started, Steve spotted the team physician and motioned him over to introduce us. Sounds of fireworks came from someplace outside the stadium, and Steve carried on an exchange with Kerry and people around them before concluding it was nothing to worry about. Later in the game when the "lineman" carrying the first down marker was close by where we were standing, he handed his pole momentarily to someone else and ran over to say hi and visit with Steve.

The map in Figure 4.2 along with the image (Figure 4.1) and interaction (Transcript 4.1) are clear markers of another key positioning: Steve is palpably *no-longer-a-doctor*. When the player was injured on the field, Steve walked down the sideline to consult with others but did not run out onto the field with the medical personnel. When Steve reported to us what happened, he positioned himself as a knowledgeable outsider: "It's looking bad. First thing . . . they think he broke his tibia." Notice here that the pronoun is "they" (referring to the coaching staff and the medical team), not "we." Yet Steve used a somewhat specialized way of referring to the player's anatomy. He identifies a specific bone (tibia) rather than a typical phrasing (e.g., "he broke his leg"). Both nonverbally—by where he walks and where he doesn't walk—and verbally—by deploying specialized vocabulary but reporting it in third person, Steve was walking the line not only between the field and the stands, but also between being an insider to the team and an outsider. More subtly, Steve was reporting the injury to Kerry, Cassie and me on the side-lines. The families of other members of the coaching staff and medical team were typically in the stands watching the game, not on the sidelines (and none had a PhD candidate video recording their interactions). The three of us being there marked Steve's positioning as someone who was disabled and might need extra supports.

Although his access and actions ultimately made it clear that he was not one of the team physicians, his past history, presence in some insider spaces, and knowledge of sports, medicine and the community gave him greater insider status than the people sitting in the stands. Having observed Steve in many settings (as both clinician and researcher), I was struck that evening that Steve was displaying greater fluidity in his communication with people and in managing multiple activities on the sidelines than I saw in many set-tings. He was keeping track of the game; supporting the team with avid cheering; popping in and out of discussions with Kerry and me about key players, their standings and their recruiting chances; periodically responding to Cassie by laughing at her antics and answering her questions; and moving freely around the sidelines to get a closer look at the action on the field and to visit with different people. In contrast with reports from family gather-ings, where people saw him as getting overwhelmed and eventually seeking solitude, Steve seemed both comfortable and in command in these spaces, accepting his positioning and accepted and supported by others.

Using Communicative Resources to Build Identities in Figured Worlds

We began our observations of communicative resources in Part 1 by attend-ing to what communicative resources people were using to communicate. The first three chapters established that SDA focuses on complex multi-modal uptakes of diverse semiotic resources orchestrated in real time by real people. Taking up notions of figured worlds and positioning highlights that as individuals improvise their actions and responses, they are also shaping and reshaping their identities. These notions then lead us to ask: *How are communicative resources indexing potential identities?*

In analyses of communicative resources around *Cindy Magic* in Part 1, we began to see ways that communicative resources like *modes of address, constructed dialogue*, and *social voices* evoke figured worlds to index and develop identities. We saw, for example, how Paul, Nora and Anna had developed a repertoire of *social voices* (recognizable ways of *speaking as* someone) to inhabit different characters (e.g., Mary, Jane and Elizabeth Magic; Cruella de Vil) in the figured world of *Cindy Magic* in contrast to their ways of inhabiting roles (e.g., Nora as older sister, daughter; Anna as younger sister, daughter; and Paul as dad) in the figured world of the family. Critically, multiple figured worlds are available and at least partly inhabited in any interaction. Embodied physicality is another resource central to position in interactions, as illustrated in examples in this chapter of inclusion or exclusion based on embodied characteristics like gender, race, and ability to walk. Here we will introduce two additional communicative resources, *registers* and *narrative*, that play prominent roles in indexing potential identities.

Sociolinguists have long attended to regional differences (dialects) in the forms of language people use. For example, when I speak my varieties of English, I index my identity as an American. Some of my dialectal resources (in syntax, pronunciation, lexical choice, and usage) also index the years I spent in Oklahoma. Sociolinguists have also identified *registers*—sets of finer-grained distinctions marking, for example, levels of formality or participation in occupational and social spheres of activity. Registers are often named by the activities and social roles they index (e.g., medical registers, polite registers, sports registers). In SDA, registers are better conceptualized as embodied arrays of signs (e.g., talk, gesture, proxemics as discussed in Chapter 1) linked to particular social identities and sociocultural activities. Drawing on the work of anthropological linguists (Agha, 2007; Hanks, 1996), we consider how such *discourse registers* work to index, invoke, acknowledge, challenge, and negotiate potential identities and social roles linked to people's positioning in figured worlds.

Researchers have also long recognized the powerful role of narrative in organizing human experience and displaying cultural categories that exemplify individual qualities and social roles (e.g., Basso, 1996; Bauman, 1986; Bruner, 1990). Of particular interest to us is how personal narratives (stories people tell about themselves and others in everyday events) provide rich resources for identity work across the lifespan (Miller et al., 2007). Everyday interactions are often filled with personal narratives, from brief anecdotes to fully developed narrative performances. In their book, *Living Narrative*, Ochs and Capps (2001) focus on five dimensions to trace the different ways personal narratives emerge in and are shaped by everyday conversations:

- *tellership*—how people are involved in recounting and telling the narrative;
- *tellability*—how remarkable the narrated event is and how skillful the telling is;
- *embeddedness*—how embedded or detached the narrative is from surrounding interaction;
- *linearity*—how clearly and coherently the narrative elements emerge in the telling; and
- *moral stance*—how clear and stable values, or moral purpose, are in the narrative.

These dimensions highlight how people are positioned in the figured worlds of the narrative as well as how the functional system of the narrative telling figures people as certain kind of tellers or audiences. A wide array of communicative resources may be called on to navigate these dimensions of narrating, so the disruptions caused by acquired communication disorders typically reshape the ways both tellers and audiences engage with conversational narratives.

Indexing Steve's Identities: Mixing Registers, Blending Identities, and Claiming Authority

Steve's blending of social roles in figured worlds was clearly displayed in our conversations with him on the sideline. Over the full observation at the football game, Steve displayed the discourse register of an avid *sports fan*. When the home team received the opening kick-off, Steve was already absorbed, shouting encouragement from the sidelines "COME ON. COME ON NOW!" and shaking his head at missed plays. Steve and Kerry coordinated much of their cheering (e.g., Steve: "There we go, good job good job!" Kerry: "Good cut back"). Only minutes into the game, the home team made a long touchdown run and Steve burst into cheers with the rest of the crowd, saying "BEAUTIFUL PLAY! . . . Yeah all day long, all day long . . . all day long" as Kerry applauded enthusiastically. Steve also told me about specific players as they ran by, identifying them by their names and jersey numbers and telling me about their chances of being recruited by college teams.

Early in the first quarter, the home team recovered a fumble and a player appeared to be injured on the field. Alert to such incidents, Steve started heading to the other end of the field before most of the stadium realized there was an injury. Kerry, Cassie, and I stayed where we were. Members of the Sports Medicine Project joined the coaches on the field and attended to the injured player. Steve's lapel microphone picked him up asking someone "What's the story (about the guy) that's injured?" The two have a brief discussion about what they can tell from the side lines, "I think it's his leg." Steve finds someone else to ask, "Is he hurt bad?" and then commiserates with them about there being such a bad injury so early in the game. Steve stays at the other end of the field trying to find out more about what is going on. Pretty soon, we see the player carried off the field on a golf cart and the crowd settles into subdued applause. As he watches from the sideline, I hear him say to no one in particular, "Boy I just love the team doc. Love it. Unfortunately, I just can't do that I guess. Just can't do it." Another round of applause and the announcer acknowledges the injured player. Steve stops someone coming off of the field, addressing them by name and asking: "Hey D—what's the story out there?" Transcript 4.1 starts when Steve returns to report to us what's going on: "It's looking bad. First thing . . . they think he broke his tibia." Kerry responds: "Broke his leg, ouch." Over these interactions, Steve was blending fan and sports medicine registers and orienting to narratives (both in seeking the story of the injured player on the field and in his comments that index a life story that positions him as *no-longer-a-doctor*).

As we continued to have a long discussion about the probable injury (e.g., Kerry "The tibia, now is that the big bone?") and what hospital they will take him to, a narrative emerges about the injured player—how it happened, how badly he's injured, how he will be cared for (probably taken to an ER), and how sad it is that this happened especially this early in the game. In Ochs and Capps (2001) terms, this emerging narrative is marked by distributed *tellership* (the telling distributed across Steve, Kerry, and me), high *tellability* (an injury on the field being a matter for serious concern), high *embeddedness* (with the narrative emerging in the interaction as opposed to being a bounded, separate story), fairly high *linearity* (the story moving from injury to assessment to treatment at the hospital, although many details were still not known), and a *moral stance* highlighting good sportsmanship (the opposing player's injury being a source for concern, not celebration) and the value of medical intervention (physicians standing by). In this interaction, Steve's statements identified the medical issue, but the narrative world was evoked more by the contributions made by Kerry and me. This event also highlights Steve's changed status. As our conversation continued (beyond the excerpt in Transcript 4.1), Steve repeated the comment caught earlier from his microphone: "Gal' I just love to play the- the team physician like that I guess I love it I love to and unfortunately I just can't."

Steve was deploying a multimodal array of communicative resources that positioned him as a partial insider to the world of high school football, as no-longer-a-doctor, as a parent and husband, and as a participant in my research. Physically, he moved freely along the home team's sidelines, not sitting in the stands. When he sensed trouble on the field, he quickly moved down the sidelines to where the play happened. He asked others what happened and got information about the injury. When he returned, he offered us a diagnosis. My questions all seemed oriented to getting the story (whom he talked to, where the player was going now). Steve offered answers. Jointly, we co-produced a narrative. However, Steve also deployed an array of resources that marked his identity as *no-longer-being-a-doctor*. He did not join the medical team and coaches on the field. He bemoaned his inability to practice medicine, first to himself when he was down the field and then to Kerry. By where he went and where he didn't go, by what he said and did and what he didn't say and do, Steve positioned himself and was positioned in multiple figured worlds across this short stretch of interactions on the sidelines.

Note on Methods: Language Ideologies and Systematic Transcription

As a concept *figured worlds* highlights people's beliefs about who *figures* into everyday interactions—who has what rights to be in what spaces, to participate in activities, and to take on particular roles in functional systems. Anthropological linguists use the term *language ideologies* to describe beliefs people hold about language use in interactions. Kroskrity (2004) notes that language ideologies are diverse, are held both explicitly and implicitly, and guide people's engagement in and evaluation of communicative interactions. Language ideologies involve not only attitudes and beliefs about language, but also ways of naming languages, dialects, types of speech, genres, and speech acts. It is important to recognize that language ideologies inform all of our interactions and interpretations, including the beliefs of clients and participants we are studying, our own beliefs as researchers and clinicians, and the beliefs of people reading our clinical and research reports. Being aware of our language ideologies is particularly important when we are making decisions about collecting and analyzing interactional data. Where Chapter 1 introduced the importance of developing a theoretically grounded approach to transcribing interactional data, this note highlights the importance of developing and using *transcription keys* to guide systematic analysis of interactions and to guard against smuggling unexamined ideologies into our analysis.

Broadly, a *transcription key* lists the conventions you are using to represent the communicative resources you have identified as important for interpreting a specific interaction and have systematically attended to during the transcription process. Developing a transcription key is an iterative process, developed in repeated passes through the data. In my research lab we begin with a preliminary transcription key that we update and finalize for each data set. Our consensus transcription process broadly involves three passes through the data, with a goal of updating the transcription key at the end of each pass and finalizing it on the last pass. Grounded in SDA our preliminary transcription key (see Chapter 1) describes the organization of the transcript and participants' speaking turns (e.g., like a musical score), the identifiers for each participant (e.g., initials of their names), and how different communicative resources are presented, including: spoken language (e.g., standard orthography); speech production patterns (e.g., phonetic transcription); prosody (e.g., punctuation marks); silences (e.g., measured in seconds); non-speech vocalizations (e.g., in square brackets); marked use of social voices and registers (e.g., font styles); and visible gestures and actions (e.g., temporally located with an asterisk in the person's speaking line and described later). Although there is value in using transcription conventions that are relatively standardized especially when sharing transcripts with other clinicians or in research publications, it is important to remember there is no right or wrong way to represent a specific communicative resource. The goal of transcription is to develop thick descriptions that support interpretations that are systematically tied to the data.

A well-done analysis requires researchers to carefully list conventions in the transcription key, to systematically attended to those features throughout the transcription process (updating transcripts as conventions are finalized), and to use the same conventions for all participants (including clinicians and researchers). Casual attention to communicative resources and poorly operationalized transcription systems lead to inaccurate interpretations and smuggle in researchers' language ideologies. A classic example is the use of *eye-dialect* (like "He wuz gonna get'em."). As a literary device, novelists use eye-dialect to build up a character's identity and social positioning by playing on language ideologies and stereotypic linguistic forms. As such, eye-dialect is often used to mark less preferred dialects (e.g., Spanglish, African-American English, Southern American English) or as indication of characters' education levels and socioeconomic class. Early conversation analysts (i.e., researchers who follow CA approaches discussed in the Note on Methods in Chapter 1) were initially trained in sociology (not as sociolinguists) and chose to use eye dialect to capture the sounds of talk. However, eye-dialect does not offer a technical system of phonetic representation, and it has routinely been applied unsystematically (e.g., using "know" for standard dialect speakers even though the k is clearly silent; writing "anybuddy" for "anybody" to mark an informal register). The effect of *ad hoc* use of eye dialect is not only a lack of precision, but also stereotypical representations of people's identities (see Green, Franquiz, & Dixon, 1997; Roberts, 1997).

Inconsistent and *ad hoc* marking of speech forms threatens the validity of any analysis, but is especially problematic for SDA, where the goal is to analyze the communicative patterns of functional systems. A stereotypical analysis of interactions including individuals with communication disorders might represent speech productions errors (e.g., false starts) only when they reify the category of the disorder (e.g., stuttering), but then overlook similar disfluencies in the talk of researchers or other communication partners. Thus, systematic analysis of a full range of communicative resources being used by everyone in an interaction is a critical first step for understanding the diverse ways communication success and communication disorders are distributed in interaction.

Chapter Summary: Recognizing Identity Work in Interaction

In this chapter, we have begun to apply SDA to analyze interactions involving people with communicative disorders. We do not need different kinds of tools to do this work, but we do need to think carefully about what tools will best highlight important patterns in the communicative interactions and how to apply those tools. The study of communication disorders highlights the importance of attending to identity work, a dimension of interaction that is often taken for granted. To focus analysis on identity, we introduced the new but theoretically related concept of figured worlds, and used these three guiding questions:

- *What social identities and roles are associated with these sociocultural activities?*
- *How are people positioning themselves and others in this sociomaterial space?*
- *How are communicative resources indexing potential identities?*

As people re-negotiate their rights and responsibilities of communicative access and participation, it becomes particularly important to attend to positioning practices, language ideologies, and communicative resources centrally involved in identity work (e.g., registers and narratives).

Both as diagnostic and social categories, communication disorders position people outside of the "normal range" of human abilities and physical forms. Such categorizations can dominate identity work, positioning people rigidly and stereotypically only in terms of their deficits. However, people can dynamically re-imagine identities in figured worlds, rework functional systems, and adopt new communicative practices. For example, consider the social movements that have reinterpreted deafness as a cultural difference rather than a deficit. Likewise, Nancy Bagatell (2010) traces a shift away from seeking a cure for autism spectrum disorder (ASD) to a focus on optimizing successful development and building sociomaterial spaces that support social participation for all individuals, including individuals with ASD. Such moves challenge not only medical models, but also our own practices as we recognize and embrace new forms of communicative diversity in sociocultural activities and sociomaterial spaces.

I close this summary by returning to Larry's words in the epigraph of Part 2. Figured worlds may provide at least part of the answer to Larry's (unstated) question of why so many of his friends and family could no longer talk with him. Too often, figured worlds are inflexible and unexamined. If Larry's friends interpreted his silences through their routine understandings of how conversations should go, then they might interpret his lack of response as uncomfortable disinterest, the way they would react to the non-responsiveness displayed by an able-bodied communicator. Instead, they needed to imagine new *figured worlds*, as I will emphasize in Chapter 5.

Reflective Observations

1. *Tracing figured worlds in everyday communicative interactions.* Review the data you collected for the reflective observations in Chapters 1 and 3, and write up a brief analysis of the *identity work* in these interactions by providing preliminary responses to the three questions outlined in this chapter:

    a. Identify a range of possible social roles and identities associated with the figured worlds in the interactions. Be sure to attend to all sociocultural activities at play here.

    b. Trace ways that people are positioning themselves and others in particular social roles and assuming specific rights and responsibilities. How are identities accepted or contested? Give specific examples.

    c. Describe how communicative resources are indexing different identities, and discuss examples of ways different registers, social voices, modes of address, and embodied enactments are signaling different identities or social roles.

2. *Comparing identity work across interactions.* A core assumption of SDA is that identity work is a part of all interactions. Thus, compare the preliminary analysis of the identity work at play in your interactional data (from item 1) with analyses completed by others (either published data, or analyses from other members of your class or research group). Discuss similarities and differences in how identity work is being managed in the different interactions.

3. *Creating a transcription key.* Revise your transcription key to include codes that trace identity work in your data. This revision may include attending to changes in discourse registers as well as changes in manners of enacting different communicative resources. Develop a consistent convention for transcribing these communicative resources and list them in your transcription key.

Suggested Readings

By focusing on functional systems and figured worlds, SDA is especially useful in documenting the diverse ways people with communication disorders are positioned in everyday interactions. In addition to the articles referenced throughout this chapter, here are three readings that offer detailed analyses of the roles of communication partners. As you read through these studies, pay particular attention to how interactions are represented, if the article includes a transcription key, and how consistently transcription conventions are used.

1. "Conversational frameworks for the accomplishment of meaning in aphasia" (Goodwin, 2003a). In this chapter, Charles Goodwin analyzed the diverse multimodal communicative resources used by adult family members to support conversational interactions with his father, Chil, who had chronic global aphasia.

2. "Interactional differences in Alzheimer's discourse: An examination of AD speech across two audiences" (Ramanathan-Abbott, 1994). In this article, Vai Ramanathan analyzed family stories told by a woman with dementia and found that the narratives she co-told with her husband were much more disrupted than ones she told with the researcher.

3. "Semiotic remediation, conversational narratives and aphasia" (Hengst, 2010). My analysis of conversational narratives collected during interviews with adults with aphasia and their family members highlights how shared histories support narrators both in telling specific stories and in building identities through the stories they tell.

Notes

1. All study participants and patients throughout Part 2 are referred to by pseudonyms.
2. For details on P.L. 94–142: www2.ed.gov/about/offices/list/osers/idea35/history/index_pg10.html

Chapter 5

Recognizing Interactional Success With Communication Disorders

This chapter explores the challenges to, and potentials for, successful communication inherent in functional systems that include people with communication disorders. Too often, communication troubles are simply attributed to the person with the communication disorder. However, as we saw in Chapter 2, *situated discourse analysis* (SDA) recognizes that communicative interactions are distributed accomplishments. Thus, successful communication emerges through the moment-by-moment alignments of functional systems as people work to accomplish goals, coordinate participation, and deploy meaningful communicative resources.

If you ask people what is needed for successful communication, a common answer is likely to be shared language. However, everyday communicative interactions often involve strangers with diverse language backgrounds, and all of us have encountered words and discourse registers in our primary language that we are unfamiliar with or only partially understand. For example, you might struggle with legal language in formal contracts or specialized terminology in unfamiliar disciplines (physics, mathematics, philosophy). From a multimodal perspective, we also have varying familiarity and abilities in understanding visual, mathematical, and musical representations, as well as the typical arrangements of sociomaterial spaces. Consider, for example, the ease with which you navigate your local grocery store (e.g., reading signs, recognizing pricing, understanding checkout conventions), and yet how baffling and difficult it may be to shop for food the first time in another country. Instead of conceptualizing communicative competence as a catalogue of isolated traits all participants need to possess, SDA invites us to trace the distributed processes that support communicative success with whatever experiences and abilities individuals bring to an interaction.

Communicative competence is not a single, settled, uniform thing, but a complex, in-flux patchwork of partial and incremental understandings as people muddle through everyday interactions. Jan Blommaert (2010) describes that patchwork as people's *communicative repertoires* of language use around *bit competencies* with *linguistic codes* (e.g., languages), *communicative modes* (e.g., written or spoken), *discourse registers* (e.g., vernacular or formal), and *sociocultural domains* (e.g., professional discourse, sociocultural activities). As an example, Blommaert describes his varied competences with the four languages he uses regularly—Dutch, French, German and English. When using Dutch (his first language), he can routinely and successfully shift among a variety of vernacular and formal forms in both spoken and written modes. Although he learned both German and English later, his bit competencies in the two are very different. When using English (his primary language for academic work in sociolinguistics), he has considerable facility with giving conference presentations, writing articles and books, and discussing academic topics with colleagues and students. However, he struggles with many everyday uses of English, such as shopping. His use of German, on the other hand, remains limited mainly to what he needed to know to pass his school exams. Blommaert observes that tests designed to determine a speaker's *general* proficiency in a given language (even with subscores for speaking, listening, reading and writing) miss the point: "they overlook the very specific nature of language use, of the various chunks and pieces of language we deploy for specific tasks" (p. 104).

SDA shifts our attention to the *distributed communicative repertoires* of functional systems, an approach particularly important for understanding the complexities introduced by communicative disorders. As Larry noted, interacting-in-unanticipated-ways due to his paralysis also made apparent the limited competencies of some of his communication partners. Although highly competent in aligning with Larry's pre-ALS communicate repertoires, some people apparently could not summon the practices needed to communicate with Larry when he was no longer able to give rapid, verbal responses. The ways acquired communication disorders disrupt the communicative practices and competencies of communication partners has also been documented by researchers and clinicians who specialize in treating patients with Alzheimer's disease and the associated declines in cognition, or *dementia* (e.g., Davis, 2005; Hamilton, 1994; Orange, 2001; Ramanathan-Abbott, 1997). Familiar communication partners (e.g., family members, friends, caregivers, co-workers) play particularly critical roles in the communicative lives of individuals with such complex and evolving communication disorders.

Focusing on successful everyday communication among partners managing communication disorders highlights the importance of attending to the communicative *flexibilities* available in functional system, the key roles communication partners play in negotiating successful communication, and patterns of change across all participants as people adapt to the unanticipated-patterns-of-interaction typical of communication disorders. In this chapter, we explore how people with communicative disorders and their communicative partners engage in the distributed work of successful communicative alignment. The data I present here were collected to support the development of augmentative and alternative communication (AAC) technologies for face-to-face interactions by detailing the everyday communicative environments of young adults on our campus (current or former students) who self-identified as potential AAC users (Hengst, McCartin, Valentino, Devanga, & Sherrill, 2016). These data allow us to explore the *mobility* of functional systems as people navigate public spaces, *communication brokering* as partners augment each other's social roles to mediate successful interactions, and *interactional discourse resources* participants orient to in everyday interactions. The notions of communicative repertoires and bit competencies invite us to recognize the communicative diversity of all interactions and develop more precise accounts of communicative success and trouble in interactions involving people with communication disorders.

The Case of Jessie: Navigating Sociomaterial Spaces

Using ethnographic methods we interviewed participants about their everyday interactions and collected video-recorded observations of them navigating campus activities and spaces (Hengst et al., 2016). Here we focus on the second campus observation of Jessie, one of the five participants who self-identified as having cerebral palsy, and Karen, a personal assistant he worked with regularly and well.

At the time these data were recorded, Jessie was a 30-year-old doctoral student. I had met him two years earlier through our joint service on a campus committee charged with identifying and addressing campus accessibility issues for students, faculty, staff, and visitors with disabilities. Jessie was invited to serve on the committee because of his dual expertise as a student in disability studies and a disability stakeholder, that is, a person with a disability on campus. In interviews, Jessie reported that he had been diagnosed with cerebral palsy (CP) as an infant and had used assistive technologies, including motorized wheelchairs and special education services, throughout his schooling. Jessie's primary communication disorder was a *dysarthria* marked by a slow initiation of speech and reduced intelligibility on all utterances. He reported he had used an AAC device to support face-to-face interactions when he was younger, but had abandoned it years before we met. He could not recall which device he had used and had no plans for using one in the future—it was his position that people needed to learn to be diverse listeners who could adapt their interactions to his patterns of talk. He reported that, although people did have difficulty *understanding* him when he spoke, they often seemed to have even more difficulty *letting* him speak—that is, giving him the interactional space and time he needed to take his speaking turns.

The data excerpt we will focus on was taken from a campus observation that included Jessie going to the tech store to buy a remote-control device to use when he was teaching or presenting talks. Figure 5.1 displays two photos from this day—the first shows Jessie and Karen in the research office sitting together with a researcher as they make plans for their observation,

(a)

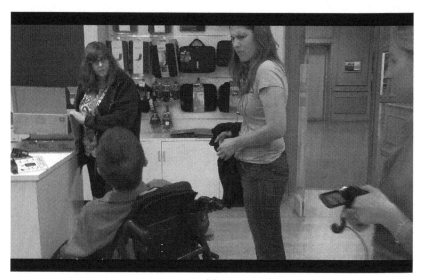

(b)

Figure 5.1 Two photos from Jessie's second observation: a) Jessie (center) and his personal assistant Karen during an interview with researchers just before that day's observation; b) Jessie (front) and Karen (right) talking with a clerk (left) at the tech store.

Source: Hengst et al., 2016.

and the second shows Jessie and Karen interacting with the tech store clerk. Transcript 5.1 is an excerpt of the interaction that Jessie and Karen had with the store clerk (in that second photo). For the research, we were particularly interested in understanding how Karen mediated Jessie's interactions with others.

Transcript 5.1 The transcript shows speaking lines for 3 people throughout, J for Jessie, PA for his personal assistant and Z for the store clerk, plus one researcher (H). (Note: several research assistants are also present, but not represented in this transcript; see Hengst et al., 2016).

J:	I would wonder if you had uhm if you sold uhm the X to change the slides or change the
PA:	
Z:	

J:	pictures clickers [..2..] clickers Clickers.
	[looks at PA] [looks at Z]
PA:	CLICKERS! Oh clickers I'm
Z:	The wireless- speakers?
	[looks at J] [looks at PA, then back at J]

J:	No, when you have a presentation.
PA:	sorry. Oh yeah, if you're giving a presentation
	[clicking gesture]
Z:	The I-Clickers
	[Z looks at PA]

J:	yeah.
PA:	like [.1.] if you have power point up and you need to li- right? Actually I could
	[lifts hand as a screen] [clicking gesture]
Z:	

J:	
PA:	totally use one of those [.1.] do you guys sell those?
Z:	Uhmm I think we have them at the
	[points to back wall, shifts body]

J:	
PA:	oh I'm sorry What is THAT? I don't even know
	[points to display]
H:	sorry sorry
Z:	back [.1.] over here [.1.] uhm.
	[gathering walks to back of store]

J:	
PA:	what this stuff is anymore. [..2..] Yeah I see people who have those in class and like
Z:	

J:	Yeah.
PA:	Oh yeah totally
Z:	Presentation remotes. We have two [....4....] They're both uhh [.1.]
	[points to remotes on display] [picks up two remotes]

J:	Wh-what
PA:	
Z:	one's a Kensington one's a Targus [.1.] depends on what your preference is. [.l.]
	[looking at remotes]

J:	are the main differences? [loughing]
PA:	[loughing]
Z:	Well [..2..] one of them's green, one of them's red.
	[flips over remotes one at a time, looking at back of each]

J:	
PA:	Huh.
Z:	This one's the green [.1.] and this one's the red laser.
	[holds up the green remote, then the red remote]

Transcript 5.1 begins as Jessie initiates an interaction with the clerk: "I would wonder if you had uhm if you sold uhm the X to change the slides or change the pictures." When the clerk says, "The wireless-" Jessie interrupts saying "clickers." After a two second pause when no one responds, Jessie looks at Karen (his PA) and repeats "clickers," as if inviting her to help with the interaction. It seems that the store clerk doesn't understand his attempts to say "clickers," and Jessie tries two self-repetitions, which Karen finally understands, then also repeats twice. To clarify what type of clicker Jessie wants, the clerk guesses "The I-Clicker," which is a wireless device students use to respond in class to questions posed by teachers. Jessie counters by saying, "No, when you have a presentation." Karen then expands on Jessie's utterance. Using words and gestures, she acts out using an (imaginary) hand-held clicker, gesturing and gazing toward an imagined screen and saying, "if you're giving a presentation like . . . if you have power point up and you need to li- right?" Jessie confirms "yeah," and Karen then exclaims she could use one too. The clerk responds that she thinks they are in the back. As the group moves to the back of the store, Karen asks what those things are actually called and the clerk replies, "presentation remotes" and then says they carry two brands. When they get to the display, Jessie asks the clerk to compare the brands, "What are the main differences?." The clerk hesitates and then just notes one is red and one is green, which Jessie and Karen receive with laughter.

Mobility of Functional Systems

The success of everyday communicative interactions requires alignments of functional systems around multiple and shifting activities as people move through the multiple and diverse sociomaterial spaces of their daily lives. To begin to address how such dynamic success is achieved when some participants have communication disorders, we will begin by asking: ***How are accomplishments being flexibly distributed?***

As discussed in Chapter 2, everyday communicative interactions are always situated in functional systems. However, functional systems are not events neatly bounded by either time or space. People draw on immediate and long past interactions and experiences as they navigate and traverse their everyday environments. Understanding functional systems as dynamic, complex, and mobile is not new. In his now classic example of a blind man and a cane, Gregory Bateson highlights how functional systems are continually assembled and reassembled:

> If what you are trying to explain is a given piece of behavior, such as the locomotion of [a] blind man, then, for this purpose, you will need the street, the stick, the man; the street, the stick, and so on, round and round. But when the blind man sits down to eat his lunch, his stick and

its messages will no longer be relevant—if it is his eating that you want to understand.

(Bateson, 1972, p. 459)

A focus on the mobility of functional systems highlights key issues for communication and communication disorders, which have often been approached as if they were frozen and anchored matters. First, functional systems are not fixed, but dynamic and mobile, continuously being assembled and reassembled (e.g., as the blind man moves from walking on the sidewalk to sitting at a table in the restaurant). Second, social roles and responsibilities of people shift both within and across functional systems. Third, the availability and prominence of potential tools and resources continually shift. Fourth, experiences of functional systems are always perspectival—the blind man's experience of interactions in the restaurant is different from that of the wait-staff, and both are different from the researcher's experience of the same interaction. Finally, it is important to recognize continuities as well as change. As the blind man in Bateson's example sits at the lunch counter, he remains blind and his blindness factors into how the functional systems around eating, ordering, and paying will play out.

Considering the theoretical and methodological implications of mobility in his research on high school students' literate practices, Brice Nordquist (2017) highlights the permeability of presumed boundaries between locations and the reach of activities across time and space. For example, rather than limiting his research on students' writing to classrooms, he traced students' movements over the course of their days. He found, for example, that a group of students, including a focal student he was following, routinely collaborated on schoolwork during bus rides to and from school although they didn't acknowledge this collaboration to teachers for fear of being accused of cheating. His current research on dual credit high school programs in New York City (Nordquist, 2018) is tracing a multilingual group of students whose activities and roles morph as they socialize and do school tasks during hours-long commutes (walking and riding subways) to and from school.

Jessie's Case—Making Plans and Navigating Spaces

The University of Illinois has a large campus (about 700 hectares) with complex indoor and outdoor spaces that students, faculty, staff, and visitors routinely navigate. At the center of the main campus is a grassy quadrangle (or quad) surrounded by many of the original campus buildings, including a large, multipurpose Student Union at one end of the main quad. The quad serves as a commons for foot traffic, public events, and hanging out to study, play games, or just socialize. In initial interviews with the participants, we used a static campus map to identify where they spent most of their time and what areas of campus they frequented. Not surprisingly, their answers were diverse, with little overlap. Although the Student Union did not emerge as a highly frequented place, we selected it as a focal point for the campus observations because participants all knew where it was, most had visited it at least once, and it was close to our research lab. The Union also provided opportunities for participants to engage in multi-party interactions in a variety of public spaces (e.g., elevators, multiple food vendors, a coffee shop, a tech store, a computer lab, a bowling alley and pool hall, and study rooms) and allowed us to travel together across the quad to get there.

Given that this was his second observation, Jessie (and the research team) knew what to expect. Jessie came prepared with plans of what he wanted to do, and he invited Karen, a personal assistant he worked well with, to join him in the study. As was typical, the team met with Jessie and Karen first in the research lab to plan the observation. Jessie was asked to select an activity from our list of things to do at the Union (e.g., visit the bowling alley to find out about wheelchair access to the lanes), or any other similar activity. Jessie chose to use this second observation to run an errand—he wanted to sell his used books at the temporary book stall set up on the quad outside the Union. The group (Jessie, Karen, and three research assistants) went together from the research office to the book stall at the end of the quad. After Jessie sold his books, he suggested another errand in the Student Union. He wanted to buy the remote-control device to advance his slides when he was teaching his classes. So the group moved from the quad to the Tech Store. Finally, the group returned to the research office, passing the time with small talk about their personal lives.

In many ways Jessie was in control of this session, making decisions about where the team went, what their goals were, and how long they stayed. Lasting about 86 minutes, this campus observation was the longest of the 16 collected in the study. It included a total of seven active participants: Jessie, Karen, and two unexpected participants (the clerks in the bookstall and the tech store) along with three research assistants (who helped with recording and also secured permissions from unexpected participants). Except for length, it was typical of the 16 observations, which ranged from 4–9 participants, lasted an average of 41 minutes (range of 8–86 minutes), and were almost always marked by frequent transitions across sociocultural activities and sociomaterial spaces on campus. Given our interest in AAC devices (which are often extensively programmed for expected interactions in fixed sites), the mobility displayed in these brief observations was striking.

Brokering Social Roles and Successful Participation

Some language researchers use the term *brokering* to describe the diverse, routine, and variously named ways people support one another's participation in communicative interactions[1] (Dorner, Orellana, & Jiménez, 2008;

McQuillan & Tse, 1995). Applied linguists have explored ways minority language communities draw on communication brokers to navigate both the language and the social practices of unfamiliar regulations (e.g., getting a driver's license). In immigrant families, for example, children who attend English speaking schools will often be called on to broker interactions for their parents (De Fina, 2012; Perry, 2009). This is also common among the deaf community, where a hearing child raised bilingually with ASL (as a home language) and English (as a school/community language) will broker for their parents (Pizer, Walters, & Meier, 2013). Brokering describes a range of roles. For example, real estate agents broker the processes and terms of buying and selling homes, and the digitally adept may broker online transactions for those unfamiliar with computers. Brokers use their verbal and nonverbal resources, as well as experiences with sociocultural activities and roles, to mediate interactions. In less marked ways, brokering is a routine part of everyday interactions as we help others navigate unfamiliar social situations or activities, highlight points of connection between strangers, and share our expertise with others. To understand how success is distributed across people, we ask: *How are people brokering one another into social roles and successful patterns of participation?*

For our purposes, brokering offers a way to describe how communicative competence and success are distributed across people especially in functional systems involving diverse communicators. In *Hawking Incorporated*, Mialet (2012) provides a thick description of what I would call both the immediate and extended brokering that was routine in the communicative life and professional career of the famous physicist, Stephen Hawking. Hawking was diagnosed with ALS as a young adult. He began using a computerized AAC system in 1985 and continued using successive devices until he died in 2018. The devices gave him a digital voice and allowed him to select, store and speak words. They offered him a remarkable freedom to speak publicly and professionally (e.g., in televised documentaries, public engagements). However, his successful use of AAC in public spaces hid the enormous and distributed supports that brokered that success.

Through her ethnographic research, Mialet (2012) documented the people, practices, institutions, and artifacts that collectively assembled Hawking's identity and communicative success. She offers "a thick description of the network of competencies—the computer/the synthesizer/the personal assistant/the graduate assistant/the nurses—that transforms a man deprived of speech and movement into 'the genius we all know'" (p. 6). Hawking could preprogram his AAC system to efficiently voice lectures; however, using it to produce spontaneous utterances was a laborious and slow process. He could at best produce only 15–20 words per minute, a rate that disrupted the timing of everyday interactions (i.e., typical spoken language rates are 100–200 words per minute). To broker successful public appearances, Hawking's audiences and interviewers were routinely asked to submit questions in advance. Answers were written into the device by Hawking but also by his assistants. These constraints made follow-up questions so difficult they were typically not even entertained. (Recall that Larry, who also had ALS, likewise used alone time to type out things to tell/ask his family and friends, but he did not have a team to join in co-authoring.)

Beyond planning ahead for face-to-face interactions, Hawking relied on teams of people, to maintain his computerized AAC system. That maintenance included students and personal assistants working daily to charge the computer batteries and correctly connect access switches, and computer engineers designing and continuously updating the hardware and software of his AAC system. As digital technologies advanced and components of his original AAC system became outdated, Hawking was not impressed with the "better" voices and was determined to keep his trademark voice—the voice so many people recognized as his. Maintaining that distinctive voice involved a tremendous amount of specialized engineering and programming. Mialet also documented the mundane (and "unaided") ways he carried on everyday communicative interactions with his personal network of family, friends, students, and personal assistants. These familiar people seemed to be able to carry on a conversation with him by reading his subtle gestures, knowing and anticipating his routines and preferences, and at many points simply speaking and acting for him. As the title of her book (*Hawking Incorporated*) suggests, Mialet concludes: "Contrary to the solitary genius depicted by the media, Hawking resembles a manager at the head of a company, a company that has explicitly become his extended body" (p. 22). From a communicative perspective, Mailet's analysis illustrates the range and complexity of brokering practices that were employed to build and sustain Hawking's communicative success.

Brokering Jessie's Roles as Instructor and Shopper

As noted earlier, the trip to the tech store was not pre-planned, at least not by our research team. In the planning meeting, Jessie had only mentioned the goal of selling back his books, so the researchers and even Karen were not sure what Jessie's errand to the tech store was about until they arrived. As Jessie asked the clerk for help, he was clearly having difficulty coming up with a name for the device before saying "clickers" (see Transcript 5.1). At this point, Karen, who had apparently just understood Jessie's speech, also repeats "clickers" twice, with some emphasis (as if saying, "Oh, you mean clickers"). In this way, Karen displays her own sudden recognition of Jessie's speech and uses conversational repetition to restate Jessie's word more intelligibly. As the interaction unfolds from there, we will focus on the ways that Karen, as Jessie's PA, flexibly used her positioning to broker a successful interaction and to *key* (in Goffman's sense discussed in Chapter 3) social roles that Jessie was taking up—both as an instructor (not a student) and as a knowledgeable shopper.

It could be tempting to see this interaction as a simple issue of intelligibility and to understand Karen as more attuned to Jessie's speech and able to translate his words for the clerk. However, as we analyzed the interaction, it was clear that speech intelligibility alone did not resolve the ambiguities, or misalignments, in this situation. Once the clerk understood the word clickers, she guessed, incorrectly, that Jessie must be a student looking for an I-Clicker. We cannot know, but we suspect that the clerk's guess reflected the figured worlds and social roles she imagined for Jessie (not expecting him to be a teacher or presenter). Interestingly, neither Jessie nor Karen seemed to know (or be able to recall) the name of the device he was looking for. Karen uses words and gestures to demonstrate using a hand-held remote. Saying "if you're giving a presentation like . . . if you have power point up and you need to li- right?" and acting out a narrative-like nonverbal performance where she is holding a (figured) remote with her right hand, pointing it toward an imagined screen (represented by her left hand), while gesturing with her right hand to simulate clicking the remote to advance slides on this imagined screen. Her embodied enactment works both to clarify Jessie's meaning (that he is looking for a presentation tool, not a student response tool) and to offer the clerk a different role for Jessie, a figured world where Jessie is a university instructor using presentation tools to give a class lecture.

Another striking feature of Karen's brokering role in the interaction emerges when she shifts roles to a co-shopper. Once she understands what Jessie is looking for, she enthusiastically joins in: "Actually I could totally use one of those . . . do you guys sell those?" The clerk responds that she thinks they are kept in the back of the store. At the end of this interaction Karen adjusts her stance to that of a social partner or friend as well as a co-shopper, as she and Jessie share their surprise and amusement at the clerk's surprisingly non-technical distinction between the two brands ("one of them's green, one of them's red"). Our sense was that Karen's co-participant roles (acting out giving a presentation, being a co-shopper, and engaging as a friend) all helped position Jessie in these roles too and to construct him as a person inhabiting multiple positive social roles.

Brokering highlights the diverse ways successful communication is distributed across people in functional systems. We were especially struck by the fluid and flexible interactional practices Karen displayed as she used co-participation (e.g., co-shopper) to mirror Jessie's social roles, to support their successful communication with the store clerk, and to accomplish multiple goals.

Interactional Discourse Resources and the Building Tasks of Interactional Contexts

Building on the concept of distributed communication, SDA highlights the ways communicative resources support people in successfully aligning with one another in sociomaterial spaces. In Chapter 2 we introduced Hanks' (1990) concept of *indexical ground* to help us trace the ways people actively build *interactional contexts* that situate (or contextualize) communicative resources. Contexts are never static or simply pre-fabricated; instead, people's words and actions are *contextualizing*, building contexts moment-by-moment in interaction (Goodwin & Duranti, 1992). A contextualizing move makes a proposal to others in the interaction about what is going on now and what should happen next, a proposal that can be accepted, questioned, modified, ignored, or rejected by recipients. People are, thus, negotiating interactional contexts, social roles, and sociocultural activities *through* interaction. In this chapter, we focus on the ways people deploy communicative resources to simultaneously co-construct interactional contexts and situated meanings, asking: ***How are communicative resources distributed and jointly deployed to successfully coordinate activities and meanings?***

Interactional resources include the diverse range of semiotics that people recognize as indexing particular material contexts, figured worlds and sociocultural activities. For example, if you think back to the *Cindy Magic* data (Figure 1.1), the clothes basket was an interactional resource, a material object that participants collectively aligned around. Although the basket was a critical element for one of the sociocultural activities (folding clothes), its central positioning in the living room also anchored Nora, Paul, and Anna's participation with *Cindy Magic* and the research. As we discussed in Chapter 4, indexical grounds are not random collections of things that we can reference. Instead, indexical grounds are figured worlds, with a cast of characters, a motivated collection of things, and affective atmospheres (tense, relaxed, joyous, sad), all animated by the goals of sociocultural activities. Communicative resources, like social voices (e.g., character voices and family voices) in *Cindy Magic*, function to shift and sustain indexical grounds (e.g., proposing, sustaining, or breaking out of the figured world of *Cindy Magic*). Another nice example of how indexical grounds shift can be seen in Karen moving from the role of personal assistant to co-shopper with Jessie in Transcript 5.1, a move that displayed flexibilities in the functional system.

In research that my colleagues and I have done (e.g., Hengst, 2006, 2010; Hengst, Frame, Neuman-Stritzel, & Gannaway, 2005; Hengst et al., 2016), we have identified a particular type of interactional resource that we have come to call *interactional discourse resources* (IDRs). IDRs are highly recognizable multimodal discourse patterns that routinely work to shift indexical grounds. IDRs are pervasive in everyday interactions, quickly shifting our understanding of, for example, whose words are being spoken (e.g., in *reported speech*), what time frame is being indexed (e.g., events in *conversational narratives*), and how seriously to take up the meanings (e.g., *verbal play*). IDRs are robust, deployed pervasively across the lifespan by diverse communicators, including people managing acquired communication disorders. They are *recognizable* through particular linguistic and nonlinguistic resources (e.g., as a conversational narrative may be set up with preparatory turns "Hey, did you hear . . .?"), *flexible* (realized through multiple and blended arrays of verbal and nonverbal resources), and often *fleeting* (as indexical grounds rapidly shift, jump, or get sustained through an array of resources).

In our ethnographic study of the everyday communicative environments of young adults with CP (Hengst et al., 2016), we operationally defined and analyzed five types of IDRs:

- *trouble source*—a disruption in the interaction (e.g., a misunderstanding) that shifts interactional attention to the production of communicative resources and meanings, and may include interactions focused on repairing the disruption;
- *procedural discourse*—which shifts participants to an expert-novice relationship where the expert provides information, instructions, or plans, for doing something, and which may be presented as a series of steps (e.g., setting a trip itinerary) or a list (e.g., listing or comparing brands carried in store);
- *playful episode*—which includes all forms of verbal play and humor that shift from a serious to non-serious *key* and which may include playing with the sounds and meanings of words through rhyming, punning, or teasing; telling jokes; and playing with voices through impersonations of others or acting out characters in narrative (re)tellings;
- *conversational narrative*—which reports actual or fictitious events that are displaced in time from the telling, shifting the time and often space to that of narrative events, and which may include background details, evaluations, and codas; and
- *conversational repetition*—which includes relatively immediate and interactional repetitions of one's own or another's productions of *open-class words* (as opposed to closed-class words like definite articles), and which was operationalized as the initial saying (or gesturing) and the repetition(s) that followed with no more than 3 interactional turns between each instance.

Although defined as mutually exclusive categories, it was common for a strip of interaction to include multiple IDRs. For example, when someone was (co-)telling a conversational narrative they often animated events with reported speech or emphasized emotional impact with conversational repetitions. Thus, we can attend to how communication partners are deploying IDRs and other such contextualizing resources to support successful communication by managing indexical grounds.

Gee (2011a, 2011b) offers another framework to think about how people build interactional contexts. As a linguist, he focuses on the role of language in this work. In his books, he details examples of how people use language to accomplish seven common *building tasks*. Briefly, these tasks are:

- *significance* (how the language we use signals what is significant, important, or relevant and what is not);
- *activities* (how language invokes and supports different activities and goals);
- *identities* (how language positions us and others in particular social roles),
- *relationships* (how language distances or aligns us with other participants, sociocultural identities, social groups, and institutions);
- *politics* (how language signals and enacts certain values, ideologies and power relations);
- *connections* (how language signals or ignores connections, whether cohesive links in the language used, interactional links across turns, thematic links in topics, or practical links among activities and people); and
- *sign systems and knowledge* (how language makes visible what our linguistic and semiotic repertories are or are not, how we think they should be used, what counts as knowledge, and how sign systems and knowledge relate to politics and identities).

Of course, SDA highlights the importance of attending to how people are orchestrating whole arrays of signs, not just language, to accomplish these building tasks. Recognizing communicative repertoires and bit competences as distributed, we should never imagine that building tasks are accomplished by one word, one phrase, one register alone.

Here I have introduced two approaches to analyzing how people jointly deploy communicative resources to successfully coordinate activities and meanings in functional systems. First, we can trace IDRs as resources that project recognizable indexical grounds, including how people can participate (e.g., as storytellers or audiences), what is going on, and what might be referenced through language and other means. Second, we can identify Gee's *building tasks*, highlighting the diverse work of specific utterances (e.g., to negotiate the identities, relationships, and power relationships that apply now). Both approaches focus our attention on how successful communication depends on people creating interactional contexts (or indexical grounds).

Interactional Discourse Resources in Motion: Following Functional Systems With Jessie

In Transcript 5.1, we saw a slice of interaction from Jessie, Karen, and the researchers visiting the tech store. As I noted at the beginning of the chapter, our core interest was in better understanding the mobile dynamics of functional systems that include individuals with CP, the brokering practices and roles of personal assistants in these interactions, and the way communicative success in an interaction depends on the distributed communicative repertoire of bit competencies assembled in the current functional system. To begin to map the distributed communication in these functional systems, I present here an analysis of their use of IDRs during the second observation, first presenting a quantitative analysis of the number of IDR episodes coded, and then an analysis of how specific episodes unfolded in interaction.

Our analysis (Hengst et al., 2016) focused on the five IDR categories defined earlier: *trouble sources*, *procedural discourse*, *verbal play*, *conversational narrative*, and *conversational repetition*. We coded the IDRs used by all participants in the functional system (i.e., not only IDRs the participant with CP was directly involved in producing). As expected, we found that IDRs occurred frequently in observations involving all six participants. Across the full dataset (16 observations) we identified a total of 3,272 instances of these five IDRs, with an average of 41.72 instances/1000 words (range 32.40–57.06) identified in sessions for each of the six participants. The most frequently used was conversational repetition (2,574 episodes), followed by playful episodes (220), conversational narratives (183), trouble sources (176) and procedural discourse (119). In Jessie's two sessions, there were a total of 559 IDR episodes (or 33.33 per 1000 words), with the most frequent being conversational repetition (453), followed by conversational narratives (46), trouble sources (34), procedural discourse (20) and playful episodes (6).

To see how the IDRs unfolded across activities, we first mapped how instances clustered across a contiguous strip of interaction. The density map in Figure 5.2 displays by category (i.e., not by temporal order) the number of instances of each of the five IDRs that appeared on each of the 45 pages of transcript across about 20 minutes of Jessie's second observation. Each page of the transcript represented approximately half a minute of interaction. Across this slice of interaction, all five types were identified, with a range of 1–10 identified per page. Only 5 of the 45 pages had a single category of IDR, while 16 pages displayed at least three kinds of IDRs.

We can also examine the use of IDRs in the excerpt presented in Transcript 5.1, which correspond with transcript pages 125–127 in the density map (Figure 5.2). The transcript begins with the *trouble source* (coded on page 125) and several instances of *conversational repetition* as Jessie, Karen and the clerk work to come up with and clarify the word "clickers." The second *trouble source* (coded on page 126) occurred around clarifying what type of clicker Jessie meant, as the clerk initially guessed "I-Clickers." This was also resolved in part by *conversational repetition* of "presentation" as they worked to index a device to help a person giving a "presentation"; Karen repeated this both verbally and nonverbally (by enacting giving a presentation). After they move to the back of the store, the clerk aligns around "presentation" by naming these devices "presentation remotes." At the end of the transcript we coded a brief *playful episode* when Jessie and Karen laugh at the clerk's surprisingly non-technical response "one of them's green, one of them's red";

Figure 5.2 — A density map showing number of IDRs on each of 45 pages of transcript in Jessie's second observation.

IDR Codes: T, D, P, N, R

pp.#	IDRs coded on page (stacked, bottom → top)	Activity
110	R, P	Traveling across the Quad
111	R, N, P	Traveling across the Quad
112	R, N, P, T	Traveling across the Quad
113	R, R, R, N, P, T	Traveling across the Quad
114	R, R, R	Traveling across the Quad
115	R, R, R, R	Traveling across the Quad
116	R, R, P, T, R, R	Traveling across the Quad
117	R, R, P, T	Traveling across the Quad
118	R, R, R, R, R, P	Traveling across the Quad
119	R, R, R, R, R, R	Traveling across the Quad
120	R, P	Traveling across the Quad
121	R, R, R, P	Shopping in the Union Tech Store
122	R, R, P, P	Shopping in the Union Tech Store
123	R, R, P, D	Shopping in the Union Tech Store
124	R, D, R, D, D, D	Shopping in the Union Tech Store
125	R, R, D, R, R, D, D, T	Shopping in the Union Tech Store
126	R, R, D, R, R, R, D, D, T	Shopping in the Union Tech Store
127	R, P, R, D, D	Shopping in the Union Tech Store
128	R, R, D, R, R, D	Shopping in the Union Tech Store
129	R, R, D, R, R, R, D	Shopping in the Union Tech Store
130	R, P, D, D	Shopping in the Union Tech Store
131	R, R, R, R, R, R, P, D	Shopping in the Union Tech Store
132	R, R, R, R, R, R, N, D	Shopping in the Union Tech Store
133	R, R, R, R, R, R, R, N, D	Shopping in the Union Tech Store
134	R, R, R, R, D	Shopping in the Union Tech Store
135	R, D	Shopping in the Union Tech Store
136	R, R, P, P, D, D	Shopping in the Union Tech Store
137	R, R, P, P, D, D	Shopping in the Union Tech Store
138	R, R, R, D	Shopping in the Union Tech Store
139	R, R, R, R	Shopping in the Union Tech Store
140	R, R, R, R, R, P	Shopping in the Union Tech Store
141	R, P	Shopping in the Union Tech Store
142	R, R, N	Returning to SHS
143	R, R, R, R, N	Returning to SHS
144	R, R, R, N, P, P	Returning to SHS
145	R, R, R, R, N, P	Returning to SHS
146	R, R, N, N	Returning to SHS
147	R, R, N, N	Returning to SHS
148	P	Returning to SHS
149	R, R, R, R, R, N, P	Returning to SHS
150	R, R, R, R, N, N, N	Returning to SHS
151	R, R, R, R, N, N	Returning to SHS
152	R, R, R, R, N, P	Returning to SHS
153	R, R, R, R, N, P, P	Returning to SHS
154	P, P	Returning to SHS

Figure 5.2 A density map showing number of IDRs on each of 45 pages of transcript in Jessie's second observation. Bottom row describes the general activity; the next row indicates the transcript page number (pp.#); and the top row lists each IDR coded on that page, with one letter representing one episode (R = conversation repetition; N = conversational narrative; P = verbal play; D = procedural discourse; T = trouble source).

Source: Hengst et al., 2016.

however, the clerk does not join in with the play, and instead simply uses *conversational repetition* of her description while also pointing to the two different models. Jessie and Karen do not pursue the verbal play in this interaction (but it does come up later as they reflect on what they found out about presentation remotes at the tech store). We can see here how Jessie, Karen and other participants are using IDRs then to build indexical grounds, to propose and negotiate social roles, and to align around sociocultural activities. The density map and transcript together give us a sense of the distinct and dynamic discursive texture woven together in the interactions.

Although we used IDRs in our analysis of these data, we could also trace building tasks across the interaction. For example, Transcript 5.1 opens with Jessie's utterance ("I wonder if you had uhm if you sold . . ."), an utterance where we can see Jessie beginning to build *significance* (describing the function of the device he wants) and where he uses indirectness and modals to structure a polite inquiry about the purchase (*politics, relationship, identity*). After the clerk displays uncertainty Jessie shifts to a short direct possible name (working on *significance*, but also simplifying use of language as a *sign system*). After achieving mutual understanding of the word "clickers," the clerk's suggestion "I-Clickers," displays that *significance* remains a needed building task, but that might also be read politically as a tacit presupposition of what roles Jessie was likely to play (i.e., a student, not a teacher or presenter). Karen's co-deployment of verbal and nonverbal resources to build a scene depicting Jessie as a presenter talking to a class involves marked building on all seven of Gee's building tasks. Whether tracing IDRs or building tasks, analysis of communicative success for participants, clinicians, and researchers must focus on the contextualizing work of communicative resources.

A Note on Methods: Ecological Validity and Triangulating Quantitative and Qualitative Data

By design, SDA prioritizes attention to the important issues of *ecological validity* and *trustworthy interpretations* about communicative interactions. For our purposes, *ecological validity* refers to the relationship between communicative interactions observed under research or clinical conditions (e.g., experimental protocols, clinical assessments, video observations, participant interviews) and everyday interactions found outside of those settings. Poor ecological validity is a hallmark limitation of the highly structured protocols and controlled tasks typical of most experimental studies and diagnostic protocols (Mortensen & Cialdini, 2010). Although an advantage of controlled protocols and contexts is that they focus the researcher/clinician on a limited range of relevant data, the interpretation of findings is correspondingly limited to predicting communication under controlled contexts and activities (e.g., making narrow claims about how individuals with aphasia perform on a particular naming task). In contrast, SDA optimizes ecological validity by observing people participating and communicating in everyday contexts and by loosening up the controls imposed on clinic-based and experimental protocols, which better aligns them with many everyday communicative interactions. The advantage of increasing ecological validity is that research and clinical findings can be related more confidently to everyday contexts. However, the challenge is that the ethnographic methods needed to trace and interpret complex and dynamic interactions require extensive ongoing data collection, management, and analysis. As is typical of ethnographic research methods, SDA studies often produce copious amounts of data, and *trustworthiness* of the study depends on the care researchers and clinicians give to collecting and analyzing data.

SDA relies heavily on *qualitative analyses* of ecologically situated data (e.g., observations, interviews) in order to interpret findings from multiple perspectives. Such qualitative analyses are often described in terms of narratives, that is, how researchers pull together multiple perspectives into a coherent "story" of what was happening. Researchers and clinicians can build trustworthy accounts/interpretations by respecting complexity (that there are always multiple possible narratives) and holding themselves fully accountable to the data (not smuggling in researcher biases or privileging one participant's account). However, SDA researchers and clinicians also rely on *quantitative analyses* (Miller et al., 2003) as a way of characterizing and interpreting amounts, magnitudes, and relative frequencies of observed or reported communicative patterns. In my own research I have routinely combined both quantitative and qualitative analyses. For example, in the data presented in this chapter on Jessie's observation, I combine close analysis of the sequentially unfolding interaction in the tech store (Transcript 5.1) with a broader narrative of the overall observation and Jesse's biography (drawn from interviews), and with quantitative analysis (Figure 5.2) of the five IDRs (noting totals across the full observation and offering a density map of IDRs). In the *Cindy Magic* analyses of Part 1, we also saw that change in Anna's communicative abilities were best described by integrating quantitative analysis (use of different voices, percentage of words spoken, number of pieces of clothing folded) with qualitative description of her talk and nonverbal activity across sessions along with the perceptions of her communication partners about her patterns of participation.

Qualitative and quantitative analyses are often taught as competing, even mutually exclusive, research approaches with radically different standards of evidence. However, Donald Campbell (1988, 1996), a leading methodological theorist of the social and behavioral sciences, has highlighted a wide array of threats to validity of interpretation for both quantitative and qualitative methods. To address such threats, he stressed the need to engage critically and comparatively. He came to appreciate qualitative methods, famously arguing that ethnographic case studies do not have an N of 1 (no degrees of freedom) because they involve multiple observations across time. He also increasingly criticized experimental and quasi-experimental research that settled for low-cost, low information data analyzed thinly (particularly not testing interpretations through convergent and divergent analysis of multi-trait, multi-method matrices). Campbell highlighted the importance of *triangulating* across multiple data sources and methods to build trustworthy accounts for both qualitative and quantitative analyses. SDA has often taken up qualitative and quantitative analysis as complementary methods that illuminate communicative phenomena from multiple perspectives, making them more visible and interpretable, and more relevant to clinical or other application.

Chapter Summary: Distributed Communication and Distributed Success

Everyday communicative interactions provide opportunities for forming, changing, and maintaining our enduring personal and social identities—a process that takes time (months, often years) but also has to be constructed one everyday communicative interaction at a time. Embracing communicative diversity that includes communication disorders requires identifying what communicative repertoires are typical in specific functional systems, how those repertoires are distributed across participants, and where flexibilities (realized and unrealized) exist in the functional systems and can bring together complementary bit competencies of individuals to jointly support successful communication. Much like Hutchins's (1995) example discussed in Chapter 3 of how the bridge team adapted to the loss of power, flexible adaptation of functional systems to accommodate communicative disorders may involve shifting goals, shifting patterns of alignments and brokering roles, and emergent repurposing of communicative resources. In this chapter then, we focused on these three questions:

* *How are accomplishments flexibly distributed?*
* *How are people brokering one another into social roles and successful patterns of participation?*
* *How are communicative resources distributed and jointly deployed to successfully coordinate activities and meanings?*

As a sociolinguist, Jan Blommaert has highlighted the difficulty of defining communicative competence in complex and dynamic sociomaterial spaces where multiple languages are routinely being blended and mixed in complex ways. Some of his key sites are urban neighborhoods in Europe with high concentrations of recent immigrants, spaces he refers to as *superdiverse*. In many ways the challenges of managing communication disorders in everyday interactions parallel the challenges of managing communicative superdiversity in multilingual gatherings. In *The Sociolinguistics of Globalization*,

Blommaert (Blommaert, 2010) explores how linguistic and semiotic repertoires may not easily move across contexts, across genres and goals, and across audiences: "That is, people manage or fail to make sense across contexts; their linguistic and communicative resources are mobile [i.e., flexibly deployed] or lack such semiotic mobility, and this is a problem not just of difference, but of inequality" (p. 3). Of course, superdiverse environments are also particularly rich in marked and intense communicative brokering.

Distributed success and flexibility clearly are not a local accomplishment alone. People draw on familiar cultural stereotypes and ideologies to anticipate, promote, or challenge particular patterns of success. For example, the documentary podcast *How to Become Batman* (Rosin & Spiegel, 2015) tells the story of Daniel Kish, who as a toddler lost both of his eyes to retinoblastoma Although totally blind, Daniel was not socialized into typical limits on the blind—that is, his mother did not protect Daniel from falls but let him freely explore his world. Very early Daniel began clicking his tongue and using the sound as sonar to visualize his environment (hence the name "batman"). Although he suffered a number of physical injuries in the process of developing these practices, he also became strikingly able to navigate the world (e.g., riding bikes, hiking in the woods, climbing trees, differentiating objects around him). Among the challenges he faced was sociocultural resistance to his clicking, something teachers in his schools perceived as "inappropriate" and disruptive. In Chapter 6, we will look more at the how sociocultural activities and figured worlds situate not only communicative experiences but also the long chains of learning that build recognizable resources of our everyday interactions.

Reflective Observations

1. *Identifying interactional discourse resources (IDRS) in observational data.* Follow these three steps:

   a. Study the operational definitions for the five IDRs (playful episodes, conversational narratives, procedural discourse, conversational repetition, trouble sources) used in Hengst et al. (2016, pp. 15–18). Practice identifying them in your own conversations throughout the day as well as in data sets (e.g., published transcripts, clinical sessions).

   b. Select three of these IDRs to focus on and code all instances of them in your data set. Be sure to include all verbal *and* nonverbal instances.

   c. Analyze how people are aligning within/around these IDRs.

2. *Mapping the collective repertoire of bit competencies available in functional systems.* Taking a distributed communication perspective to bit competencies challenges us to the identify the range of competencies available across functional system involving individuals with communication

disorders and then looking for where the communicative flexibilities are within those systems. To explore this idea with your data set, follow these two steps:

    a.   Catalogue bit competences available to all participants. To begin with, it may be helpful to simply chart various communicative resources by participant (much the way Table 3.2 charted use of character voices in *Cindy Magic*). Be sure to include all participants in the gathering, including participant observers (i.e., researchers and clinicians).

    b.   Discuss how this chart provides insights about how communicative success was achieved in your data and where it was not achieved, whether because of (or in spite of) the collective communicative repertoire.

3.   ***Brokering Social Roles and Successful Communication***. Although not often referred to as brokering, people routinely distribute success in everyday communicative interactions. To begin to catalogue the diverse ways we broker communicative success, keep a log of instances that you witness throughout the next week. To keep track of instances, take quick notes on the spot (e.g., in a small notebook, or as an audio-message). Then as soon after as possible, write out the details about each brokering interaction as follows:

    a.   List the date/day and time of day where you observed it.

    b.   Describe the sociomaterial space (e.g., gathering) and the immediate functional system (e.g., the people, tools, and material contexts assembled around the goals of sociocultural activities in the immediate interaction).

    c.   Describe the brokering interaction as it temporally unfolded. This may be easiest to do using a transcription-type layout.

    d.   Analyze how this interaction supported successful communication and positioned people in specific social roles in this space.

Suggested Readings

Here are three articles that provide empirical analyses of how diverse developmental pathways impact the communicative success of people with communication disorders. The articles address physical disabilities from CP, cognitive-communicative decline and dementia associated with Alzheimer's disease among multilingual individuals, and delayed spoken language associated with autism.

1.   "Slipping through the timestream: Social issues of time and timing in augmented interactions" (Higginbotham & Wilkins, 1999). In this chapter, Jeffery Higginbotham and David Wilkins explore the impact of

physical disabilities on temporal dimensions of face-to-face interactions involving individuals using AAC technologies.

2. "Alzheimer's speakers and two languages" (Nold, 2005). In this chapter, Guenter Nold examines a series of conversations between the researcher and ten different multilingual patients with dementia, focusing on the diverse ways both languages were employed.

3. "'How to go on': Intersubjectivity and progressivity in the communication of a child with autism" (Sterponi & Fasulo, 2010). As part of a special issue on "Rethinking Autism, Rethinking Anthropology," Laura Sterponi and Alessandra Fasulo provide a detailed analysis of everyday communicative interactions of a young child (5;10) with his mother and tutor at their home.

Note

1. Other researchers describe these practices as mediating (e.g., language and literacy mediators). In doing so, they are not thinking of mediation as in trying to reach agreement between conflicting parties (as in mediation of labor agreements or mediation clauses that prevent lawsuits for products); instead, they mean mediation in the sense of facilitating (of someone or something intervening in the middle of a process to make it happen). I have chosen brokering because it more clearly signals the later, aiding, assisting, and being an intermediary to enable some successful action or process.

Chapter 6

Tracing Diverse Patterns of Learning

Chapter 3 defined learning broadly as change over time in response to experience and introduced theories of *situated learning*. Situated learning aligns with *situated discourse analysis* (SDA) in four important ways. First, it conceptualizes learning as a fundamental dimension of *all* interaction, so analyses should focus on *what* (not *if*) people are learning. Second, situated learning leads not only to desirable, socially positive, and intended outcomes, but also undesirable, socially negative, and collateral (or unanticipated) outcomes; thus, analyses must trace the full range of learning outcomes. Third, situated learning recognizes that learning is always deeply situated, never an isolated process producing decontextualized skills, so analyses must focus on *learning with* particular people, resources, and sociomaterial spaces. Fourth, situating learning always happens in situated communicative interactions, so the details of everyday interactions are central to both learning outcomes (what is learned) and processes (how it is learned). While recognizing that communication within functional systems routinely involves managing all kinds of disruptions, this chapter focuses on the situated processes and outcomes of learning in functional systems that are managing disruptions introduced by communication disorders.

To focus on situated learning and distributed communication among individuals with communication disorders and their communication partners, this chapter complements the frameworks developed in previous chapters with three new concepts. Building on SDA notions of alignment introduced in Chapter 2 and socialization in Chapter 3, *common ground* focuses on how people's here-and-now communication and learning depend on jointly available environments, shared histories of past interactions with one another, and similar life experiences. Building on notions of peripheral and guided participation introduced in Chapter 3, *repeated engagement* highlights that people's motivated engagements in sociocultural activities lead to learning (i.e., changing patterns of participation). Building on the notions of indexical grounds in Chapter 2 and the repurposing of durable and emergent resources in Chapter 3, *collaborative referencing* highlights the communicative resources central to the distributed and dynamic nature of referencing.

Situated learning among people managing communication disorders must stay focused on the distributed character of communication and learning.

The data examples for this chapter are drawn from the study of discourse and aphasia introduced in Chapter 4, where we examined a community observation from Steve's case. In this chapter, we examine situated learning displayed through repeated engagement in the collaborative referencing game and focus on the case of Mary, another participant with aphasia. The chapter first describes Mary's case, highlighting her relationship with her game partner (Rob) and how the design of the game facilitated tracing learning (change over time). It then explores *common ground* as a way to trace communicative change in situated functional systems, *repeated engagement* as a way to trace changes in participation, and two interactional discourse resources, *verbal play* and *collaborative referencing*, that were fused in learning through the game play. Finally, the Note on Methods considers how *situated case studies* support *thick description* (Chapter 3) and generalizable interpretations through repeated engagement over time with participants and their functional systems.

The Case of Mary—Playing the Collaborative Referencing Game

I first met Mary at a brain injury support group I helped facilitate, and she eventually became the first person who agreed to participate in my ethnographic study examining the communicative practices of people with aphasia (see Chapter 4). Mary invited her younger son, Rob, to be her partner for the study. This chapter draws data examples from the four clinic-based sessions where Mary and Rob played the collaborative referencing game (Hengst, 2003, 2006).

At that time Mary was 47 years old, living at home with Rob, receiving outpatient speech-language therapy for aphasia, and on medical leave from her teaching job at an area middle school. About six months earlier Mary was hospitalized with a posterior left hemisphere stroke (primarily parietal and temporal lobe damage). At the time of the study, her acute hemiplegia had resolved, but she continued to have a moderate-severe *conduction aphasia* (i.e., a profile of fluently produced connected speech, relatively good comprehension, and poor phrase repetition). Her conversational speech was marked by frequent word-level errors or substitutions (i.e., *paraphasias*), long utterances (seven or more words) with good intonation, a good range of grammatical forms, and frequent hesitations and false starts as she groped for sounds and words. Her scores on the BDAE (Goodglass & Kaplan, 1983) demonstrated poor repetition (average of 28th percentile across subtests) compared to her scores in auditory comprehension (average of 50th percentile), reading comprehension (60th percentile), writing (74th percentile), spoken naming (88th percentile) and oral reading (90th percentile).

Rob was a 16-year-old high school student. He was earning good grades, enjoyed studying languages, and was planning to attend college. Across the study, Mary and Rob were both highly verbal and animated communication partners. Analysis of the amount of talk across the 12 clinic-based sessions showed that their conversations were closely balanced (measured by number of conversational turns and words) and that they both used long speaking turns, with Mary averaging 8.1 words per turn and Rob averaging 9.9. Their conversational topics varied widely, but frequently included sharing news and swapping stories about family, church, and school activities as well as managing household issues (e.g., coordinating schedules, planning meals, and running errands). Given that Rob had just recently received his driver's license (and Mary had not yet resumed driving), their conversations frequently included Rob negotiating permission to use the family car (e.g., swapping running household errands for an equal amount of personal use). Rob told me that earning some gas money (i.e., the monetary reimbursement for participating) was one of the reasons he agreed to participate in the study. Finally, Mary and Rob also reported playing a variety of board games as a family activity and when socializing with friends. Figure 6.1 is a photo of Mary and Rob in the clinic preparing to play the collaborative referencing game.

Figure 6.1 Rob and his mother, Mary, waiting for instructions to begin the collaborative referencing game. The low barrier separating them allows them to see one another and use facial expressions and gestures as communicative resources, but not to see each other's playing boards where the cards are placed.

The *collaborative referencing game* was designed to *repeatedly engage* partners in referencing twelve target cards within a game play activity. Game play involved two people facing each other over a low barrier that allowed them to easily see one another, but blocked them from seeing each other's playing boards (see Fig 6.1). Partners had identical playing boards numbered 1–12 and an identical set of 12 playing cards. Pregame set up involved identifying which partner would be the director, and then arranging the director's cards on his/her playing board (one card on each of the 12 numbered locations). The object of the game was for the director to tell the matcher how to arrange his/her cards to match the director's board, without players looking directly at each other's playing boards.

The players were instructed to play the game (working together to correctly arrange the matcher's cards), to communicate freely and in any way they wanted (e.g., using gestures, words, even showing cards), and to have fun. For my research, pairs played the game six times per session, across four sessions (a total of 24 game play trials). Within each session, pairs used the same 12 playing cards for all six trials. However, across sessions the card sets changed. In the first and fourth sessions, pairs used two different sets of 12 *tangram cards*, geometric shapes printed in black on a white background (see Figure 6.2). However, in the second and third sessions, pairs used a customized set of 12 *photo cards* of people, places, and activities that were personally relevant to them (see examples in Figure 6.3).

The design of the collaborative referencing game, with multiple game play trials within and across sessions, supported analysis of change across multiple time scales. For example, within a given trial, I could analyze how the moment-by-moment management of game play changed as partners

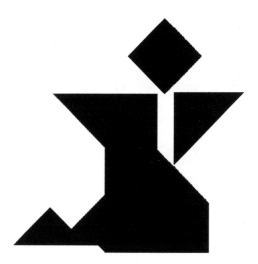

Figure 6.2 Tangram card referred to as "starman" by Rob, and referred to with a flapping arm gesture by Mary (see Transcript 6.1).

(a)

(b)

Figure 6.3 The two photo cards of dogs used in the collaborative referencing game with Mary and Rob. The top card (a) was a photo of Mary and Rob with their pet dog, and the bottom card (b) was a photo of my own dog at the time.

worked to identify and place specific cards and moved from one card to the next. Within a given session, I could analyze changes in how partners identified and placed specific cards across the six game trials. For example, Transcript 6.1 shows Mary and Rob's six *card placement sequences* for the tangram card in Figure 6.2 during their fourth session.

Transcript 6.1 Card placement sequences for the tangram card shown in Figure 6.2 across six trials of Mary and Rob's fourth session of the collaborative referencing game. Mary directed in trials 1, 3, and 5, and Rob directed in trials 2, 4, and 6.

Trial One

M:	Okay.. 1. Ahh This one is trying *to- to- come up and Ye:s:: ... yes
R:	** . 1 .* fly? **

*flapping arms   **selects   *flaps arms & shows card
correct card   **places card correctly

Trial Two

M:	I have two more. * oho:: ** I think its*
R:	Starman....3...*Star::man..2..**star::man Starman starman

*arms out   *selects correct card,
**shows card   **flaps arms   *with hands
& traces star   shoulders,
on card w/finger   flaps elbows

M:	its Where does it- * twelve? six.
R:	star ... man number six six

*places card incorrectly on 12, then correctly on 6

Trial Three

M:	O::::n the... fifth one. *We're we're talk about the arm...would Yes
R:	alright. Starman?

*flapping arms

M:	whatever it is, ... 4 ....
R:	*

*selects correct card & places it correctly

Trial Four

M:	Just a minute I'm trying to Oh *yeah yes yes
R:	S:::t arman....for twelve. Starman for twelve.

*selects correct card

M:	* For seven? Twelve.
R:	Twelve. .. 2 ..

*places card incorrectly on 7, then correctly on 12

Trial Five

M:	For the* yes, for the four. ...
R:	... starman? * number four?

*flapping arms   *selects correct card, places correctly

Trial Six

M:	...3..*. Or er- no, that*air- Yeah
R:	Starman Starman is number two. Starman Flyman. Number two

*selects correct card, places it correctly   *flaps arms

Atypically for the game, as Mary and Rob alternated director roles across trials, they each settled on different labels for the card, with Mary using a flapping arms gesture and Rob referring to it as "starman." Across the four sessions, I could analyze changes in how partners managed game play and discussed target references before, between, and after specific game play trials. Finally, across the whole data set for each case (including community observations and interviews), I was able to analyze changes in the pairs' collaborative referencing practices beyond the game play trials and these specific target cards. In short, this chapter illustrates tracing change across different timescales.

Functional Systems: Tracing Change in Functional Systems Over Time

Clark's (1992) account of *common ground* offers us a way to describe how people's experiences both impact, and emerge through, situated interactions of functional systems. Simply defined, common ground points to how the histories of experiences and knowledge people share provide relevant contexts for language use. Clark argued that successful referencing relies on communication partners interactively building and aligning around their common ground. For example, if I say, "Can I borrow the *book*?," you might decide I am either talking about the book in my hand or the one we discussed last week. If I say, "Did you see the *president* on TV last night?," you might decide that I am most likely referring to the current US president because we are in the United States and have not had any recent discussions of other presidents (e.g., of a university, a company, another country). Common ground changes as we interact, as we come to know each other better, and as events happen in the world, so it requires constant updating. We will ask first then: *How does common ground change among participants over time as they repeatedly engage in functional systems?*

In Chapter 2, we introduced functional systems as a dynamic unit of analysis that focuses on the ongoing assemblage of environmental resources and explored how communicative success in particular interactions involves ongoing alignments of people, resources, and sociomaterial spaces. In the *Cindy Magic* examples, we traced how Paul, Nora, and Anna continuously managed their embodied alignments (e.g., around the laundry basket, in front of the camera) and alignments around social identities (e.g., Paul or Elizabeth, Nora or Mary, and Anna or Jane). Common ground helps us understand people's interactional alignments around joint experiences. In analyzing *Cindy Magic*, I noted that Nora, Paul, and Anna knew how to call on certain allies (e.g., the cheetahs) to fight Cruella de Vil because they had played out such scenarios before, but did not (at first) know how to enact vampire bats (the new ally created during that episode). Common ground helps us account for the impact of common experiences on such alignments. In this chapter, we explore two ways that Clark's (1992) concept of common ground can guide us in tracing situated learning of functional systems: *co-presence heuristics* as a general process for assembling common ground in interaction and the *collaborative referencing model*, which describes patterns of change over time as people work to successfully align around what references mean.

To successfully understand everyday referencing (who or what is being referred to), people need to continuously and rapidly search to identify what experiences they might have in common with others in the interaction. Clark (1992) argued that the speed, uncertainty, and updating of referencing suggest that such searches have to rely on heuristic processes (to come up with good-enough guesses) rather than the slow, laborious process of trying to determine exactly what I know you know and you know I know. Clark pointed particularly to *co-presence heuristics*, where people search for histories of co-presence as a basis for identifying likely common experiences. In other words, we search to see if a reference might be to something in our immediate environment, to personal histories with one another, or to similar experiences we're likely to have had based on our age, gender, culture, and so on.

Clark identified two broad types of common ground: personal and communal. Similar to our discussion of indexical ground in Chapter 2, *personal common ground* is anchored in the co-experience of people and the temporal unfolding of interactional events. In the example of the book I offered earlier, our here-and-now shared sociomaterial space may make the book in my hand a likely reference for "the book." However, if we were talking yesterday about a book of interest, then we may home in on the book from that conversation as the likely reference. In contrast, *communal common ground* aligns with our expectations about what experiences we may have in common, as in the example of a reference to "the president." Similar to our discussion of figured worlds in Chapter 4, we make informed guesses about likely common knowledge and perspectives with people broadly involved in similar communities and sociocultural activities. Of course, both personal and communal common ground are updated and woven together throughout an interaction. Such ongoing updates provide a way of tracking moment-by-moment changes as the ground for potentially more sustained or robust learning.

As a psycholinguist, Clark (1992) developed his theory of common ground specifically around language use. Of particular interest for this chapter is his model of *collaborative referencing*. For Clark, all referencing is a collaborative process, so we can trace how people negotiate the meanings of referential expressions (e.g., noun phrases) by tracing the ways communication partners initiate, refashion, and accept a referencing expression in interaction. Although collaborative referencing has implications for how people negotiate language use in all everyday interactions, the collaborative processes are often difficult to trace. Highly familiar references built though personal and communal ground can make referencing seem automatic, hiding the histories of collaboration.

Drawing on a long line of barrier task protocols (e.g., Yule, 1997), Clark and his colleagues (Clark, 1992; Clark & Wilkes-Gibbs, 1986) designed a study to highlight the collaborative processes communication partners use to establish new references. To do so, they minimized common ground by:

- recruiting eight pairs of college students who were unfamiliar with one another (limiting their personal common ground);
- having one direct the other to place 12 cards depicting unfamiliar geometric shapes (i.e., tangram cards that were unlikely to be familiar from communal experiences) in order on a board;
- limiting their referencing opportunities (i.e., six trials with the same cards in one session);
- encouraging them to rely on talk alone (i.e., using a full barrier to limit use of nonverbal resources and reduce visual access to the environment); and
- instructing them to complete the task as quickly as possible (to limit side conversations).

Under these conditions, not only did all eight pairs complete the task quickly and accurately, they also displayed very similar patterns of change, or learning, across trials. On the first trial, pairs spent more time and communicative effort (words, turns) to settle on what the card looked like and how they would describe it (e.g., "it looks like an ice skater"). On each subsequent trial, pairs decreased time and communicative effort. In addition, referencing expressions became more concise and direct (e.g., shifting from a multi-turn description of what a tangram shape looked like to a direct reference, like "the ice skater"). Broadly, Clark and Wilkes-Gibbs's analysis demonstrated situated learning as communicative interactions built personal common ground around referencing target cards, which was then used in subsequent trials.

Common ground is shaped and managed by communication partners, and in any given interaction communication partners can strategically manage their use of common ground to accomplish multiple simultaneous goals. In an alternative protocol, Clark and his colleagues (Clark, 1992) encouraged participant pairs to draw on longer histories of personal common ground. Specifically, they recruited familiar partners and used photocards of locations familiar to the pair. They also recruited a third unfamiliar participant who was assigned the role of silent overhearer to the pair. The familiar partners were told the overhearer was also trying to correctly place the cards and instructed them to work together to correctly place cards, but also try to block the overhearer from correctly placing the cards. Building references around their interpersonal common ground (e.g., knowing where one worked one time), avoiding common labels, and limiting unnecessary details and descriptions, the target matchers were able to place cards with 99-percent accuracy while overhearers were only half as successful (47 percent). However, attempting to block the overhearer took increased time.

For my research (Hengst, 2003), I redesigned Clark's barrier task protocols, as described in this section, to support successful communication among pairs managing aphasia and to align the protocol with situated theories of communication: using a half barrier so partners could see each other, inviting friendly game play consistent with goals besides speed, recruiting familiar partners (usually family members), alternating the director role, using familiar photo cards for some sessions, and having pairs play six rounds on four different days. I also made several key changes to data collection and analysis. By videotaping full sessions (i.e., before, between, and after trials), I was able to trace nonverbal as well as verbal communication and analyze all the discourse (including talk that happened between trials).

Tracing Change in Common Ground Across Trials

Overall, the findings for the four familiar pairs using my game-like task (Hengst, 2003) followed the general patterns of change across sessions reported in Clark and Wilkes-Gibbs' (1986) original study. You have already been introduced to two of the pairs—Steve and Kerri (Chapter 4) and Mary and Rob (earlier in this chapter). In addition, there was Debra (a 37-year-old secretary, 6 months post a left frontal lobe stroke with residual hemiparesis and a severe non-fluent aphasia) and Monica (her 14-year-old daughter) and Ethel (a 21-year-old mother, 15 months post a hemorrhagic left frontal lobe stroke, with residual hemiparesis and a severe non-fluent aphasia) and Barnie (her 21-year-old husband). Consistent with Clark's findings, all four pairs in my study completed all game play trials, all matchers' consistently arranged the cards on their boards with high accuracy, and all pairs got faster across trials.

Evidence of learning (i.e., changing common ground) could be seen across multiple measures in this design. The time pairs took to complete trials shortened from an average of 22:49 (minutes:seconds) on first trials to 11:42 on sixth trials. The total number of words spoken by pairs decreased across the trials. The average in first trials was 2,182 words (range 1,006 to 3,876) and for the sixth trials was 1,041 words (range 432–2,366). There were similar drops in the pairs' use of significant nonverbals (which averaged 158 in the first trials and 92 in the sixth). The number of interactional turns also declined, from an average of 363 (range 237 to 526) in first trials to 219 (161 to 308) in sixth trials. Finally, the pairs almost always settled on specific referencing labels for the target cards, and those references became more concise and direct across trials.

Mary and Rob fit the dominant pattern for all these measures, averaging at least a 40-percent decline across trials in time, words spoken, nonverbals, and turns. Transcript 6.1 offers a textured portrait of how common ground developed across game play around one tangram (shown in Figure 6.1), but also displays how varied this process could be. In the first trial, Mary initiates referencing by describing the card with words ("trying *to- to- come up and") and makes an accompanying flapping arm gesture (*). Rob selects the correct card but confirms it with an array of signs (flapping his arms, saying "fly," and showing the card itself to Mary). In trial two, Rob offers a different label and gesture for the card, saying "Starman . . . * Star::man," making a gesture with his arms out (like the points of a star). He again shows Mary the card and traces on it how he sees it resembling a star. These first two trials are successful, but also establish a pattern of conflicting labels (starman vs. flying or flapping arms gesture), a pattern that we'll come to see reflects broader ways Mary and Rob participated in this functional system. Mary's flapping gesture recurs in three of the four remaining trials. In trial 5, Mary sequences the flapping gesture into the slot for a head noun following a definite article ("For the *"). Trial 5 is the fastest trial with the least number of words and turns. Trial 6 is interesting as Rob opens with Starman, Mary places it correctly, and Rob confirms the card and its number. However, Mary then contests the label ("Or er- no, that's * air"), again situating her flapping arm gesture into a linguistic slot (that's + gesture). Rob repeats his label "Starman." After Mary agrees, Rob compromises a bit with a new hybrid label, saying "Flyman."

The functional system that Mary and Rob assembled around the collaborative referencing game showed multiple, clear signs of change (learning). In a general sense, the changes closely matched the typical pattern found in barrier task designs (pairs becoming faster, settling on labels, and displaying reduced overt collaboration as measured by words, turns, and gestures). However, they also displayed very specific interactional patterns (e.g., Mary's significant use of gestures, Rob's pattern of instructing and correcting his mom, and their playful conflict, each persisting with their own label).

Participation Across Multiple Activities: Common Ground, Identities, and Relationships

Clark's (1992) design led participants to stay very focused on doing the assigned task for speed and efficiency. They did not take up the barrier task as an opportunity to build social relationships or overtly bring their own goals into these interactions. In my redesign, participants routinely and openly engaged in multiple activities and brought their own goals to the ways they negotiated game play. In other words, they were not overtly focused only on building common ground around referencing the cards, but instead displayed engagements in multiple sociocultural activities and identities. The notion of *repeated engagement* (Hengst, Duff, & Dettmer, 2010) recognizes the central role of repetition in learning, but emphasizes loosely structured and diverse patterns of repetition that emerge as individuals engage in meaningful, personally motivated activities. Repeated engagement also describes how individuals build, and have ascribed to them interactionally, social identities through an emergent process operating across multiple timescales (Wortham, 2006). Here then we will focus on this question: **How do changing patterns of participation index multiple sociocultural activities and identities?**

As noted in Part 1, sociocultural activities are complex, and participants routinely juggle multiple activities and goals simultaneously. People's patterns of participation may markedly index multiple goals. For example, consider Michael Cole and colleagues' reports (Cole, 1996; Nicolopoulou & Cole, 1993) on the Fifth Dimension, an afterschool program they organized. The Fifth Dimension uses problem-solving game worlds to support the academic success of struggling learners (e.g., children diagnosed with learning disabilities). However, their research has found that the after-school setting where children played the game led to striking differences in how players engaged in the game worlds and in what players learned.

In one study, Nicolopoulou and Cole (1993) analyzed the Fifth Dimension in two community spaces, a library and a Boys and Girls Club. They found students' engagement was shaped by these two very different sociomaterial spaces. The Boys and Girls Club encouraged flexible use of the space, so youth activities were varied, often active and loud. In contrast, the library was managed as a quiet space for reading and study. Compared with other activities in these spaces, the Fifth Dimension was an unusually quiet activity in the club and an unusually loud one in the library. However, the library space encouraged students to stay together and work on the game, whereas the club space led to more fragmented and dispersed patterns of interaction. Student groups in the library tended to stick together, meaning that they worked on the game together repeatedly, which was soon reflected in higher scores on the game's scenarios. In contrast, students at the club rarely worked together on the game more than once and tended to move to other activities when they hit problems, which was reflected in lower scores and limited evidence of change over time.

For the Fifth Dimension, the library was clearly a better site for youth learning. Ironically, the relative noisiness of students playing the Fifth Dimension meant that library staff often regarded it as too disruptive while the Boys and Girls Club staff thought the Fifth Dimension was exciting because youth became involved in a marked learning activity. In any case, the sociomaterial spaces of the Fifth Dimension game were indexed by specific patterns of participation, which led to different patterns of repeated engagement within and across episodes of game play, and resulted in different learning outcomes, including not only changes in problem-solving performance but also changes in local social identities ascribed to them.

In Chapter 4 we highlighted ways that *identity work* (typically backgrounded) situates communicative interactions involving people with communication disorders. SDA also highlights how repeated engagement and related patterns of participation in sociocultural activities shape changes in identities, including identities linked to cognitive and communicative difference. For example, Ray McDermott (1993) looked at how children's practices shaped the ways a classmate, Adam (who was identified as having LD), participated in school activities. One analysis illustrated how Adam's classmates interactionally organized attention to how he had not followed a recipe correctly in a cooking activity, adding ingredients in the order they appeared in the ingredients list rather than in the instructions:

> Looking for Adam's LD has become something of a sport in Adam's class, a subset of the wider sport of finding each other not knowing things. In the Cooking Club, many kids get things wrong without too much worry; their wrong moves only speak to not knowing how to follow a badly organized recipe. The same mistakes are for Adam a source of degradation. They speak to his LD. Adam spends his day arranging not to get caught not having information that he could get from print. His every move is designed not to have LD again ascribed to him, and, as such, his every move confirms and recreates the possibility that the label of LD will be available in the classroom for anyone to ascribe to Adam. "Where is the LD?" Behaviorally, the answer is clear. It is all over the classroom as an interactional possibility.
>
> (McDermott, 1993, p. 291)

In effect, McDermott's analysis shows how a background frame (Adam has LD) functioned interactionally to regulate how Adam's classmates, and adults in the room, shaped Adam's repeated participation in school. McDermott (1993) notes that Adam's LD was most visible in testing activities, next in regular classroom lessons, somewhat in the class's cooking club, and least of all in everyday activities.

Although not regularly named activities, repeated engagement with identity work focused on specific people (finding Adam's LD) and with backgrounded values focused on participation in specific sociomaterial spaces (keeping quiet in the library) will impact the way more recognizable and named activities emerge in interactions. These examples illustrate how subtly accumulating changes in patterns of participation that index social identities and activities differentially impact learning.

Mary and Rob's Shifting Participation Around Identity Work

Studying the interactions among familiar communication partners, recording full sessions and having scheduled interviews let me trace longer chains of interactions—that is, how Mary and Rob's game play was shaped by interactions between trials as well as by longer-term personal goals and family activities. Mary and Rob were engaged as mother and son. Rob was a strong high school student who had just earned his driver's license, and they both were grappling with the effects of Mary's stroke and continuing aphasia. Mary and I had several impromptu conversations that felt very much like moms talking about challenges of parenting. The interactions in Transcript 6.1 point to these more extended timescales and multiple identities as Mary and Rob positioned themselves as competent communicators and negotiated who got to decide what. For example, in Trial Six at the end of that transcript, Mary and Rob successfully collaborated in the card placement with a single word—Rob said "Starman" and Mary correctly placed the card. However, the interaction didn't stop there. Rob clarified the position (number 2 on the board) and Mary reiterated her preferred label with the flapping arm gesture after "that" and then the word "air." Rob repeated his label "Starman" and Mary agreed, at which point Rob seemed to compromise a bit, saying "flyman, number two."

The interaction after the initial card placement highlights the way the background activities of identity work were impacting and shaping the named activity of playing the game, which involved joint learning as changing common ground facilitated referencing. The back-and-forth of preferred labels was about who gets to decide what, who has to follow whose lead, and so on. This kind of identity work is common in families as they manage transitions of all kinds, including the changing positionings from acquired brain injuries. Mary talked with me about parenting teenagers in general and specifically about helping Rob transition from being-a-teenager to being-a-responsible-adult. She saw the research as an opportunity for Rob to follow through on his commitments by not skipping our sessions and always arriving on time. To that end, she wanted me to schedule with Rob directly (not to just go through her). She also felt it was important for her to work at making these sessions fun—for Rob's sake. Although Rob spoke to me much less about his motivations, he did report that he was glad to help his mom and was happy to receive the small payment for his participation in the study. These multiple activities, identities, and relations were visible not only in the communicative activity of collaboratively placing cards but also in use of other interactional discourse resources like verbal play.

Tracing Communicative Resources for Collaborative Referencing and Verbal Play

As pairs engaged in the collaborative referencing game, they built common ground around what the cards represented, how to manage multiple social roles and sociocultural activities, and what communicative resources to deploy. To trace change in these functional systems as participants repeatedly engaged with the game, we focus next on two types of communicative resources: initial referencing expressions (which indexed common ground around the cards) and verbal play (which indexed other sociocultural activities). Thus, we focus next on this question: **How are people's recognition and use of communicative resources changing over time?**

To trace each pair's emerging learning of card labels, Clark and Wilkes-Gibbs (1986) analyzed changes in the communicative resources participants used. Specifically, they asked 1) how directors initiated referencing for each card (what specific labels they used, how succinctly or confidently they used the label, and how much, if any, overt collaboration there was in that initiation) and 2) how much clarifying and refashioning work matchers did before completing the card placement sequence (CPS). They identified seven types of initiating referential expressions: *descriptive, elementary, episodic, provisional, installment, placeholder,* and (what I have called) *proxy.* Each type was defined by a combination of the linguistic resources and interactional patterning. Descriptive referential expressions are linguistically indefinite (e.g., "the one that looks like *a dog* with a long tail"), whereas the other six codes refer to definite referential expressions. For example, an elementary initiating referential expression includes the definite reference and any modifiers in a single intonational group(e.g., "*the dog* one again"), an episodic expression is distinguished just by having more than one intonational group ("the man, praying on his knees, in the pew"), and a proxy expression is one begun by one partner and completed by the other with grammatical form and intonational contours maintained (e.g., D: "show me the priest . . . uh"; M: "with the Bible"). In addition, I identified an eighth type of referencing expression for use of primarily nonverbal resources (e.g., "the [gesture of flapping arms]." Tracing linguistic and nonverbal resources, manners of production, and patterns of interaction allows us to trace the changing common ground between partners, of learning marked by growing evidence of confidence and effective collaboration.

As I have noted, growing common ground for a pair can also be seen in reductions of overt collaboration. To trace these changes, Clark and Wilkes-Gibbs (1986) defined a pattern of exchange that marked the most streamlined, confident referencing. In their study of college student pairs, these *basic exchanges* usually involved two turns, for example:

D: Number two is the horse
M: Okay, got it.

In these two-turn basic exchanges, where to place the card (i.e., the number on the board) was referenced either in director's initial turn (as in the foregoing example) or with the matcher's confirmation (e.g., "Okay, got it, number two"), or in some cases not referenced (i.e., simply assumed). However, in my data it was common for pairs managing aphasia to work separately on referencing the cards and the place numbers, so they often used a two-turn exchange to confirm the card and then another for the place number:

> D: Next is the horse.
> M: Okay, got it.
> D: On number two.
> M: Right.

Thus, in my analysis, I defined a basic exchange as a CPS with four or fewer turns that did not involve further clarifying or refashioning of the card reference. In addition, given that my pairs often wove other conversations into CPS's (e.g., about what they were doing after the session) and used jointly constructed labels, I identified *modified basic exchanges* as those when a) multiple turns were used for joint referencing expressions (e.g., a proxy, placeholder, or installment noun phrase); b) some turns were devoted to task management or non-task topics (e.g., talking about where to go after the session); or c) the card placement was accomplished quickly and accurately, but without *any* overt collaboration (i.e., on the 12th card placement the matcher would often simply place the only card he/she had left).

Chapter 5 introduced interactional discourse resources (IDRs), one of which was verbal play. While analyzing collaborative referencing of these pairs (Hengst, 2003), I was struck by how playful their interactions were, especially since researchers have long argued that verbal play is important for children's cognitive-linguistic and social development (Göncü, 1999; Miller, 1986; Schieffelin, 1986). Thus, I developed a systematic way to analyze verbal play and how playful episodes functioned in game play and collaborative referencing (Hengst, 2006). As with all IDRs, verbal play is diverse and pervasive, occurs across varied contexts, from the mundane everyday playfulness of children to the carefully crafted performances of professional comedians.

To capture a wide range of verbal play in the first cycle of coding, we identified *all traditional forms of verbal play including telling funny stories or jokes, playing with sounds or making puns, overt teasing of others or self-deprecating humor, as well as, all laughter, use of marked or playful voices or registers, singing or song-like intonations, and use of sound effects.* On the second coding pass, we identified specific episodes that shifted the interactional frame following guidelines:

1. a playful episode may be a single utterance or multiple utterances, but multiple-utterance episodes must be contiguous or simultaneous;
2. multiple utterances within one episode must share a common playful theme;
3. a laughter-only utterance could be part of an episode when it stood as a response to a playful utterance or action, but laughter alone was not counted as a playful episode.

Significantly, these guidelines allowed us to combine into one episode multiple utterances connected by the same theme (e.g., a knock-knock joke, a funny story, a punning duel), and to differentiate such extended episodes from a series of unrelated playful utterances (e.g., such as when the director of the game would make joking, but unrelated, comments about each card directed one right after the other). Playful exchanges on the same theme that were temporally disconnected would be identified as separate episodes, capturing the way that participants would often return to, or recycle, jokes or playful teasing. Finally, nonverbal responses (e.g., laughter, groans) to playful utterances could be included in a playful utterance, but laughter-only utterances (e.g., nervous laughter) that were not linked to playful utterances or actions would not be counted. By clearly identifying the boundaries of each playful episode, we could also identify which participants used their utterances to initiate or make substantive contributions to the episode. After recoding, 1,005 playful episodes were identified from the collaborative referencing game data for the four pairs.

Tracing Collaborative Referencing Around "That Mean Dog"

As Mary worked to make the research sessions fun for Rob, a clear example of this emergent reorganization of roles can be seen in how Mary and Rob managed a distinction between two photo cards (shown earlier in this chapter in Figure 6.3) used in the second and third sessions.

The excerpt of interaction in Transcript 6.2 is from the first round of game play in the second session. It focuses on a sequence of turns where Mary (as the director) was instructing Rob to select the photo card of my dog (see Figure 6.3b) and place it on number 12 on his playing board. While directing Rob in selecting and placing this card, Mary also used this card to initiate an extended episode of playful teasing directed at me in the observation room where I was watching the pair). She began referencing the card simply as "the other dog," producing an *elementary* initiating referential expression. However, when Rob sought clarification ('oh, her dog"), Mary quickly switched to referencing it as "that mean dog." Using verbal, prosodic, and gestural resources, she acted out a playful insult (as if behind my back) and worked to pull Rob into conspiratorial "teasing" over a series of interactional turns. Because of this extended interaction, this trial was not coded as either a basic or modified basic exchange. When I reentered the room at the end of the trial, Mary continued this teasing frame—saying boldly to Rob (but so I could overhear) "The old dog-" before switching to an ingratiating voice and addressing me directly "oh, I said this is the wonderful dog." Continuing the playful frame, I responded with an exaggerated "Thank you."

Transcript 6.2 Excerpt from the second collaborative referencing session with Mary and Rob, during the first trial using photo cards. This excerpt shows interactions around identifying and placing the photo of my dog (see Figure 6.3b).

M:	game. Now| its a- okay and number twelve
R:	its alright. We're going to have to play that game sometime.

M:	is the other dog. That mean dog.**Shhhh *Her* mean dog. But
R:	mhm Oh, her *dog. Oh oh our dog? Is-
	*R selects card **looks at observation window, finger to lips

M:	don't let her know about it. No her mean dog. No *Her
R:	Her dog? is it-? our dog or Julie's- oh. Our dog?
	*nod

M:	mean dog. Julie's
R:	Oh wait a s- wait a second mom. ... Are you talking about- Julie's okay.* And
	*R places card w/ a snap

M:	shhhhhhh She's finding them
R:	you're saying mean dog and I'm like "are you talking about our dog?"

M:	out it! okay. The:: C:::: ... har- with the little cor- corner.
R:	Oh shhh*okay (she can't hear it).
	*okay gesture

Clearly, Mary knew I was not only watching and listening through the mirror, but also recording these interactions with multiple cameras with the intention of transcribing her words, which is what made this so playful and mischievous. At the same time, this playful management of multiple frames actually confused Rob. Rob's initial uncertainty may have reflected the uncertainty resulting from Mary's aphasia, as he knew through repeated interactions that she often did produce paraphasias in her speech. In Transcript 6.2, Mary indicates it is "her" dog three times and then clarifies Julie's dog, before Rob confirms the reference and places the card. In fact, he said later that he just couldn't believe his mom was saying bad things about someone else's pet.

Although not as elaborate as this initial episode, Mary returned to this playful teasing repeatedly with this photocard, not only throughout the session this day, but again in the next session, where there were nine more playful episodes around the "mean dog" theme. In fact, the phrase "mean dog" stabilized as the label for this card. Moreover, when Mary and Rob used it, they would engage in playful prosody and/or gestures—emphasizing the insult or feigning secretiveness (e.g., by whispering and covert glances at me) so much so that the tone itself began to signal the card. Adeptly layering what was often a fleeting playful frame onto the referencing task itself, they made playfulness part of the reference for this photo card. Mary's use of "that mean dog" was a surprising way to identify this photo. It shifted the indexical ground from Rob and Mary playing the game and working on correctly selecting and placing the target card, to Mary working to make the sessions fun by conspiring with Rob to tease me. This teasing was also shifting our relationship to a more friend-like stance than simply researcher-participant.

Humor often is effective when it plays with frames and boundaries (e.g., Bateson, 1972; Goffman, 1981; Sherzer, 2002), and teasing shifts interpersonal boundaries—insider/outsider, friend/foe. Teasing has the potential to enhance insider status—as it relies on people not taking it too seriously (e.g., Straehle, 1993). It is important to note that verbal play and shifts among social roles were not limited to the mean dog episodes. In Transcript 6.1, we saw Mary and Rob playfully contesting each other's labels for the card that was either "starman" or the flapping-arms gesture. In addition, during game play, Rob began practicing his high school foreign languages (Spanish and German) to reference numbers and respond to Mary—a move Mary complained about since, in addition to her aphasia, she did not speak either Spanish or German.

Note on Methods: Building Generalizable Knowledge From Case Study Research

Case studies have been a key basis for theory and research on the brain and communication disorders over the past 150 years. Broca's descriptions of "Tan" (e.g., Selnes & Hillis, 2001), the case of Phineas Gage (e.g., Damasio, 1994), and patient "H.M." in the literature on amnesia (e.g., Manns, 2004) are famous examples of hallmark cases that have documented patterns of cognitive, linguistic, and physical disruptions experienced by individuals with brain damage. Decades and even centuries later, these cases continue to inform our categories and theories. Arguing for the critical role of rich case studies in developing scientific accounts of brain-behavior relations, neuropsychologists like Luria (1968, 1972) and Sacks (1970, 1984) have offered rich, clinical case study narratives that provide thick descriptions of the impacts of brain injuries on the lives of individuals.

Research methods typical of SDA are well designed to support case based research. A critical first step in conducing case study research is to define the case (Dyson & Genishi, 2005). As displayed throughout this book, case study research can be defined around specific individuals with communication disorders (e.g., the case of Steve); around target activities (e.g., the case of *Cindy Magic*); and around particular sociomaterial settings (e.g., the case of the collaborative referencing game). Defining the case guides researchers/clinicians in formulating specific questions, and designing ways to collect and analyze data. For example, the data from Mary and Rob (presented in this chapter) were drawn from the broader study of discourse practices and aphasia (introduced in Chapter 4). In that broader study, I defined the "case" around understanding communicative practices of routine communication partners, and especially how the partners succeeded in communication despite aphasia. To support both group and individual analysis, I recruited eight participant pairs managing aphasia and followed the same data collection protocol for all eight cases. The research questions focused on how the pairs communicated successfully across these different settings. Looking at Mary and Rob playing the collaborative referencing game, I can articulate a case within the broader case. The game provided a consistent sociomaterial space and repeated engagement in collaborative referencing, putting referential practices and partners' patterns and relationship into sharp relief. Building thick description (through systematic discourse analysis) and drawing on other research on collaborative referencing (Clark, 1992) and game play also supported making general interpretations about issues like how partners build indexical common ground over time and the ways they might manage multiple activities in such interactions.

It is not unusual to hear the claim that case study research is not generalizable. In a narrow statistical sense, generalizability refers to properties of a sample (particularly size and randomness) as a representation of the total population; however, those statistical properties (which offer no guarantee of the meaningfulness or truth of a conclusion) are often conflated with the idea of generalization. In statistical terms, a sample of one (n = 1) offers no basis for representing the population. However, science (as the critical pursuit of grounded knowledge) often engages in systematic investigation and knowledge building from single cases or small samples.

When paleontologists discover a single skeleton of a dinosaur, they don't sigh and ignore it. When astronomers see a black hole sucking up one star, they don't throw up their hands because they cannot study a hundred such events. In the same way, situated cases studies can support generalizable understandings from repeated, in-depth observation and analysis of what is possible, of within-case trajectories (whether this is a trajectory of development or recovery), of relations to other cases, and of rich patterns of complex interacting variables. As we noted in Chapter 5, Donald Campbell (1988) eventually concluded that rich case studies have a number of degrees of freedom, not an N of 1. Case-based research should not be dismissed because it doesn't fit the standards for population-based, inferential statistical analysis of experimental designs. The strength of case-based research is its complementary contributions: thick description of phenomena, repeated observations under varying conditions, and concrete, specific instantiations of theories and population-based accounts.

Thus, case study research focuses on documenting what is possible while population-based research focuses on identifying what is typical. As we will see in Part 3, clinical work is best understood as a specialized form of case-based research in that it requires clinicians to form "*thick descriptions* of their clients' (dis)abilities in relation to the activities and practices of their everyday life worlds" (Hengst et al., 2015). Clinicians and rehabilitation teams are called on to collect diagnostic, treatment and case history data relevant to specific clients, and interpret those data in relation to professional literature, including population-based evidence, clinician expertise, and client's communication needs and goals. Gould (1996) and Rose (2015) have noted that much scientific research has been over-focused on central tendencies and under-focused on variation. After all, in a normal bell curve distribution, over 80 percent of the individual items (scores, people, whatever is being measured) are not at the center (the mean/median), and in some cases it is possible that no item falls at that exact number. Our goal is not simply to know how all clients with aphasia perform in an abstract way. If we want to understand how *this* client will perform in *specific* clinical, educational, professional, and other everyday activities, then the methods and reasoning needed will be much closer to those of case study research than of population-based experimentation.

Chapter Summary: Recognizing and Tracing Situated Learning

Situated learning is ubiquitous—we never stop learning from and being formed by our experiences. In this chapter, we have focused on how people with communication disorders and their everyday communication partners change and develop diverse patterns to successfully communicate and get things done through their repeated engagement in functional systems that both provide some stable goals (e.g., the game) and allow for a range of sociocultural activities and roles (e.g., carrying on family goals, having fun). In this chapter then, we asked questions specifically to focus our attention on how people and functional systems are learning/changing through repeated engagements:

- *How does common ground change among participants as they repeatedly engage over time in functional systems?*
- *How do changing patterns of participation index multiple sociocultural activities and identities?*
- *How are people's recognition and use of communicative resources changing over time?*

It is important to note that sociocultural activities don't just blend seamlessly in interactions. Within this game-like context, a marked and focal goal was to successfully label and place target cards. However, that referencing goal was often backgrounded, disrupted, or even openly flaunted by playful or mischievous teasing. In other words, playful episodes did not always support referencing or the transmission functions of language use. We saw that kind of disruption in Rob's uncertainty during the game when his mom starting calling my dog "a mean dog," and as I noted, in Rob's shifts into French and German, which were quite disruptive to interactions with Mary. However, such playful episodes did foreground important social, interpersonal, and interactional functions of communication. Indeed, these game sessions, although done for research in a clinical space, had a natural, comfortable, everyday feel, a characteristic due in no small part to the way that playfulness indexed social identities and roles (e.g., familiar partners) and sociocultural activities (e.g., a friendly game, not a test). Where Clark and his associates only found referencing emerging in their collaborative referencing task, this design allowed us to see a wide range of communicative resources (reported speech, verbal play, narratives, etc.).

Reflective Observations

1. *Analyzing how backgrounded activities are shaping communicative interactions.*

    a. Compare the two observations you have collected for your mini-ethnography project. First describe the diverse activities/goals evident in each session. Then analyze how different patterns of participation and use of resources index these sociocultural activities, and how they shift and blend across the interaction. How do various alignments around these different activities enhance or inhibit what the functional system is accomplishing?
    b. Select three articles and review if/how they attend to backgrounded activities in their analysis of communicative interactions. What would you need to do to extend these analyses (e.g., access to more observation or interview data, use of different tools to analyze the interactions)?

2. *Analyzing data for patterns of collaborative referencing.* Although we used the collaborative referencing model as a conceptual tool to trace the development of referential expressions in the collaborative referencing game, it is also a useful tool to see how people use and develop situated common ground in everyday interactions.

    a. Using the collaborative referencing model, re-analyze Jessie and Karen's interaction with the clerk in the Tech Store (Transcript 5.1).
    b. Use the collaborative referencing model to analyze interactional data from your mini-ethnography project.

3. *Analyzing multimodal communicative resources.* It is important to remember that communicative resources are continually combined and recombined in everyday interactions and re-purposed to index different activities, figured worlds, and common ground.

    a. Identify a gesture, action, or word that occurs frequently in your data. Now, analyze all occurrences of that resource and how each occurrence is specifically situated, for instance, how it is orchestrated with different resources, produced by different people, and indexing different activities and identities. Discuss how these differences may impact learning.

b.   Identify a gesture, action, or word that you use frequently. Keep a log of your everyday uses of this resource and analyze the diverse ways you deploy it at different moments, in different interactions, and in different sociomaterial spaces.

Suggested Readings

Empirical research focusing on people's repeated engagement in everyday interactions provides us with diverse examples of situated learning in functional systems. Given the centrality of tracking change in CSD, it is critical to develop rich toolkits for tracing communicative change in and across functional systems. Here are three articles (in addition to the articles cited throughout this chapter) that provide thick descriptions of case studies of people's repeated engagements with everyday communicative activities.

1.   "Collaborative discourse facilitates efficient communication and new learning in amnesia" (Duff, Hengst, Tranel, & Cohen, 2008). In this article Melissa Duff and her colleagues trace the communicative resources and practices used as communication partners managing amnesia successfully completed repeated rounds of the collaborative referencing game.

2.   "Examining interactions across language modalities: Deaf children and hearing peers at school" (Keating & Mirus, 2003). In this article, Elizabeth Keating and Gene Mirus explore how hearing-oriented participation frameworks in school settings disrupt the ways deaf children interact and structure limited communicative success with their hearing peers.

3.   "Negotiating communicative access in practice: A study of a memoir group for people with aphasia" (Miller, 2019). In this article Elizabeth Miller traces moment-by-moment changes in interactions, as communication partners managing aphasia flexibly adapt resources and shift modes to successfully contextualize their talk and actions.

Part 3

Using Situated Discourse Analysis to Understand and Design Clinical Practice

> Paul would dutifully join his speech therapist in the library for an hour each day, emerging exhausted and demoralized, having punished his brain in an effort to fill in blanks, list words within categories (How many flowers can you name? None. . . . How many animals can you name? None . . .), link words with pictures, and attempt to perform other language skills. She tried teaching him to ask himself: What category is a word in? What color or shape is the object? If he could exclude many competing things, his quest would be clearer. Despite their simplicity, he found the exercises demanding and at times impossible.
>
> (Ackerman, 2011, p. 184)

Part 1 of this book introduced conceptual frameworks and tools of *situated discourse analysis* (SDA), and Part 2 explored the implications of those frameworks and tools for understanding the complexities of everyday communicative interactions and communication disorders. In Part 3 we turn our attention to clinical practice, using those SDA frameworks and tools to analyze and understand the situated nature of clinical interactions and clinical approaches to intervention.

Clinical work involves a widely recognized set of sociocultural activities organized around the goals of diagnosing and treating communication disorders. People's familiarity with how clinical goals are routinely accomplished not only shapes the functional systems that emerge in clinical spaces but also impacts how the success of particular client-clinician interactions is distributed. Thus, we begin Part 3 by using SDA to examine traditional sociocultural activities and figured worlds of clinical work. In the last two chapters we then examine how understanding the complexity of everyday communicative interactions might be used to re-design and optimize client-clinician interactions. We will focus in particular on how clinicians can utilize or build *rich communicative environments* (in everyday and clinical settings), how clinicians can productively function as flexible and authentic communication partners with clients, and how repeated engagement in meaningful and successful communicative interactions can promote learning (for individuals with communicative disorders and their routine partners in everyday functional systems).

Diane Ackerman's quote in the epigraph highlights the consequences for clients when clinicians rely on limited off-the-shelf treatment activities and a restricted communicative repertoire. Shortly after Ackerman (2004) finished her book on brain research (*An Alchemy of Mind*), her husband, Paul West, also a well-published author, suffered a massive left hemisphere stroke. In her memoir *One Hundred Names for Love* (2011) Ackerman documents Paul's recovery from that stroke. Paul's acute diagnosis was global aphasia, with spoken language limited to a stereotypic utterance (*mem mem mem*). He was given a poor prognosis for significant recovery. Ackerman (2011) reflected: "In the cruelest of ironies for a man whose life revolved around words, with one of the largest working English vocabularies on earth, he had suffered immense damage to the key language areas of his brain and could no longer process language in any form" (p. 18). Beyond his struggles, Paul was very unhappy living on the rehabilitation unit, so six weeks after his stroke Ackerman moved Paul and his therapy program home. She arranged to continue Paul's daily speech therapy sessions, but found that what happened in those few hours a week was not only far from enough to help him overcome his aphasia, but also too often misaligned with Paul's knowledge, life experiences, and interests.

Ackerman reflected on how the therapists didn't know Paul very well and often missed what was creative in his multilingual labels and playful responses. Instead of tapping into the potential richness of Paul's home setting, their home therapy sessions mirrored the hospital-based treatments he had received early in his recovery. The therapists brought structured tasks and worksheets with them and focused on correcting or reshaping his aphasic errors. Ackerman recalled a session when a therapist was asking him to name items in postcards depicting famous works of art. Paul was struggling with the task, and most of cards "left him speechless or uttering the wrong words." When they got to one showing Raphael's famous painting of two baby angels leaning on chubby elbows over a balcony, Paul said, "Chair-roobeem." The therapist patiently corrected him, "No, . . . these are angels, AINGELS" (2011, p. 191). Ackerman found herself explaining that *cherub* is an Old English word for a baby angel, and *cherubim* is its plural form.

During his daily home sessions with his speech therapists, Paul struggled to give the "right" answers and show improvement on the therapy tasks. However, as the epigraph from Ackerman indicates, these sessions routinely left him despondent—"exhausted and demoralized" with minimal improvements to show for his efforts. To create opportunities for more meaningful interactions, Ackerman hired an aide and designed a home program centered on creating a rich environment throughout Paul's days. Her program was grounded in what she had learned while researching her book about how the brain works, in her knowledge of her husband, and in her own desire to reconstruct their life together. Several years later, Paul had returned not just to writing daily but also to authoring and publishing books.

Relationships between brain injury, behavior, diagnostic testing, and therapeutic intervention are complex. For example, in the mid-twentieth century, Sperry pioneered a surgical procedure, a complete *callosotomy*, to treat severe cases of intractable refractory epilepsy. For people with that form of epilepsy, seizure activity in one hemisphere spreads to the other hemisphere. The callosotomy severed the *corpus callosum*, a primary path of communication between the left and right hemispheres of the brain. The surgery stopped seizure activity from spreading across the hemispheres. Sperry partnered with Gazzaniga to study behavioral outcomes among patients who had undergone this surgery.

In controlled settings and with carefully designed tasks, researchers documented striking effects from severing inter-hemispheric communication (Doron, Bassett, & Gazzaniga, 2012; Gazzaniga, 1967). For example, if different visual information was simultaneously provided to patients' left and right hemispheres and they were asked both to name what they saw and to select the item from a group of objects, patients would *name* the object that was processed in their left hemisphere while at the same time *selecting* the different object that was processed by the right hemisphere. Or, if an object was displayed so it would be processed only by the right hemisphere, patients would correctly *pick up* the object, while at the same time *saying* they could see nothing.

From a rehabilitation perspective, however, what was striking was the often-cited observation that "complete severing of the corpus callosum had surprisingly little observable effect on the behavior of these patients in the real world" (Doron et al., 2012, p. 3). In other words, although the neurological consequences of severing the corpus callosum were permanent, and striking evidence of breakdowns could be elicited years later on tasks carefully designed to isolate the hemispheres, the effects of the surgery were largely invisible when the patients were functioning in the world, in distributed systems that could flexibly adapt and reorganize. The clinical research work with these so called *split-brain patients* highlights the power of carefully structured tasks and interactions to make highly visible an individual's isolated skills and deficits. However, it also highlights the limits of such controlled tasks.

These research designs did not predict or account for the striking success split-brain patients had in everyday functional activities. Although communicative disorders typically do have observable effects in everyday worlds, highly structured patterns of interaction can amplify the problems and increase their visibility. In many ways then, such formal assessments resemble McDermott's observation (see Chapter 6) that making Adam's LD visible had become something of a sport for his fellow students, but it was most marked by testing. To forge tighter connections between diagnosis, treatment, and everyday activity, we need to focus on situated communication, to shift our practices to identify what is possible, to support creative redistribution of cognitive-communicative success within functional systems, and to marshal flexibilities of clinicians in understanding how they can support that success.

Part 3 will shed light on how therapy sessions like those Paul participated in are interactionally structured, how participation frameworks can be examined and re-designed, and how rich communicative environments can support change. Chapter 7 analyzes figured worlds of clinical work, focusing on how people routinely participate in client-clinician interactions and how assessment is central to the figured world of the clinic. Chapter 8 focuses attention on ways that clinicians can shift from traditional communicative roles and take up more flexible roles as communication partners. Chapter 9 explores the importance and potentials of optimizing clients' participation in *rich communicative environments* both inside and outside of clinical spaces. As usual, each chapter includes reflective observations (now using SDA to reflect on clinical discourse) and suggested readings that focus on SDA approaches to understanding and designing clinical interventions.

Chapter 7

Situating Clinical Practice and Clinical Discourse

The clinical work of speech-language pathologists is essentially a matter of face-to-face communicative interactions between clinicians and clients. This chapter uses *situated discourse analysis* (SDA) to characterize typical clinician-client interactions in the institutional spaces of clinical activity. The goals and cultural practices of CSD emerged broadly from two institutional sources: earlier work of *speech correctionists* in schools (e.g., St. Pierre & St. Pierre, 2018; Van Riper, 1939) and medical models used in hospitals (e.g., Helm-Estabrooks & Albert, 1991; Sohlberg & Mateer, 1989). Both were grounded in identifying the correct way of communicating (e.g., right/wrong speech patterns, standard language forms, and proper displays of social etiquette) and launched lines of research designed to better understand the specific physical abilities and skills people need to achieve normative communication goals.

Combining diagnostic models from medical settings, models of testing from schools, and didactic (school-like) practices to teach correct usage and appropriate communicative norms, clinical work has thus been designed to "normalize" the disabled (to help them fit in) and to relieve any communication burdens that might be put on non-disabled society. Foucault (1972) traced the historical emergence of *disciplinary institutions* (schools, hospitals, psychiatric asylums, prisons, monasteries, the military). He noted their common forms of discourse (e.g., valuing ranked categorical identities and utterances based on them) and ways of organizing sociomaterial spaces (e.g., special spaces for specific categories of people as in hospital wards, classrooms divided by grade, and therapy rooms). Assessment practices are central to producing such ranked categories and to highlighting norms and deviance from norms. Central then to clinical interactions are *power dynamics* that naturalize the clinician's authority to direct clients' activities and distinguish what is a disorder from what is a difference (see Damico, Simmons-Mackie, & Hawley, 2005).

In Chapter 7, we explore the sociocultural activities and figured worlds of clinical spaces, the expected (and dominant) patterns of participation between clients and clinicians, and how communicative resources are deployed to establish and sustain clinicians' control of clinical interactions.

We focus particularly on the *clinical stance*, that is, the interactional dynamics that support clinician-control over what happens in clinical sessions, what goals are addressed, and how those goals are accomplished. Clinical communicative repertoires are typically quite standardized and restrictive, leading clinicians to, in effect, limit communicative opportunities for their clients. We will begin by looking at interactions from a discourse elicitation protocol (Hengst & Duff, 2007) that was designed to change clinician practice, but in the initial pilot failed to do so. In Chapter 8, we will return to these data and see the successful implementation of the protocol.

The Case of Susan—Initial Pilot of Mediated Discourse Elicitation Protocol (MDEP)

Drawing on SDA, I worked with Melissa Duff to design a clinical-research protocol that would preserve the interactional dimensions of more complex, collaborative forms of everyday interaction (as opposed to seeking linguistic forms through highly controlled clinical discourse). We designed what we referred to as a *Mediated Discourse Elicitation Protocol* (MDEP, which we call the "Med-DEP") and piloted it with Susan, a patient with chronic, dense amnesia (Hengst & Duff, 2007). The protocol included narrative discourse, using three story-generating prompts (a frightening experience, a historical event, a personal/family story). The goal was to elicit personal narratives in a conversational framework. We chose story generation because it was assumed to be more demanding than tasks that required clients to describe story sequences using picture prompts or retell stories from verbal models. We focused on personal narratives because they were a well-documented type of discourse common to everyday talk across social and professional settings (e.g., Ochs & Capps, 2001). The goal here was to analyze Susan's abilities to use narrative discourse in recalling and talking about past events. The excerpt presented in Transcript 7.1 begins four turns into the narrative discourse tasks, immediately after Melissa has given the first story prompt—"Can you tell me the most frightening experience . . . that you've had in your life?"

The protocol called on Melissa to shift from more clinical control in the set up and instructions to a more reciprocal, everyday role during the discourse elicitation tasks themselves. However, during this initial pilot Melissa struggled to make the shift to a more everyday communicative stance. The results are apparent in Transcript 7.1. Melissa's turns are short and mainly directive or reflecting (i.e., repeating Susan's words). Overall, the narrative discourse task, including all three prompts, was 46 turns long. Melissa's instructions to Susan were minimal ("Now I'm going to have you just . . . tell me some stories") and did little to motivate the task, to indicate how the task was related to research or clinical goals, or to clarify what aspects of storytelling (e.g., accuracy, performance) were important here. Most critically, Melissa didn't establish the reciprocal frame of a communication partner.

Transcript 7.1 Susan's response to the frightening story prompt during initial session piloting the MDEP. Transcription Key: # Turn number; **S** = Susan; **M** = Melissa; . (period) = turn final intonation; , (comma) = turn continuation intonation; ? (question mark) = questioning intonation; : (colon)= prolonged sounds, each : about half a second;—(dash) = abrupt stop; . . . (ellipses) = pauses of less than a seconds, with . . . 3 . . . indicting longer pauses indicated numerically as number of seconds; and [ ] = descriptions of gestures (see Hengst & Duff, 2007, p. 42).

#4 S: hm ....10.......... the only thing that comes to mind is going on this silly roller coaster and [shakes head "no"] and I couldn't hardly get out [laughs]

#5 M: Well tell me about that.

#6 S: It was just so scary that ..2.. my knees just buckled when I tried to get out of it in the car [laughs] when it was over with, ..2.. that's about it, I never had any major ....4.... burglars or robbers or anything like that. [shakes head "no"]

#7 M: Well tell me more about this roller coaster.

#8 S: Just .....5..... I'm sacred of heights ...3... and (uh) ...3... that was probably my big thing, going through loops and everything, it was a great huge big roller coaster, the scariest thing ever happen in my life is this ..2.. this problem [laughs & nods head "yes"]

#9 M: What problem is that?

#10 S: No memory [shakes head "no"]

#11 M: No memory.

#12 S: No memory, ...3... yeah, ...3... like ... being stranded somewhere and ..2.. not having a clue how to get home or ..2.. remembering telephone [shakes head "no"] numbers or, ...you know ......6......

#13 M: So these things have happened ... to you or you're afraid they're going to.

#14 S: No::::, I'm- I've- [nods head "yes" then shakes head "no"] my family's been wonderful.

#15 M: Mhm

#16 S: They ... don't want me out their sight [laughs and shakes head "no"]. They have just absolutely been wonderful, ...but I'm always scared that it's going to happen you know? Ronald caught me one time, ... I just stood where I was supposed to stay and wait for him you know and he was late, and when he came up I had a little tear in my eye and he felt so bad [laughs] yeah, but I know if I just stood there he would be there you know?

Sociocultural Activities of Traditionally Designed Clinical Spaces

Using SDA, we begin our exploration of the sociocultural activity typical of clinical spaces by asking the fundamental question introduced in Chapter 1 of what is going on in the communicative interaction of those spaces. As was discussed in Chapter 5, we also need to begin with a focus on the contextualizing work participants do to build contexts and roles. We cannot assume that clinical activity is simply whatever happens in a clinical space; that clinical spaces will display simple, singular activity; or that participants' roles can be taken for granted. Thus, to examine communicative interactions between clients and clinicians, we begin with the question: *What are the sociocultural activities and social roles in clinical spaces?*

As laid out in Chapters 1 and 4, sociocultural activities are most easily described by the work being done (i.e., the goals) and by the *figured worlds* associated with accomplishing those goals. Sociocultural activities and figured worlds *presuppose* how specific goals should be accomplished and the social roles involved. We can look to professional organizations, such as ASHA (the American Speech-Language-Hearing Association), to outline the professional roles of SLPs (speech-language pathologists). As set out by ASHA (www.asha.org/about/), clinical work must be grounded in the precepts that communication is a human right and the work of SLPs is to support individuals with communication disorders in achieving their communication goals. To do that, SLPs are professionally trained to diagnose communication disorders in individuals across the lifespan and to implement treatments designed to eliminate, mitigate, or compensate for communicative impairments. SLPs may also be involved in counseling/educating patients, family, friends, teachers, and others about communication disorders and specialized accommodations clients need. Like all sociocultural activities, clinical interactions are complex, multiple, and dynamic, with people routinely working to accomplish a variety of easily named and recognizable goals along with less easily named or recognizable goals (e.g., identity work). Clinical spaces and activities are quite recognizable (in part because of their overlaps with the institutional spaces of school and medicine), alerting people to *anticipate* specific patterns of interaction (see Goody, 1995).

Central to the figured worlds of clinical work is a *power dynamic* that privileges the clinician's expertise and control over that of the client (Damico et al., 2005; Leahy, 2004). The routines of clinical interaction are strongly patterned on routines from didactic approaches used by teachers in schools (e.g., Mehan, 1979; Minick, 1993) and medical models designed to eliminate or mitigate impairments. Like teachers, clinicians rely heavily on directives, questions and prompts, and evaluative patterns of interaction. Like students, clients are expected to comply with the tasks given and to be motivated to excel in them. In this figured world, clients and their families (much like students and their families) are not expected to understand the content, and families are viewed as biased (non-expert and interested) reporters of their family member with a communication disorder. The figured world of clinical practice then sets up interactions between the clinician as an expert-in-charge and the client as a person-needing-help (Simmons-Mackie & Damico, 1999).

As a form of *medical labor*, the design and organization of clinical work is strongly shaped by billing/funding decisions. Much as chores routinely regulated the length and development of *Cindy Magic* episodes (see Chapter 3), funding for therapy routinely regulates the goals, length, and conduct of clinical interventions. In medical settings, activities related to billing and meeting expectations for billable hours are central to clinical work. In schools, services may also be charged to Medicaid and other insurers, especially for costly services and devices that SLPs might be involved with (e.g., feeding/swallowing; AAC devices). Many clinical routines are centered around the need to document diagnoses and progress for such third-party payment. When clinicians keep records of client responses during formal assessments and use the data to score, interpret and report a client's performance compared with developmental or standardized norms, they are often simultaneously enacting school-like practices (where assessment is tied to learning) and business-like practices (e.g., documenting client contact, writing referrals, submitting billing information).

A striking example of the consequences of current funding systems is that SLP services typically are quite limited (e.g., an hour a day counts as intense therapy). Given that we know intensity is central to learning, interventions designed primarily to optimize impact would not be so limited. To get a sense of how funding shapes school interventions, compare SLP services in schools to the time, energy, and resources devoted to other specialized activities such as high school sports, where teams attend daily practices, preseason training campus, and post-game debriefings; individual team members might also attend weight training sessions; and players are cheered by cheerleading squads and school-wide pep rallies.

Clinical work calls on clinicians to function as *session managers*. Clinical sessions are routinely organized with a few minutes of introductions and relaxed conversation designed to build rapport and put the client at ease, followed by assessment and/or treatment tasks, and ending with wrapping up, which might include reviewing what was accomplished, reporting how the client did, setting out homework goals, and scheduling future sessions. Comparing different clinical approaches to treating clients with cognitive-communication disorders especially associated with traumatic brain injuries, Ylvisaker and his colleagues (Ylvisaker, Hanks, & Johnson-Green, 2002) characterized five key dimensions (or sub-activities) of planning and implementing interventions:

- *focus and goal*—what the clinician works to accomplish;
- *assessment*—what is involved in assessment and how results are used to organize treatment goals and monitor progress;
- *treatment modalities and methods*—how the clinician implements treatment;
- *organization of treatment*—how the clinician moves the client along to greater success; and
- *setting, content, and providers*—who participates in interventions, what materials are used, where treatment sessions are held, and who implements therapeutic supports.

Using these dimensions, the technical report describes typical intervention practices.

Broadly, Ylvisaker and his colleagues note traditional approaches seek to simplify activities, focus clients on specific skills, and limit unexpected responses. The clinician focuses on identifying behavioral dysfunctions or deficits based on the client's pre-morbid abilities or in comparison to normative data for typical performance of age-matched peers. The treatment aims to eliminate or mitigate the impact of some underlying impairment(s). Formal measures and controlled observations are used to establish treatment goals (e.g., fixing the deficit) and to monitor client's progress. Traditional approaches may use a variety of controlled treatment tasks designed to isolate and practice (or drill) specific skills and to teach compensatory strategies. Regardless of modality (computer programs, paper/pencil worksheets, auditory-oral drills), treatment is organized incrementally, beginning with simple isolated tasks and moving to progressively more demanding tasks as the client improves. Treatment tasks are designed to target underlying skills in the most generalizable way, so not customized to specific functional or personal content. Clinical interactions are typically controlled one-on-one interactions that take place in a quiet setting with minimal distractions.

There are clinical alternatives to these traditional practices that take a more situated and distributed perspective. As Ylvisaker and his colleagues (Ylvisaker, et al., 2002) noted, *contextual approaches* are designed to target functional systems by using environmentally aligned supports to accomplish meaningful activities. For example, in my role as a staff SLP on an interdisciplinary ALS team through the neurology department at the University of Minnesota Hospital and Clinics, the position where I worked with Larry (who wrote the epigraph at the beginning of Part 2), I was charged with helping families and patients adjust their expectations, attitudes, and goals to the changing/declining communicational consequences of ALS, changes that simultaneously altered their social roles and relations. As a terminal disease marked by progressive paralysis that affects respiratory, laryngeal and oral muscles, ALS leads to dysarthria and dysphagia, which in the most severe cases leaves people unable to speak or swallow. This clinic's approach was to offer multi-professional team support to patients and their families as a unit, helping them adjust to and compensate for the patient's deteriorating condition. This approach was reflected in billing practices—patients were charged for the clinic visit, not charged by each team member. As an SLP on the team, my role was to help clients and their families develop evolving communicative strategies to compensate for loss of function and to be successful communication partners. Such strategies included providing patients and caregivers with AAC (alternative and augmentative communication) systems (including using paper and pencil, eye blinks and eye gaze boards, prerecorded phone messages, and sophisticated computer systems). To assess situated needs and design relevant interventions, I and other team members routinely visited homes. To be successful, clinicians engaged in family-centered and community-based service delivery approaches, routinely altering their clinical stance to better support clients and their families in articulating and achieving their communication goals.

The Grip of Traditional Clinical Activities: Piloting a Protocol

Transcript 7.1 captures a stretch of interaction between the clinician (Melissa) and client (Susan) during an assessment session piloting the MDEP (Hengst & Duff, 2007). This interaction was situated in multiple activities with multiple goals and indexed multiple social identities. Melissa was a PhD student, a licensed SLP with 5 years of experience, and a clinical coordinator in a university Amnesia Research Lab. We were piloting the MDEP protocol to support Melissa's research along with other projects in the Amnesia lab. Susan was a 54-year-old wife, mother, and former hairdresser who had had profound amnesia for four years following an anoxic incident. Formal testing placed her language and intellectual abilities within normal limits, but indicated severe memory impairment. Susan was a long-term participant in the Amnesia Research Lab and was identified as a potential participant for piloting this protocol because of her comfort in that setting and the ease with which she conversed with Melissa. It is important to note that the protocol was not intended to be only a research tool, but also a protocol that could be used for clinical assessment.

We had developed the MDEP with the goal of eliciting four types of *interactional discourse* samples typical of everyday interactions. As the clinician, Melissa thus needed to shift from a stance of clinical management to being an engaged audience to Susan's conversational narratives, or an interested novice wanting to learn how Susan makes her favorite sandwich. Although we expected the MDEP to capture difficulties patients might have across different types of discourse, we also anticipated the interactional samples would capture how Melissa and Susan worked together to distribute successful communication. Consistent with assessment protocols more broadly, the MDEP was implemented by Melissa in a specified order as a one-on-one interaction in a quiet clinical setting with minimal distractions. Because we were piloting the MDEP for research, the session was video recorded to support more detailed discourse analysis.

As we reviewed what happened in this pilot, Melissa and I were both surprised she had found taking up a reciprocal interactional frame difficult to do in the clinical setting. She reported feeling conflicted. Trained to limit her input during testing and to prompt the client to talk, Melissa could not bring herself to break out of that clinical stance, something we will explore in more detail as we discuss patterns of participation and communicative resources. As can be seen in the transcript, the interaction proceeded reasonably smoothly. Melissa worked through the basic prompts. Susan responded in anticipated ways (e.g., telling a story when asked about a story). The research activity, indexed by the video recording, also meant that, although Melissa had her clipboard, she took very few notes during the session.

Patterns of Client-Clinician Participation in Assessment

The activities, goals, and social roles of clinical spaces shape, and are shaped by, people's patterns of participation. Clinical spaces are designed to support one-on-one interactions between the clinician and client. Clients typically come to the clinician's space, leading to the construction or selection of spaces for therapy that are small and relatively private. Of course there are exceptions (push-in sessions in schools, home treatment for early childhood services, and the ALS team where patients came to one clinic to work with diverse professionals). As we noted in Chapter 4, it is particularly critical to attend to how people are socially and materially positioned in particular functional systems and figured worlds. Given that clients are positioned as in need of help and by definition as someone whose communication is in some way limited or problematic, the second question we will consider is: *What are the patterns of participation by clients and clinicians in clinical spaces?*

Assessment protocols and formal tests are one central pattern of participation. As with the split-brain research discussed in the introduction to Part 3, to document how specific physical impairments may disrupt behavior, assessment protocols must be carefully designed and tightly controlled. Designed to make deficits apparent, cognitive-communication assessments likewise dictate highly scripted and controlled communicative interactions between clinicians and clients. For example, the *Recent Memory Screening Test* (RMST) is designed to assess the abilities of adults to recall details of a story. The test specifies how to set up a physical space without distractions, where to sit in relation to the client, what specifically to say to set up the task, how to engage (conversation-like), what responses can be counted as correct, and how to interpret the client's score. Assessments of a child's receptive vocabulary (e.g., the *Peabody Picture Vocabulary Test-Revised*) likewise instruct clinicians how to respond, including how many times prompts can be repeated. The goal of such scripted interactions is to standardize clinician behavior, to stabilize measurement of client discourse, and especially to direct the client to specific responses the clinician can evaluate as correct or adequate. Scripted interactions are designed then to ensure the clinician knows what to expect, to limit distributed communicative patterns typical of non-scripted interactions, and to minimize emergent and creative dimensions of communication. Of course, if the goal is to assess a client's ability to engage in distributed, creative, everyday communicative interactions, then the restrictions built into assessment for specific tasks need to be lifted (just as split-brain patients' performance on controlled tasks did not reflect their experiences and abilities in everyday environments).

From the perspective of SDA, the notion of *stance* (Goffman, 1981; Ochs & Capp, 2001; Agha, 2007) is central to these institutional patterns. Bucholtz and Hall (2005) define stance as "the display of evaluative, affective, and epistemic orientations in discourse" (p. 595), highlighting it as an interactional resource central to building identities, social relations, and contexts (the indexical grounds of interaction). The stickiness of the clinical stance for traditional assessment becomes especially apparent when clinicians shift from diagnosis to intervention, but the scripted, restricted patterns of participation are tacitly adopted as a stance for all clinical interactions. If clinicians simply follow the script, they can achieve a technical proficiency, but they will not be able to flexibly adjust their patterns of participation to assess and support clients' interactional success.

In fact, as Kovarsky, Kimbarow, and Kastner (1999) note, the interactions that structure treatment tasks routinely focus on constructing and indexing the incompetence of clients rather than supporting their communicative success. Studying a group treatment session for individuals with traumatic brain injuries (TBI), they documented how clinicians controlled interactional patterns in ways that alienated clients from the task. For example, as a memory treatment, a group of TBI clients was directed to play a game called "Going to the Moon." The first person was supposed to name an object beginning with A that they would take to the moon, the second person was then supposed to identify a new object beginning with B and say the object the first person gave and then their own object. When one of the clients indicated he would take vitamins to the moon, the clinician hesitated, then noted that they were on "I," so his object had to begin with "I." Kovarsky, Kimbarow, and Kastner note that the game could be viewed as a "competency-lowering communicative practice" (p. 304) as it involved arbitrary rules (what does the alphabet have to do with planning for a trip to the moon?), discouraged personal relevance and experience, and was not utilized to provoke discussions of participants' rationales for their choices. In many ways, this "memory game" treatment is indistinguishable from a memory test, pointing again to the influence of assessment practices and stances on therapeutic interactions.

Reacting against the way clients are positioned in typical clinical interactions, some researchers and clinicians interested in interactional dimensions of discourse (see Damico, Oelschlaeger, & Simmons-Mackie, 1999; Lesser & Perkins, 1999) have turned to conversation analysis (CA, see Chapter 1). CA approaches argue that to assess client language, "natural" samples of conversations should be recorded in the course of everyday activities and that clinicians should not participate in those conversations. While traditional approaches seek the controlled conditions of clinical settings to isolate client competence, CA-based approaches reject clinical spaces as artificial, understand clinicians as competency-limiting agents, and assume clinical discourse is necessarily asymmetrical. In contrast, they take everyday settings as natural, imagine everyday partners as competency-supporting agents, and assume everyday discourse is naturally symmetrical. As discussed in Chapter 6, SDA argues instead that particular environments (settings like homes and clinics) may contribute to, but do not automatically produce, particular activities, functional systems, and forms of participation. Rather than assume non-clinical spaces are egalitarian and symmetrical, SDA recognizes everyday communicative spaces can ostracize and suppress people.

Indeed, power dynamics play out in all interactions as people continually negotiate their positioning in social roles and identities. We saw this in Goodwin and Alim's (2010) research on girls' talk on playgrounds (Chapter 1). Analyzing an intervention motivated by a similar confidence in everyday spaces, Dean, Adams, and Kasari (2013) describe a social-skills intervention organized in a school for Cindy, a 7-year-old girl with ASD who was paired over lunch with three other girls (typically developing peers) who volunteered. At the beginning the adult facilitator would discuss possible activities with the girls, encourage them to socialize and have fun, and make sure they were starting lunch, but then would withdraw to leave the girls on their own. As the researchers analyzed narratives told by the girls in the group, they found the three volunteers' narratives were shorter, thematically more varied, and often (60 percent of the time) cooperatively engaged with. In contrast, Cindy's narratives were longer, more thematically focused, and only infrequently (20 percent of the time) cooperatively engaged with. In other words, left on their own, the peer group highlighted Cindy's ASD and the three peers increasingly censured Cindy's storytelling. Despite the peers' lack of engagement with Cindy, the researchers' analysis located the problem solely in Cindy's narrative practices and did not consider how Cindy's narratives had been shaped by her peers' inflexible participation. One of the key problems identified was that Cindy had strong interests that led to multiple stories on those topics. Is having interests a social deficit, or should it have been understood as a difference? In any case, pairing Cindy with her peers over lunch did not automatically result in competence-enhancing interactions for Cindy (or her peers).

Clinician-Client Interactions—Examples From Clinical and Schools Settings

Next we will look at three examples that examine patterns of client-clinician participation, highlighting the dominance of the dominance of a pattern combing clinician control, collaborative reticence, and a clinical stance of asymmetrical power and evaluation. The first focuses on a professor's recollections of SLP sessions designed as drills to help him recover from aphasia and improve his word retrieval. The second describes a phonics lesson layered onto a book reading activity for a grade school child. Finally, we look again at the interaction between Melissa and Susan in Transcript 7.1.

The retired professor I discussed in Chapter 4, whose stroke left him with chronic anomic aphasia (and who used the "oh, in English, what do you call it?" strategy to request a spoon at a restaurant), told me another story in our conversations that illustrates the power dynamics of clinical interactions. In one of his speech-language therapy sessions, his therapist, a young man, was showing him cards and the professor was naming them, "house . . . dog." The therapist was giving typical feedback and moving the task along, "Good, now what's this?" Shown a picture of a pair of men's dress shoes, the professor recalled hesitating. He knew what they were, but the right word just would not come. The therapist prompted: "Do you remember it? It starts with sh-?" The professor replied: "No, that's not right It's . . . ah, it's . . ." The therapist completed the sentence "shoes," but the professor insisted that shoes wasn't right. The therapist assured him that it was a drawing of a pair of men's shoes, asked if he recognized them, suggested he must have worn shoes like that with his suits, and said just to call them shoes for the task. The professor told me that he never did think of the right word but also refused to say "shoes" during that therapy session. At the end of the story I asked if he had meant "wingtips." He was almost sure—formal, black shoes with designs cut into them. In any case, years later he was still frustrated with that interaction and at not being able to convey to his young therapist that not just any word would do. This story clearly echoes Ackerman's story in the introduction to Part 3 of her husband doing a similar task (naming pictures) and being corrected when the word he said (cherubim) didn't match what the therapist expected (angels).

Another example of clinical controls can be seen in Ukrainetz's (2006) account of what she identified as *contextualized language intervention* grounded in sociocultural theory. Although sociocultural theories typically construe contextualization as a matter of aligning with the motivations of activities and people, Ukrainetz's approach is highly didactic, calling for explicit scaffolding of children's productions within instructional tasks and for targeting isolated language features, grounded in theories of language as a system of rules (phonemic, syntactic, and perhaps pragmatic) the child possesses. Ukrainetz argues that school intervention needs to be grounded in motivated sociocultural activities like storybook reading. However, she uses storybook reading not as the basis for imaginatively entering into the figured worlds of the story or following student uptakes wherever they go, but instead as a prop for tightly controlled whole-part-whole instructional sequences. She illustrates this approach with a transcript of an interaction in which the SLP begins by reading a bit of a story ("This is a boy named Fred. He hates to go to bed. He hides out in a shed . . ." p. 452). The SLP then interrupts the story for direct instruction on phonemic awareness: identifying the rhymes ("all those words rhyme, Fred-bed-shed"), asking students to isolate sounds ("What's the first sound in Fred?"), and then directing the student to count the phonemes in individual rhymed words from the story ("Let's count the sounds in Fred"). There may be reasons to count the sounds in "Fred," but an SDA approach would insist that the activity in that case is *not* storybook reading, but language drills on phonemes (see also Hengst, 2015).

Melissa's first pilot, as seen in Transcript 7.1, displays the stance that typically marks clinical interaction. Melissa is professional and friendly, the clinician-in-charge, but not an engaged audience for Susan's narrative telling. Melissa directs and elicits, but offers quite limited supports. Critically, Susan knows how to fit into such school-like tasks, where stories are told to be assessed, not appreciated or taken up as an invitation for others to share their stories. The participation structure of the interaction is visible in the resources used (as we see later), but it may be most apparent in *what does not happen*. For example, there is no overtalk. Melissa does not jump in during long silences or tell any stories (e.g., of her own experiences with roller coasters or of what frightens her). For her part, Susan does not ask why Melissa is asking these questions or requesting narratives. Susan does not break through into marked narrative performance with animated voicing, poetics, constructed dialogue, and highly detailed representations of scenes and settings (Hymes, 1975, 1981).

The power of the clinical stance—centered on asymmetrical expertise, evaluation, and interactional reticence—is strikingly pervasive in clinical settings and inflexible in interaction. The clinicians in these three examples were persistent in keeping clients on task and resistant to shifting their stance to follow the client's lead. The professor's therapist never acknowledges that there might be another word to better describe the picture. Although setting out to illustrate the power of everyday storybook reading for school-based intervention, Ukrainetz seems to not notice that the activity quickly morphs back into a highly directive, test-like drill. Melissa sets out to pilot a mediated discourse elicitation protocol after extensive development work but finds she just cannot bring herself in the moment to shift from the clinical stance to reciprocal stances aligned with the forms of discourse being elicited.

Communicative Resources in Typical Clinical Interactions

Given the strong focus in many clinical interactions on language and scripted interaction, it is important to attend not only to what forms of language appear in clinical interactions, but also to the broader arrays of signs and discourse patterns and how they are interactively and emergently deployed. In clinical interactions, clinicians and clients deploy resources differently. This difference may certainly be due in part to more limited or disrupted communicative resources available to individuals with communication disorders, but it also serves to index and reinforce the familiar and anticipated clinical dynamic that presumes the clinician is in charge. For example, throughout a session, clients are positioned to respond to the clinician's questions and prompts while clinicians are positioned to direct clients and provide *feedback* about how well clients are complying with the agenda and accurately responding to the task. The question we ask here is: *What communicative resources are clients and clinicians using in their interactions?*

Conversation analysis (CA; introduced in Chapter 1) has focused on *adjacency pairs*, highly recognizable patterns of turn initiations and responses (e.g., *question-answer, greeting-reply, directive-acknowledgement/refusal*). The power of adjacency pairs to structure interactions and establish roles is worth noting. For example, when someone asks you what your name is, you might answer almost automatically, unless you actively resist this familiar dynamic. Think about how telemarketers use the power of questions to control interactions. The default response to the first part of an adjacency pair (e.g., a question) is the second part (e.g., an appropriate answer), and CA has observed an interactional preference for people to comply with expectations to complete these familiar patterns. The person who initiates an adjacency pair (e.g., by asking a question or offering a greeting) is then momentarily bidding for control over the interaction.

Of course, *adjacency pairs* do not occur in isolation. For example, speakers routinely monitor listeners' *backchannel* responses (e.g., head nods, eye contact, verbal agreements "right" "okay") to gauge their ongoing alignments and to identify possible trouble sources (e.g., a speaker could not hear or understand the listener's reply, or the listener disagreed with or wanted to alter what the speaker initiated). When a trouble source arises in an interaction (see Chapter 5), a *repair sequence* may be prompted (often discussed as an optional third part of any adjacency pair). Repair sequences involve identifying the problem (or misunderstanding) and resolving (or correcting) it before returning to the original adjacency pair (e.g., answering the question originally asked). Trouble sources can be identified by speakers mid-turn, prompting them to *self-repair* by, for example, adding clarifying details; or trouble sources can be identified by a listener using their turn to ask for, or propose, a clarification (*other-initiated repair*). Although repair sequences are typically managed within a few turns, they may become extended exchanges, especially for communication partners managing aphasia or dementia (e.g., Laakso, 2003; Orange, Lubinski, & Higginbotham, 1996; Samuelsson & Hydén, 2017).

Patterns of clinician/teacher control of topic, response, and accuracy have been partly stabilized in a highly recognizable three-part discourse pattern (*initiation-reply-evaluation; IRE*) that combines question-answer and repair sequences. Broadly, this IRE discourse pattern has been identified as a hallmark of instructional discourse in schools (e.g., Mehan, 1979) and of language therapy in clinical settings (e.g., Davis, 2014; Horton, 2006). Critically, a teacher/clinician *initiates* the exchange with a *display question or prompt* (i.e., one they know the answer to), the student/client *responds* with an anticipated answer, which the teacher/clinician then *evaluates*. A simple example of this three-part sequence would be:

Teacher: What is the capital of Illinois? [pointing to map]
Student: Chicago
Teacher: No, remember, Spring . . . .

In this hypothetical exchange, the teacher initiates the sequence with a *display question*, the student replies with an incorrect city, and the teacher indicates it is wrong and offers a hint. In effect, any response from the instructor that does not specifically accept the answer (like, "yes," "good," "correct") indicates the answer was not adequate. For example, the teacher could say "no," "well," "um," or use nonverbal responses such as sighing, looking back at or tapping Illinois on the map, or just giving a quizzical look (e.g., cocking her head and raising her eyebrows). An initiation can be a directive as well: "Name the capital of Illinois." In this example, the teacher also uses her evaluation turn to initiate a correction (i.e., an instructional repair) to the student's error, prompting the student to give another response. In this way, IRE discourse works to establish and reinforce a particular hierarchy between experts/novices, teachers/students, or clinicians/clients. For example, the student cannot respond by saying, "Good question. Why don't you look that up in the atlas?" although that would be a response the teacher could give to a student asking the same question. In any case, initiations are not done to get answers to questions the asker is curious about, but to prompt others to display their knowledge in a manner easily evaluated by the clinician/teacher.

Studying *clinician feedback* during sessions with aphasic clients, Simmons-Mackie, Damico, and Damico (1999) found clinicians' negative evaluations of client's responses were frequently indirect (e.g., asking for a repetition rather than explicitly critiquing a response) and that, if given directly, feedback was often vague. The success of such indirect and vague feedback in changing client productions depended on the client interpreting them within a clinician-client framework. For example, if the clinician was silent after a client response, the client was expected to take the silence as a negative evaluation (e.g., an off-task or inaccurate response), indicating the need for the client to try again. In their study of the group sessions for adults with TBI mentioned earlier, Kovarsky and his colleagues (1999) also observed that clinicians used their feedback to keep clients focused on therapeutic topics and goals (e.g., clients' cognitive-linguistic abilities/disabilities) by offering frequent and marked evaluations of the form of client productions (e.g., "that doesn't begin with the right letter," "remember, you need to go in alphabetical order") while minimizing response to broader issues related to content (how do people pack for trips) and game play (setting up house rules).

In summary, as a communicative resource, IRE discourse patterns function as an interactional discourse resource (IDR) that establishes relevant indexical grounds. IRE discourse proposes an expert-novice relationship (e.g., teacher-student, parent-child; clinician-client) with the goal of testing or evaluating the novice's knowledge or abilities. It is a highly recognizable discourse pattern that supports the institutional positioning of schools and clinics. In the epigraph to Part 3, we saw IREs playing out in Ackerman's account of Paul's sessions—where Paul's "cherubim" was wrong, not because he struggled to say it smoothly, but because it didn't conform to a clinical indexical ground where the clinician was expert and expected answers she knew. From an SDA perspective then, doing IRE discourse does not just index clinical or instructional discourse, it also builds clinical spaces, roles, and activities.

Communicative Resources in Clinical Assessments

Next we will consider the communicative resources used in two clinical settings. First, we will look at Maynard and Marlaire's (1992) research that examined clinicians in schools giving a formal test of learning abilities to students identified as having problems with school success. Then we will return to Melissa and Susan's interactions during the first pilot of the MDEP.

Maynard and Marlaire (1992) video-recorded testing sequences where clinicians administered the *Woodcock Johnson Psychoeducational Battery* to children identified as having problems with school learning. The researchers' approach to transcription and analysis was grounded in CA frameworks. In the test administration, in one task, clinicians would say a word separating syllables with a pause and ask the student to say the word. Here is an example of an interaction:

Part 1; testing prompt:	Fing? ger. (Line 6)
Part 2; reply:	Finger. (Line 7)
Part 3; acknowledgement:	Goo::d. (Line 8)

(Maynard & Marlaire, 1992, p. 180)

The test then fits into the IRE pattern. The initiation is a word spoken with unusual prosody and timing. What the student is supposed to do with "Fing? ger" is not specified in this initiation but the earlier directions to the student established a repeated pattern of initiations on this part of the test. The student repeats the word with more usual prosody and timing. The clinician then offers an evaluation of the student's production—note the elongated prosody of the vowel (as marked by the use of colons) in "good."

Here is an example that goes less smoothly:

1. CLI: Roh::duh.
2.   (1.2)
3. CHI: Rohduh.
4. CLI: Inkay. Roh::duh
5.   (3.8)
6. CHI: Roh::
7.   (0.2)
8. CLI: Can you say it fast?
9. CHI: Rohduh
10. CLI: Oka::y.

(Maynard & Marlaire, 1992, pp. 182–183)

The parenthetic with numbers mark pauses or silences in seconds. The clinician offers an initiation in line 1 that is followed by a relatively long pause, and then the child's answer. In line four, the clinician says okay (transcribed using eye-dialect[1] as "inkay," perhaps something like hm::kay), but then repeats the initiation. The 'okay' could be understood as a positive evaluation, but when spoken atypically and followed by repetition of the prompt and then silence, it is meant to be interpreted as a negative evaluation. After a marked silence (3.8 seconds), the child repeats the first syllable, including the elongation of the vowel from the clinician's utterance in line 4. After a short pause, the clinician asks the child to say it fast. The child does, but maintains the two-syllable form, not uttering the intended word, "road." The clinician again says in line 10, "Okay," elongating the final vowel, but scores the response as incorrect. The preference for vague negative evaluation is clear here: the child's three answers never get a clear negative evaluation. It is also worth noting that the test item "road" is not a two-syllable word like other items in the test (finger, candy, mother). The child's responses are all one-word utterances intended to repeat or repeat with some transformation the words of the clinician.

Maynard and Marlaire (1992) also note that the embodied behavior of the clinician and the child contribute to the clinical contextualization of these interactions. The child and clinician sit across from one another at a small table. On the table is a test book, propped up so that the clinician can read the prompts and the child cannot. They note that the child displays signs of attentive alertness, maintaining a stiff posture and keeping eye gaze on the teachers. The clinician focuses eye gaze mostly on the test book.

In Transcript 7.1, Melissa and Susan are also engaged in an assessment sequence that displays clinical controls and IRE-like sequences, but it is more elaborated and open-ended than the school assessment Maynard and Marlaire analyzed. Just before this transcript, Melissa had said "Can you tell me the most frightening experience . . . that you've had in your life?" Susan mentions a scary roller coaster ride, noting she had not had major frightening experiences like burglaries or robberies (turns 4–8). Susan then suggests (in turns 8–16) the scariest experience has been her amnesia. In turn 12, she narrates being stranded somewhere and not knowing how to get home, but the story is skeletal. Mellissa asks if she had been stranded or feared it could happened. Then Susan narrates a particular time when she was left waiting. As noted earlier, Melissa sustained a typical clinical stance instead of taking up the reciprocal stance the MDEP asked her to assume. Melissa did not follow up on details of these narratives or respond to their emotional tones. That is, she did not display the kind of active listenership expected from a conversational partner truly interested in the story being told. Melissa's clinical stance is visible in turns 5, 7, 9, 11, and 13 as she instructs Susan to say more and requests clarifications. It is also worth noting that she did not jump in on some long silences (10 seconds in Susan's turn #4; 5 seconds in turn #8, and 6 seconds in turn #12). Melissa also didn't reciprocate by sharing any stories of her own (e.g., about her own experiences with roller coasters). For her part, Susan never broke into an animated performance of either story by setting the scene, narrating a detailed sequence of events, or using engaging storytelling elements (e.g., changing speaking prosody, including gestures, using reported speech).

Overall, the absence of the intended reciprocal stance in Melissa's interactions with Susan, the failure to actually pilot the protocol throughout, is a testament to the power of the institutional space of clinical interaction, to the professional socialization Melissa had experienced into the figured world of the clinic, and to the well-developed of the communicative resources for the clinical stance. The interactions also display Susan's socialization to the role of client/student. She cooperates and follows directives, never becoming animated or displaying engagement in the topics. Although not captured in Transcript 7.1, Susan repeatedly asked how she was doing, seeking confirmation she was doing what Melissa wanted, and commented how hard it was to remember things. The IRE-like sequences here functioned as an IDR (interactional discourse resource) building the interactional contexts and social roles of traditional clinical-school discourse. The muted production and reception of Susan's stories showed they did not function as typical conversational narratives (another IDR), but fit into the IRE pattern of offering up an answer to be evaluated.

Note on Methods: Clinical Spaces Are Specialized Everyday Spaces

The institutional spaces of clinical work have been designed to support clinical activities and relations, to align with our expectations about how that work gets done, and to structure assessment. However, the communicative interactions that occur in these spaces, even between clients and clinicians, fall within the range of what is possible in everyday interactions. In other words, clinical spaces are not "artificial" spaces that make everyday interactions untenable (as we will see in Chapters 8 and 9). From the perspective of SDA, all communicative interactions are situated, and clinician-client interactions are no exception. Thus, the tools of SDA we have explored in other settings all operate (or can operate) in the institutional spaces of the clinic. Indeed, management of multiple activities and forms of participation through use of an array of communicative resources is precisely how institutional spaces and practices are indexed and built in interaction.

The power of institutional spaces (school, hospital, therapy room) has been a key focus of SDA research. Several early ground-breaking studies focused on the interactional dynamics of psychotherapeutic interactions in an effort to understand talk therapy (Labov & Fanshel, 1977; Scheflen, 1973). Mehan has studied the power dynamics of IRE discourse in classrooms (Mehan,

1979) and of disciplinary stances of expert assessment in Individualized Education Plan (IEP) meetings (Mehan, 1993). An extensive line of work has also explored the asymmetrical relations between doctors and patients sustained in part by hospital settings (e.g., ten Have, 1991). As we have seen in this chapter, the power of the communicative resources and figured worlds of clinical practice borrows heavily from people's socialization to other disciplinary institutions, especially school. Minick (1993) and Cole (1996) note that cultural psychological studies across the globe have repeatedly found that participants who have not attended schools do not perform as expected when they are tested. Asked a simple syllogism (e.g., "All the bears in Novarsk are white. I saw a bear in Novarsk. What color was the bear?"), unschooled participants are unlikely to give the expected answers (e.g., "White"). However, they don't respond with a random color ("purple"), but most often refuse to comply, to fall in with the expectations of IRE discourse. Instead, they answer on practical grounds ("I can't say, I have never been to Novarsk"). Clinical discourse may be initiated then by clinicians, but it is important to recognize that its success as a collaborative achievement depends on client compliance as well as clinician control.

SDA has also focused attention on the ongoing negotiations of control and authority in everyday interactions, an issue particularly important for understanding and managing clinical interactions. In a chapter on language and power, Damico, Simmons-Mackie, and Hawley (Damico et al., 2005) review sociolinguistic theories of power relations and the complex dynamics of negotiating power in everyday interactions. They argue clinicians must recognize the complexity of interactional power, use their clinical power to meaningfully address the goals of specific clients, and take responsibility as the person in authority for the success or failure of clinical encounters. As a starting point, they outline five ways that power differentials routinely manifest in everyday interactions. *Forms of address*—honorifics (*Your Honor, Sir*) and professional titles (*Dr. Jones*)—routinely signal a person's authority. People positioned as more powerful (e.g., a teacher) will often use less formal address (e.g., a person's given name) with someone positioned as less powerful (e.g., a student). *Speaking rights*, who is positioned as having rights to initiate and maintain a speaking turn, also index and build power. *Topic selection* is also typically controlled by the person positioned as dominant in an interaction. *Asking questions* is another interactional resource often used to control speaking rights and topics in interactions. Finally, *evaluative statements* signal the presumed right to pass judgement on someone or something (e.g., a mother telling a child "say please").

The power dynamics of institutional interactions are visible in the resources used (e.g., forms of address, questions, evaluative statements), but again may also be apparent in *what does not happen*. As we saw in Transcript 7.1 in Melissa's silence as Susan sought stories to tell and in Susan's compliant, but anxious, willingness to be assessed. Nevertheless, it is important to recognize that the communicative resources clinicians use to control and dominate interactions are assembled from the same kinds of communicative resources and practices people use to dominate and control everyday interactions.

Summary: Recognizing and Managing Authority in Client-Clinician Interactions

In this chapter, we shifted our attention to examining communicative interactions between clinicians and clients engaged in clinical work. Using SDA, we explored the powerful pull of traditional clinical practices that set clinicians up as the experts in charge of everything, using the following questions to guide our analysis:

* *What are the sociocultural activities and social roles in clinical spaces?*
* *What are the patterns of participation by clients and clinicians in clinical spaces?*
* *What communicative resources are clients and clinicians using in their interactions?*

In our article on clinicians as communication partners (Hengst & Duff, 2007), we noted a growing body of research on clinical discourse practices of SLPs that points to ways client-clinician interactions suppress the competencies of clients and limit the roles of clinicians. Responding to Kagen's (1998) article on supported conversation, Holland (1998) argued that clinical training approaches may actually make it harder for SLPs to carry on meaningful conversations with aphasic adults. Kagen had documented that laypeople were able to successfully adopt supported conversation techniques to improve their interactions with aphasic adults, whereas SLPs found such strategies difficult to implement. Holland suggested SLPs' poor performance could (in part) be accounted for by the way professional socialization pulls clinicians away from being effective communicators in conversational interactions with clients. Theoretical and methodological traditions in CSD often define conversational interactions as nontherapeutic, privileging instead use of isolated linguistic forms produced by individual speakers. Thus, clinicians are trained to focus attention on client talk by adopting an impersonal, distanced clinical stance. Indeed, according to Holland, the common sentiment among clinicians seems to be that although conversation with clients may be important for building rapport, it is not an integral part of therapeutic procedures.

That most client-clinician interactions resemble the controlled and scripted interactions designed to assess a patient's communicative deficits suggests that therapeutic interactions are tacitly modeled on and optimized for assessment. Regardless of what we call it, we are testing and evaluating. Client-clinician interactions will look different when directed at non-assessment activities—counseling, treatment, clinical business. In the next chapter, we use SDA to focus on ways of expanding the communicative repertoires of clinicians and changing the clinical stance as a means of supporting communicative diversity in clinical spaces.

Reflective Observations

1. *Analyzing control.* Much of clinical work involves managing clinician-client interactions, from initiating specific interactions to indexing specific goals and sustaining specific social roles. Think about the diverse ways you manage everyday communicative interactions—which is the source of communicative resources honed for clinical interactions. Now re-watch the observations you recorded for Chapter 1 and analyze the diverse ways people shape, manage, and control the interactions.

2. *Using IREs.* Select an assessment or treatment protocol to practice with a classmate and video-record your practice. Analyze how you used initiation-response-evaluation (IRE) patterns to implement the protocol. How did you use nonverbal resources to support the IRE patterns?

3. *Analyzing response patterns in clinical interactions.* For this reflection you will need to obtain a video recording of a clinical treatment session. If you are in a clinical program, you may be able to arrange this through your program. If not, there are clinical videos available online (e.g., Courtney Warner's vlog: www.youtube.com/watch?v=tFCK01_Arbs).

    a. Watch the session and observe the different ways that the clinician and client respond verbally and nonverbally to each other's turns, communicative offers, or actions.

    b. Analyze the clinician's responses to the client—what resources does the clinician use, what activities and social roles do the responses index?

    c. Analyze the client's responses to the clinician—what resources does the client use, what activities and social roles do the responses index?

    d. Compare the patterns of responses used by the client and clinician.

Suggested Readings

To understand typical practices of clinical interaction (in CSD and other fields), it is valuable to examine the empirical research that has developed since the 1970s. Here are three articles that offer detailed, critical analyses of communicative interactions in clinical spaces.

1. "Procedural display and classroom lessons" (Bloome, Puro, & Theodorou, 1989). David Bloome and his colleagues analyze procedural display in classrooms, the interactional patterns students and teachers align to in order to contextualize their actions as doing lessons and other events in school.

2. "Communicative accessibility in aphasia: An investigation of the interactional context of long-term care facilities" (Azios, Damico, & Roussel, 2018). Jamie Azios, Jack Damico, and Nancye Roussel examine how institutional dynamics in long-term care facilities (LTCF) limit communication opportunities and experiences of residents with communication disorders.

3. "Social role negotiation in aphasia therapy: Competence, incompetence, and conflict" (Simmons-Mackie & Damico, 1999). Nina Simmons Mackie and Jack Damico analyze a communication breakdown between a clinician and client during a therapy session.

Note

1. As discussed in Chapter 4, use of eye dialect is a common practice in CA, but one that is problematic both as a representation of phonetic and phonological processes and as a representation of people.

Chapter 8

Clinicians as Communication Partners Supporting Success

In contrast to the impersonal, directive clinical stances we identified as typical in Chapter 7, this chapter focuses on ways that clinicians can be effective and flexible communication partners who support communicative success. This chapter will focus particularly on taking a *situated discourse analysis* (SDA) approach to clinical assessment while Chapter 9 will turn to treatment. As discussed in Chapter 7, clinical training has typically emphasized learning specialized and tightly scripted patterns of interaction. Designed to support clinicians in reliably diagnosing disorders, these scripts aim to isolate the client from (or strictly control) communication supports and to require responses that make apparent the types and degrees of their impairment. However, it is rare for attention to be given to identifying client strengths (beyond the absence of specific impairments) or creating interactional contexts that simulate everyday interaction or even optimize communicative success. As we saw in Chapter 7 with Melissa's first pilot of the *Mediated Discourse Elicitation Protocol* (MDEP), clinicians trained in such scripted interactions are likely to struggle if asked to shift to being communications partners who flexibly align with clients and broker successful interactions with them and others. Thus, we will explore how the notion of distributed communication can inform and support clinicians in shifting their stance and aligning as communication partners, even in assessment activities.

A distributed communication perspective calls upon clinicians to be mindful of the complex, dynamic, and situated nature of all client–clinician interactions. We will begin with a data example from the second pilot of the MDEP, which was much more successful than the first pilot discussed in Chapter 7. We then turn to *activity frames* in clinical functional systems, the stance of a *communication partner* in clinical spaces, and communicative resources that build interactive *involvement*. The Note on Methods highlights how SDA offers a rich toolkit for being a *reflective practitioner*, which is central to ongoing professional development.

The Case of Susan—Second Pilot of Mediated Discourse Elicitation Protocol (MDEP)

In this chapter, we turn to the second pilot of the MDEP (Hengst & Duff, 2007). The MDEP discussed in Chapter 7 was designed to preserve the interactional character of four different types of discourse (conversational, narrative, picture description, and procedural). The original MDEP specified two key interactional roles for the clinician: *clinician-manager*, who is in charge of keeping the client on task and moving the session forward, and *communication partner*, who functions as an active, engaged participant in the discourse tasks being assessed. However, as Chapter 7 documented, Melissa struggled in the first pilot to enact the communication partner role and the discourse samples elicited from Susan fell far short of what Melissa knew Susan was capable of from many conversational interactions with her outside of clinical tasks.

The video recording of the first pilot allowed Melissa and me to analyze what happened and talk through how the interactions unfolded. Based on our review, we realized we needed to better specify the clinician's dynamic role in the elicitation process. We revised the protocol to focus Melissa on recognizing and acting on the different goals during the session by continually asking herself: *What is the current activity? What clinical goals does this activity address? How should I collaborate with the client to accomplish this activity?* Transcript 8.1 displays Susan's narrative beginning right after Melissa had said: "the first story I want you to tell me is about your most frightening experience."

Comparing Transcript 8.1 to Transcript 7.1, we see striking differences in the interaction. In contrast with Susan's fragmented skeletal attempts at telling narratives and Melissa's directive clinical stance in Transcript 7.1, Transcript 8.1 displays Susan sustaining an animated, detailed narrative and Melissa being an engaged audience for the storytelling. From the perspective of assessment, the second protocol was more successful than the first in the sense that more, and more varied, discourse was elicited. Overall, the second session was twice as long as the initial pilot (45 minutes, vs. 19 minutes), with Susan and Melissa producing more than double the turns and words they did in the first session. From Melissa's many interactions with Susan, the second protocol also seemed more in keeping with Susan's everyday communicative practices. Given Susan's dense anterograde amnesia, I want to remind you that although Melissa and Susan had had many interactions over several years Susan never remembered having met Melissa and did not recall having done the first pilot of the protocol. It is also intriguing that in Transcript 7.1 turn #6, as Susan began thinking about possible frightening experiences, she said, "I never had any major . . . 4 . . . burglars or robbers or anything like that," yet in the second pilot her first story (an intact memory formed before her amnesia) was exactly a story of a frightening

Transcript 8.1 Susan's response to the frightening story prompt during second session piloting the MDEP. Transcription Key: # Turn number; **S** = Susan; **M** = Melissa; . (period) = turn final intonation; , (comma) = turn continuation intonation; ? (question mark) = questioning intonation; : (colon)= prolonged sounds, each : about half a second;—(dash) = abrupt stop; ... (ellipses) = pauses of less than a seconds, with ...3 ... indicting longer pauses indicated numerically as number of seconds; and [ ] = descriptions of gestures (see Hengst & Duff, 2007, p. 46).

#14 S: Frightening experience ...3... frightening experience ...3... have I had one of those. ....4.... okay ..2.. it was no- not too frightening, but uhm, I was working at the beauty shop ..2..

#15 M: Mhm

#16 S: a:::nd everybody had gone to leave and there was about nine of us ... that worked in there

#17 M: Mhm

#18 S: and everybody had gone and I was there with keys to close up and I was working on my last customer

#19 M: Uhm

#20 S: and it was like ... nine o'clock at night, ... a::nd there was a door at both ends [gestures as if pointing at doors] ... of the shop, that went straight through [moves hands side to side] the shop again, a::nd when I look up ... and there was a man standing there and the door was locked you and it was like ..2.. "Can I help you?" you know

#21 M: Oh my gosh!

#22 S: It was like "Ohhh! Gosh what is this!" ... and we had already had the cash door open a::nd ... [moves hand as if opening drawer] yeah

#23 M: Mhm

#24 S: everything opened and you could see there was no money

#25 M: Right

#26 S: You could see that from the outside even but uh ..2.. he's standing there and he's he's really nervous you could tell he was shaking and and I was ... a little alarmed and my customer was very alarmed you know and ...

#27 M: Oh well, at least there was someone else there.

#28 S: Yeah [nods head "yes"]

#29 M: For a minute I was thinking it was just you.

#30 S: Yeah, but she was like a hundred years old so [laughs:::::::::::]

#31 M: [laughs] So she was useless to you?

#32 S: Yes, mh [nods head "yes"] and finally I ge- I- you know ... "Can I help you?" ... Uhm, ... very nervously he says "Yeah I need uh change for the vending machine." I said "Okay [nods head "yes"] I can do that you know" I said "that's all I got is change."

#33 M: Mhm

#34 S: I said "I don't have any bills you know." So I- I gave it to him and ..2.. and I let him out cause I had to unlock the door you know and uh ...3... my customer immediately got up and called her husband and told him what happened you know ... he came straight down ... with his handgun [laughs]

#35 M: Oh wow

experience with a robber at a beauty shop where she had worked. The framing of the task (which we will examine later) seems to have affected not only the way Susan communicated within this interaction, but also the way she drew on her memories.

Sociocultural Activities Organizing Client-Clinician Interactions

SDA recognizes that all communicative interactions are shaped (at least in part) by the expectations people bring to the interaction, expectations about what is happening, what goals people are working to accomplish, and what roles people should take to achieve those goals. Certainly clinicians' expectations about their roles in defining and supporting client success play a powerful role in shaping clinical interactions. In Chapters 4 and 5, I introduced the notion of figured worlds and explored ways that figured worlds shape expectations and contextualize interactions (i.e., actively build the context, roles, and activities that people are engaged in). To understand the sociocultural activities of clinical interaction then, we begin with the social matrix from which clinical interaction emerges and ask: *What is being accomplished by clinical functional systems?*

As outlined in Chapter 7, traditional clinician-client diagnostic goals are heavily influenced by a figured world in which competence is imagined as the isolated traits of an individual. Thus, the goal of the clinician is to prompt the client's individual performance by limiting any assistance in, or influence on, the client's performance. In contrast, SDA understands communicative success as distributed within functional systems. As discussed in Chapters 2 and 5 in particular, success and failure alike are distributed accomplishments and all individuals display a range of performances depending on the functional systems they are *acting-with*. From the perspective of distributed communication then, any role the clinician plays will inevitably affect a client's communicative performance.

SDA's concepts of sociocultural activity and distributed communication challenge the assumption that clinical assessment requires a stance of detached reticence and disengagement. In the context of diagnosis, it is important to not think of distributed communication and being a communication partner as always having a positive impact on interactions, that is, only as a means of enhancing or augmenting someone's baseline performance. Recall Kovarsky et al. (1999) observation that typical clinical roles too often represent a "competency-lowering communicative practice" (p. 304). Likewise, if the aim of assessment is to assess the range of a client's communicative performance and to inform decisions and strategies for supporting participation in everyday communicative interactions, then sampling only through IRE discourse (see Chapter 7) and resisting cooperative interactional practices will result in assessments that offer limited validity and usability. Nevertheless, communicative assessments have typically been designed, like the experimental tests for split-brain patients, primarily to throw a spotlight on patterns of deficit and to support diagnostic categorizations.

To assess clients' range of communicative performances, to sample how clients participate in everyday communicative interactions, and to explore diverse ways clients might be more successful in those interactions, clinicians should aim instead to partner with clients in strategic ways. For these key goals, the most productive role a clinician can play in the diagnostic process is to elicit meaningful discourse samples by acting as a communication partner rather than staying rigidly in a directive clinical role. Of course, as we saw in the *Cindy Magic* examples that anchored the three chapters in Part 1, multiple sociocultural activities are routinely at play in interaction. A key question for clinicians then is how different clinical *activity frames* can be effectively juggled—how they are nominated, established, sustained, challenged, and abandoned in pursuit of clinical assessments.

Tracing Shifting Goals in Clinical Interactions During the MDEP: The Second Pilot

Table 8.1 displays a framework that we developed before the second trial of the MDEP in order to support Melissa in enacting the role of communication partner. While we had initially identified two activity frames centered around two roles, *clinical management* in a clinician role and *discourse sampling* in the role of communication partner, we realized as we reviewed the video recordings of the first pilot that *transitioning* between these frames and roles represented a distinct activity frame and called on distinct management of roles. Table 8.1 then lists the three goal-directed activities (clinical management, target discourse sampling, and transitioning) that were part of this clinical-research session, identifies the clinical goals of each activity frame, and specifies the collaborative role the clinician should work to enact with each. To support making interactional choices at any point throughout the session, the framework focused Melissa on three questions: What is the current activity? What clinical goals does this activity address? How should I collaborate with the client to accomplish this activity?

The first activity frame in Table 8.1 is *clinical management*, which should be understood as a dimension, whether foregrounded or backgrounded, of all client-clinician interactions. This frame acknowledges the clinician's professional responsibility to display and use her position in ways that serve clinical, institutional, and (potentially, as in this example) research goals. In this frame, the clinician is expected to take charge of the overall session and provide expert judgments. Two core goals shaped communicative patterns and resources that we identified for this activity frame. First, clearly displaying

Table 8.1 Revised protocol for the MDEP with greater specification of activities, goals, and clinician roles

Activity frame	Clinical goals addressed in activity	Clinician's collaborative role in accomplishing activity
Clinical management	1. Set research/session goals 2. Present task instructions and prompts 3. Evaluate client responses, progress 4. Provide clinical expertise 5. Respond to client questions and concerns 6. Obtain recordings of interactionally produced discourse samples	Clinician-controlled discourse marked by 1. Clinician provides overt, explicit, instructions, directions and feedback. 2. Topics discussed focus on session goals, form and content of client utterances, and explanations of communication, communication disorders, diagnosis, and treatment. 3. Clinician works with client to develop shared understanding of, and motives for, activities in the session.
Target discourse sampling	Four target discourse types: 1. Conversational 2. Personal narratives 3. Picture descriptions 4. Procedural	Clinician in communication partner role, marked by 1. Clinician responds to content of client talk and provides appropriate reception (e.g., conversation partner; narrative audience; listening to client picture description; taking notes on procedural expertise). 2. Topics discussed are personal and social in nature. 3. Clinician provides interactional support and follows client's lead.
Transitioning	1. Make shifts in activities visible 2. Create opportunities for nonprompted talk 3. Create and maintain conversational framework for session through use of small talk	Clinician has fluid role—shifting between clinician-controlled and communication partner: 1. Formally marks end of current target task 2. Makes conversational small talk 3. Responds to conversational offers by client 4. Introduces next task/prompt

Source: reprinted from Hengst & Duff, 2007, p. 44.

the managerial stance allows both parties to more easily differentiate clinical management activity frames from other session frames. Second, overt and direct explanation of clinical (or research) goals provides an opportunity to build common ground and better motivate the tasks. During our evaluation of the first protocol session, it appeared that Susan interpreted the discourse tasks as memory assessments and thus worked to shape her narratives as memory displays (e.g., recalling story details) instead of as conversational stories. Overt discussion of clinical goals could reduce and channel client guesses about task motivations and, thus, facilitate client and clinician collaboration. Third, explicit discussion of the clinical (and research) activities creates opportunities to collaboratively negotiate goals of the session, positioning the client as an active, empowered participant rather than assuming passive compliance as the only available stance.

The second activity frame for this session was *target discourse sampling*, which was the specific clinical-research goal for this session. Attending to potential goals for each of the discourse types being elicited was central to motivating the clinician roles in the sampling. Telling a story is partly motivated by an audience displaying engagement in hearing the story. Procedural discourse makes sense when your interlocutor is motivated to learn from your expertise or follow your instructions about a procedure. Casual conversation is motivated by participants' swapping stories and opinions, making conversational offers and responding conversationally to offers made by others. In preparing for the second pilot of the MDEP, Melissa and I identified and imaginatively role played where these discourses emerged in everyday settings (e.g., getting a recipe from your mom; sharing stories with co-workers at the start of the day) and what roles, affective stances, and communicative resources characterized those everyday uses of these types of discourse.

The third activity frame, *transitioning*, highlights the importance of attending to the work of, and opportunities for, shifting activity frames throughout the session. We particularly focused on recognizing that this activity frame is not limited to pre-defined moments between targeted tasks, but may be initiated by the client (or clinician) at any time during the session. For example, in the first session, when Susan commented on her poor memory or the inadequacy of her responses to task prompts ("I don't know if I'm doing this right"), Melissa could have identified that utterance as a cue for the transitioning activity frame by ratifying a shift to clinical management and overtly restating the goals of the task (e.g., "There are no right answers here. This isn't a memory test."). Similar to clinical management, whether foregrounded or backgrounded, the interactional work of transitioning within and across different activities should be understood as a critical for all functional systems, including clinical.

Melissa reported a striking change in her communicative roles in the second MDEP pilot, and we can see clear evidence of that change in the interactional data. First, Melissa reported that during this second pilot session she did not work to limit her talk time, which was reflected in the more even distribution of words spoken. Melissa actually produced more words (3,315) than Susan (2,602), while still eliciting longer, more varied, richer discourse samples from Susan. Second, Melissa reported that she worked to explicitly coordinate goals with Susan throughout the session. She initiated conversations with Susan about the research project and goals. For example, Melissa framed the narrative task by telling Susan that she wanted to hear her tell stories, not test her memory. She focused Susan's attention on what it meant to be a good storyteller by asking her who the good storytellers were in her family. On the few occasions across the interaction when Susan did mention her memory deficit, Melissa transitioned to a clinical frame to overtly restate the research goals.

The difference in these two sessions is clearly displayed in the narrative samples. For example, in comparing the second pilot to the first, we found that Susan and Melissa devoted more than four times as many turns (199 turns) to the narrative discourse tasks as they did in the first session (46 turns). Transcript 8.1 displays a stretch of interaction in the second activity frame, discourse sampling, where Melissa aimed to enact the role of communication partner. Throughout the 37 turns of this storytelling, Melissa displayed her active engagement in Susan's emerging conversational narrative. She did not display (or need to display) the kind of directives, long silences, or simple repetitions that marked Transcript 7.1. When we turn to discussion of communicative resources, we will also see that Susan's narrative was markedly more animated and elaborated. In Hymes's (1975, 1981) terms, there is evidence that Susan broke through into performance, meaning that she actively animated the narrative, not offering a thin, cooled-off narrative telling. Melissa received Susan's narrative performance in reciprocally engaged fashion.

Examining Clinicians' Patterns of Participation in Clinical Interactions

SDA assumes that patterns of participation for all participants in an interaction emerge and change with the shifting goals and resources available to the functional systems. As communication experts, SLPs are expected to be strategic, hence flexible, communicators in the functional systems of clinical spaces. In Chapter 7 we highlighted IRE (initiation-reply-evaluation) exchanges and *display questions* as interactional patterns that clinicians (and teachers) use to maintain control. A clinical stance focused on the accuracy of the response or the manner of production was evident in the original pilot (Transcript 7.1), where Melissa was disengaged from Susan's narrative discourse she was seeking to elicit. Being a communication partner involves taking a very different stance, more like brokering roles discussed in Chapter 5. Brokering involves working collaboratively for success, monitoring how things are going, stepping in to provide support where needed, and stepping back to let successful interactions unfold. Brokers, in other words, align with others by being attentive, flexible, and oriented to assist interactions. To explore how clinicians can utilize their expertise to flexibly fulfill the responsibilities of their professional roles in clinical spaces, we ask: *How can the clinician partner support the client's successful participation?*

Being a communication partner is not a given, not tightly anchored to specific sociomaterial spaces. As we noted in the last chapter, CA approaches to clinical practice have sometimes assumed that people in everyday settings are naturally flexible partners who partner and broker successful communication whereas clinicians hold institutionally powerful roles that severely limit their flexibility, setting them up to be professionals-in-charge, not communication partners. However, we can all think of people we have interacted with in informal settings who are not flexible communication partners, people who receive our conversational moves with hostility or apathy, dampening our excitement and interests, and working (intentionally or not) to shut down our discourse. SDA perspectives, on the other hand, see clinicians as capable of flexibly managing multiple communicative stances.

In my experience, most practicing clinicians are strong communicators and have moments (perhaps at the edges of their clinical interactions) where they engage actively and animatedly with clients. Those moments show that a directive clinical stance is not a given situationally, but instead built interactively. SDA offers tools that help us understand how clinicians can strategically and flexibly wield particular stances for motivated reasons. As communication experts, SLPs should strive to be the most aware and flexible communicators in the clinical space, able to broker successful communication and be communication partners.

Melissa's Participation in MDEP Sessions

Unlike the typically assumptive, vague, and indirect ways that have been documented as clinicians seek to exert clinical control and display expertise (see Chapter 7), the MDEP calls for overt and direct clinical management. As seen in Table 8.1, the clinician is expected to display, through verbal and nonverbal means when she is exercising her professional control of the session (e.g., managing clinical business of scheduling, billing, directing tasks, and so on). However, in the target discourse sampling frame, the MDEP calls for the clinician to instead align as an appropriate *communication partner* for whatever type of discourse is being elicited.

For the *conversational discourse task*, the clinician aims to create opportunities for the client to engage in a social back-and-forth interaction. Conversational discourse happens in all kinds of settings and with participants who range from being strangers to close friends and family; it tends to be marked by shared and shifting topics. The clinician's role then is to be an active partner, flexibly following a line of conversation or introducing a new line, engaged in swapping stories, observations, personal experiences and interests, and opinions.

For the *narrative discourse task*, the clinician aims to create an opportunity for the client to not only produce a narrative, but also break through into narrative performance of a rich, detailed story. Narrative discourse occurs in diverse sociomaterial spaces, and narratives can be briefly offered amidst other interaction or can become extended performances. The clinician's role as audience is critical in encouraging the client to break into a narrative performance. To do this, the clinician needs to be engaged with, and responsive to, the content and emotional valence of the story event. Narrative performances in everyday settings often lead to others' narratives, story swapping, so the clinician may offer as well receive narratives.

For the *descriptive discourse task*, the clinician aims to solicit the client's opinion or observations about a target picture. Descriptive discourse emerges in everyday settings when people talk about absent objects or images, when images are complex and interesting (e.g., art works), and when people are unsure what is being depicted (e.g., trying to figure out where a picture was taken or who the people in it are). The clinician's role then is to allow the client to have the first say, to listen attentively with interest and curiosity, and to follow up by offering observations of her own.

For the *procedural discourse task*, the clinician aims to create opportunities for the client to display expertise by outlining or describing a procedure. Procedural discourse occurs in everyday conversational settings, such as getting a recipe from a friend or explaining how to use a new piece of equipment. Speakers often recite the procedure in a manner that allows the listener to accomplish the steps in the procedure in the moment or to write them down for future use. Listeners often seek confirmation of the procedure by restating the steps. Thus, the clinician's collaborative role in the protocol includes writing down the procedures presented by the client and reading them back to the client for confirmation.

Compared to the first session, Melissa felt her interactions with Susan throughout this second session had "loosened up." She experienced the session as one that flowed easily from task-to-task and topic-to topic. At various times both Melissa and Susan took the conversational lead. As the communication partner in the target discourses, Melissa confidently took on diverse interactional roles. This was apparent in the way Melissa responded to Susan's initiations, which often led to brief side conversations during which both Melissa and Susan made comments and offered stories. Critically, Melissa reported that their interactions during this second session were more consistent with her conversational engagements with Susan outside of the clinic room.

In reviewing the videotape, there was clear evidence that Melissa shifted her stance to accomplish target activities. As the clinician in charge, Melissa took a directive and open stance at the beginning and end of each target task to move through the protocol and to clarify what she was, and was not, looking for (e.g., "There are no wrong answers here, all I am interested in . . . is to see how you communicate"). During the conversational task, Melissa made comments, offered opinions, and told stories to shape the discourse into a back-and-forth, or swapping, pattern. She introduced topics by sharing her own experiences (e.g., "My dad uhm.1. he had a truck, he didn't have to go . . . you know cross-country, he pretty much stayed in the Midwest"), by reintroducing past topics (e.g., "one of these past times when you were in you told me that you used to work in a . . . salon"), and by following up on emerging topics. Susan's talk was likewise more varied. She responded to topics Melissa raised, initiated topics of her own, and made fewer comments that expressed concerns about her memory impairment or the accuracy of her responses.

Deploying Diverse Communicative Resources to Support Clinician Client Interactions

To successfully build the contexts for any sociocultural activity and to enact particular social roles and participation frameworks in mobile, shifting functional systems, people have to deploy and recognize diverse communicative resources, both drawing on and emergently establishing common ground. The communicative resources for clinical activities are drawn from the resources used in various sociomaterial spaces (i.e., they are not unique to clinical spaces), but those resources need to be deployed and repurposed for clinical goals. As we turn to considering what communicative resources are associated with diverse clinical practices, we ask: *How can the clinician flexibly draw on and use diverse communicative resources to support client-clinician interactions?*

One of the central challenges of the MDEP, with its goal of generating reciprocal patterns of collaborative discourse, is defining what resources contribute to being a communication partner and characterize collaborative discourse. Observing that many everyday conversational interactions can be categorized as *high involvement* (animated, fluent, highly collaborative), Deborah Tannen (2007) details some key *involvement devices*, including participatory *displays of listening*, patterns of *conversational repetition* that build coherence and produce poetic effects (e.g., alliteration, rhyming, assonance, and other sound repetition; parallel syntactic structure; repetition as affective savoring), *constructed dialogue* and animated *voicing, narrative performances*, and even offering and savoring *descriptive details*.

Central, for example, to high involvement are displays of participatory listening. *Backchannel* responses are a key way to display listening as they align with a speaker's continuation (i.e., not vying to be recognized for full turns). Backchannel includes utterances (e.g., *um-hm, yeah yeah, ah, no,* and *oh*) that listeners make as others speak (overtalk) or in short pauses in the other's talk. Backchannel is particularly important in telephone calls, where a listener's total silence for an extended time will typically lead a speaker to ask if the other is still on the line. Jakobson (1990) identified one of the central functions of language in interaction as *phatic*, by which he meant the function of signaling connection, that the channels of communication are open and working. Of course, backchannel can also be communicated nonverbally by gaze, nods of the head, facial expressions, and rhythmically coordinated embodied movement.

Strategic and Overt Use of Communicative Resources: High Involvement Narratives in the MDEP

If we return to Transcript 8.1, we can see involvement devices and signs of high involvement in both Melissa's and Susan's discourse. As Susan settled on a frightening story to tell, presented a description of the scene, and set up the story events to follow (turns 14, 16, 18), she began to display patterns of conversational repetition (e.g., three tokens of "frightening" in turn 14; three tokens of "work" as a verb in turns 14, 16, and 18; repetition of the critical set up that "everybody had gone" in turns 16 and 18; three repetitions of "I was" in turns 14 and 18). Melissa provided backchannel responses to signal her involvement in the unfolding narrative (turns 15, 17, 19). In turn 20, Susan narrated the initial frightening event ("a man standing there"), and dramatized the telling with an array of signs: use of gestures (pointing to imaginary doors, moving her hands side to side) and constructed dialogue in the form of direct reported speech ("'Can I help you?'").

In turn 21, Melissa's backchannel reaction ("Oh my gosh!") marked heightened affective involvement in the story. Susan seems to align with Melissa's response by creatively recasting it as her own response (spoken or thought) within the story to the stranger's sudden appearance: "Ohhh! Gosh what is this!" Susan continues to produce a high involvement narrative. Consider, for example, the sequence of constructed dialogue across turns 32 and 34 and the likely hyperbole of line 30 as she describes the customer with her ". . . she was like 100 years old so . . . ," a comment punctuated by both Melissa and Susan laughing. Throughout the storytelling, Melissa responded to the narrative by mirroring story emotions and elaborating conversationally on story details (as in turn 27, "Oh well, at least there was someone else there"). At the end, beyond Transcript 8.1, Melissa not only agreed that it was a scary story but even imagined a more dramatic setting for the tale ("I picture it being a dark night"). Throughout the telling, Susan capitalized on Melissa's affective displays of involvement to construct a successful, dramatic narrative performance.

Given the clinical goal of eliciting a diagnostic sample of Susan's narrative discourse, contrast this complex, animated story with the thin sketches of Transcript 7.1, where only turn 16 offered more than a vague fragment of narrative. In turn 16 in Transcript 7.1, we do find some involvement devices, some conversational repetition (e.g., "I just stood there") and detail ("I had a little tear in my eye") but there is no constructed dialogue and the narrative is still vaguely contextualized (e.g., we don't know where and when this event happened). It is interesting that this bit of more engaged narrative followed the only backchannel response in that stretch (Melissa's, "mhm" in line 15), but Melissa offered no verbal backchannel throughout Susan's relatively long turn 16, even though it has two marked pauses in it. In short, the second pilot of the MDEP elicited a longer, richer, more interactional, and more animated narrative than was elicited in the first pilot.

Melissa displayed other communicative resources in other activity frames. To build clinical management she explicitly stated, established, and negotiated clinical goals; openly took responsibility for management of institutional issues; and provided direct and specific evaluations of Susan's performance as needed. Likewise, during transitioning, Melissa overtly marked shifts in activities both verbally (e.g., "okay, now we need to move on to the next task") and nonverbally (e.g., picking up a clipboard, changing posture). In short, Melissa flexibly shifted between explicit and marked use of resources for clinical management (as opposed to the directive but vague clinical stance noted in multiple clinical settings in Chapter 7) and implicit but systematic use of relevant and appropriate communicative resources for aligning as a communication partner with Susan across the four different discourse tasks.

Note on Methods: Becoming a Reflective Practitioner

Donald Schön (1983) has identified the importance of reflective practice to professional expertise and ongoing professional development. Being a reflective practitioner requires open, critical attention to your professional practices combined with a desire to continually improve both your individual mastery of the practice and the professional practice itself. In a scoping review, Caty, Kinsella, and Doyle (2015) noted that in spite of broad agreement in health science professions that reflective practice is important to the development of both expert practitioners and expert practice, "the scholarship on reflection and reflective practice in the field of speech–language pathology is limited" (p. 418). Central to those limits was a lack of clear definitions for reflection and of clear conceptualizations of practice.

Schön (1983) highlights the difference between typical notions of technical expertise and reflective practice. Technical expertise is conceived as professionals first learning specialized technical knowledge and then simply applying that knowledge to what are presumed to be standard cases. However, in modern professions, the problems and domains of application turn out to be much more complex, so technical practice calls instead for knowledge-driven curiosity, inquiry, and experimentation. This is where Schön's reflective practitioner becomes essential. To support complex evolving forms of expertise requires a professional who is reflexive about their knowledge, who anticipates the need for inquiry, and who approaches their clients and cases expecting to need to learn and experiment to be effective.

SDA offers a rich set of tools for undertaking reflective practice, as the process of developing the MDEP illustrated. The first pilot of the MDEP described in Chapter 7 was carefully prepared. Melissa had developed a deep understanding of amnesia, had extensive experience as a clinician and as a research assistant engaged in assessments in the Amnesia Research Lab, and had participated actively in planning the MDEP pilot. Nevertheless, although the preparation was a model for technical expertise, the pilot was not a success, as was detailed in Chapter 7. Applying principles of reflective practice, Melissa and I analyzed what happened and why. Melissa left the pilot with a clear sense that the MDEP had not gone as planned. However, it was only through close analysis of activity frames, interactional roles, and communicative resources from video recording of the initial pilot session that we could understand in detail what went wrong and work out alternatives. Neither of us had anticipated how powerful Melissa's socialization (and Susan's) was to the clinical stance.

Table 8.1 outlines the protocol we developed to support her (and other clinicians) in effectively implementing the MDEP. Specifically, we realized we needed to more sharply define the different activities incorporated into the session, to specify the clinician's role in each of them, and to highlight the importance of openly marking and actively managing transitions within and across activities. This example then offers a general roadmap for reflective clinical practice in CSD. Recording and analyzing clinical sessions (or everyday interactions) can support clinicians in planning and implementing interventions and can develop deeply situated understanding of problems and challenges (whether for clients in their interactions or for the clinician in their professional practice). Grounded in SDA, this continuous, open-minded inquiry, reflection, and adjustment can then be used to improve both clinical practice and professional mastery.

Summary: Reflecting on the Clinician's Role in Building Clinical Functional Systems

In this chapter, we revisited the MDEP pilot from Chapter 7, analyzing how we redesigned the protocol to help Melissa shift from the typical clinical stance for assessment (emphasizing control and isolation) that had undercut our efforts to assess discourse as distributed communication. As this chapter has illustrated, the reflective analysis of the first pilot and the redesigned protocol (Table 8.1) that emerged from that analysis succeeded. In the second pilot, Melissa functioned as a communication partner for the discourse tasks, managed clinical tasks more explicitly, and engaged in transitioning between activity frames as a distinct activity frame in itself. For her part, Susan communicated in markedly richer, more engaged ways on the discourse tasks. Reflecting on the second pilot, Melissa reported that Susan's communication in the assessment matched Melissa's experience with her in everyday settings. The following questions focus on how functional systems, patterns of participation, and communicative resources contributed to this dramatic change in the discourse elicitation:

- *What is being accomplished in clinical functional systems?*
- *How can the clinician support the client's successful participation?*
- *How can the clinician flexibly draw on and use diverse communicative resources to support successful client-clinician interactions?*

Overall, this chapter has illustrated how SDA can support engaging in reflective practice that contributes to specific clinical interactions with a client, improves clinical practices (in this case further elaborating the MDEP), and builds professional expertise (increasing Melissa's flexible mastery as a clinician). It also illustrates the potential of rethinking communicative assessments from the perspective of SDA. Theoretically, SDA is grounded in a recognition of the distributed nature of communication. That recognition suggests that the interactive contexts of communicative assessments should be designed to mirror the communicative resources and roles typical of everyday interactions. Finally, SDA approaches suggest that beyond categorical diagnosis, assessments should be designed around the goal of sampling clients' performances in ways that offer ecological validity and that can, therefore, inform interventions focused on the functional systems and figured worlds of clients' everyday communicative lives.

Although Chapters 7 and 8 have focused on communicative interactions as part of a diagnostic assessment, it is important to recognize the implications are broader. As Chapter 7 pointed out, much of the basic clinical stance, including in therapeutic interactions shaped around IRE drills, has been modeled on and motivated by the values and practices of traditional assessment. As we will note in Chapter 9, Table 8.1 can be easily adapted to therapeutic interactions where clinicians aim to partner in a targeted kind of communicative interaction while also managing the clinical activity and transitioning among multiple activity frames. In the final chapter, we will use the full array of SDA tools to describe how clinicians can design interventions as *rich communicative environments*.

Reflective Observations

1. *Analyzing client-clinician interactions during a clinical session*. Arrange to observe a clinical session, or record one of your own. It is important

for this reflection to observe and analyze the full session. Then, using Table 8.1:

   a. List the activities (e.g., managing clinical business; specific clinical activities; transitioning activities) as they occurred chronologically across the session.

   b. Describe what goals are being accomplished and how the clinician is collaborating with the client to accomplish those goals.

   c. Describe how closely these client-clinician interactions align with the collaborative roles described in Table 8.1. Give specific examples.

2. *Analyzing clinical skills for brokering client success.* Review the procedures for collecting interactional discourse samples using the Mediated Discourse Elicitation Protocol (MDEP), and arrange to record a session where you use it to collect a discourse sample from a friend or a client.

   a. Use SDA to analyze the quality of the interactional discourse collected.

   b. Reflect on how comfortable or uncomfortable you felt deploying the MDEP and discuss why.

3. *Analyzing the flexible use of communicative resources in successful clinical sessions.* Arrange to record yourself in clinical sessions with several different clients and analyze how flexibly you recognize and adjust to using diverse communicative resources. To prepare for this reflection, review the discussion of communicative resources in Parts 1 and 2 (e.g., semiotic modalities, typified social voices, interactional discourse resources, durable and emergent resources, building tasks, and discourse registers). Use the following prompts to analyze and reflect on your flexible (or inflexible) use of communicative resources in this clinical session:

   a. Identify all instances of agreement or confirmation between you and the client. How were each of these signaled? How were they received?

   b. Identify all instances of clinician feedback to the client. How was each of these signaled? How was each taken up the client?

   c. Identify all instance of client feedback to the clinician. How was each of these signaled? How were they taken up?

   d. Reflecting on your analyses for a, b, and c., consider how you could expand your communicative repertoire to more flexibly recognize/ signal agreement and other types of feedback.

Suggested Readings

A wide range of SDA research in institutional settings (schools and clinical spaces) offers insightful guidance about options and stances clinicians can take to enhance communicative interactions and engage in reflective practice. Here are three articles that illustrate the range of approaches found in that research and that point to concrete ways to change clinical practices.

1. "Illustrating a supports-based approach toward friendship with autistic students" (Vidal, Robertson, & DeThorne, 2018). In this article Veronica Vidal, Scott Robertson, and Laura DeThorne analyze a supports-based approach in a school setting to enhance socializing among peers, including an autistic student.

2. "Reflections on Dobermanns, poodles, and social rehabilitation for difficult-to-serve individuals with traumatic brain injury" (Ylvisaker & Feeney, 2000). In this article, Mark Ylvisaker and Tim Feeney highlight the importance for clinicians of interacting with their clients as people and adapting interventions to fit with the individual life trajectories and identities of each client. Using the metaphor of comparing the temperament of a "Doberman" with that of "Poodle," they argue that interventions designed for one will inevitably fail if applied to the other.

3. "Positioning readers in one-on-one conferences" (Hikida & Lee, 2018). In this article, Michiko Hikida and Jungmin Lee explore the interaction between race and disability as they analyze teachers' one-on-one literacy conferences with their students in school.

Chapter 9

Designing Rich Communicative Environments in Clinical Spaces

In this chapter, we consider how *situated discourse analysis* (SDA) can guide clinicians in designing, participating in, and supporting interactions that optimize clients' learning and the ongoing reorganization of their communicative lives. Drawing on theories of *situated learning*, Chapter 3 described learning as a ubiquitous dimension of all interactions, not something that can be turned on and off and certainly not something that only happens when intentionally targeted (as in schools and clinics). Understanding that communication is fundamentally dynamic and routinely involves managing disruptions, we began in Part 2 to consider how particular functional systems re-organize around disruptions introduced by communication disorders and how situated learning is primarily achieved through people's *repeated engagement* (Hengst et al., 2010) with others in meaningful, motivated activities rather than by isolated individual repetition under controlled conditions. In Chapter 9, we turn our attention to the potential of using SDA to create *rich communicative environments* in clinical spaces that support clients' situated learning and address clinical goals.

The concept of rich communicative environments (Hengst, Duff, & Jones, 2019) integrates SDA with long-standing neuroscience research documenting the positive impacts *enriched housing environments* have on lab animals' abilities to learn new tasks and recover from injuries (e.g., Greenough, 1976; Hebb, 1949; Van Praag, Kempermann, & Gage, 2000). In contrast to small, unadorned cages for individual animals, enriched housing provides environmental complexity by housing animals in social groups in large cages filled with toys and other objects that they can traverse and manipulate. The environmental *complexity* of enriched housing also supports *voluntary participation* as individual animals can manage their own engagement with the complex sociomaterial environment. Researchers have also highlighted the importance of *optimization* of such environments, noting that both too little social contact (e.g., isolation) and too much social contact (e.g., overcrowding) will have detrimental effects. Reviewing the evidence that enriched housing environments have positive effects on learning, neuronal structure and function, and recovery from brain damage, Hengst et al. (2019) observe that "there is no treatment approach that has been more well replicated to improve function in rodent models of acquired brain injury than housing in a complex environment" (p. 218).

To translate the research findings from lab animals to humans, it is critical to focus on the power of meaningful complexity, voluntary participation, and optimization of experiential quality for specific individuals, in specific settings, and at specific times. Drawing on this work, we have begun to describe rich communicative environments as ones that:

> are likely to include multiple participants who are engaged in multiple activities, who actively use diverse multimodal communicative resources (including language, gestures, physical tools, and instruments), and who take up and shift among various communicative roles (such as people switching between storytellers and audiences as they swap stories).
>
> (Hengst et al., 2019, p. 221)

This chapter then will explore *complexity, voluntariness,* and *optimization of quality* as design principles to assemble rich communicative environments for clinical practice.

In Chapter 6, I described the game-like protocol informed by SDA and situated theories of learning I used to study collaborative referencing between communication partners managing aphasia. As described in Chapter 6, I redesigned the game protocol to support the emergence of rich communicative environments (Hengst, 2003). For example, I recruited familiar communication partners who brought long intertwined histories that they could draw on to successfully complete the game-like task. I encouraged the pairs, together voluntarily and already in multifaceted relationships, to engage in diverse and open-ended communicative interactions (e.g., minimal rules and "have fun") and to use of a wide range of communicative resources (e.g., lowering the barrier and explicitly indicating that participants could write, gesture, and show cards). In this redesigned protocol, familiar communication partners managing chronic aphasia demonstrated the classic pattern of change across trials (i.e., getting faster, decreasing communicative effort; developing specific, streamlined labels for each card), but also displayed a wide range of types of discourse practices (e.g., narratives, verbal play) that some have argued occur only in "naturalistic settings"—that is, outside of research and clinical spaces.

The power of this collaborative referencing game to support learning was strikingly documented in Duff's adaptation of the research design to explore memory systems supporting learning (Duff, Hengst, Tranel, & Cohen, 2006). Participant pairs in that study included four individuals with hippocampal damage and profound declarative memory impairment (amnesia, an impairment in forming explicit memory) interacting with familiar communication partners and four comparison pairs, neither of whom had amnesia but otherwise demographically matched with the original pairs.

Duff further modified the redesigned protocol (e.g., extending the number of trials to 24 to maximize the chance of learning in patients with hippocampal amnesia) and assessed the duration of learning effects (e.g., assessing memory for labels at 30 minutes and 6 months).

Although the participants with amnesia could not recall ever having met the experimenter or playing the game, they demonstrated remarkable learning. In fact, the focal pairs displayed a *rate* of learning across trials that did not differ from the comparison participants. Moreover, the participants with amnesia displayed impressive recall of the labels they had developed in the game after delays of 30 minutes and 6 months (and even at 30 minutes they had no memory they had played the game). Finding that the redesigned barrier task protocol supported creative, complex communication and language use in people with chronic aphasia and robust new learning in people with chronic amnesia encouraged us to begin adapting our research protocol for clinical intervention.

This chapter then explores how to marshal SDA to design successful clinical interventions. First, we focus on designing intervention activities within clinical spaces by building *rich communicative environments* and structuring clients' *repeated engagement* with meaningful activities in those environments (Hengst et al., 2010). Second, we turn to the notion of *affinity spaces* (Gee, 2003) to stress the importance of designing opportunities for clients to build *common ground* and support successful participation in targeted everyday activities. Finally, I introduce the concept of *interactional correlates* as a way of linking isolated clinical techniques (e.g., cuing, repetition) and targets (e.g., naming) to communicative resources typical of everyday interactions. The chapter begins with a description of the initial pilot study designed to translate the collaborative referencing research protocol into a clinical intervention. In the Note on Methods, we will explore *participatory design* research methods to guide the ongoing development, implementation, and assessment of rich communicative interventions.

The Case of Dave: Translating the Collaborative Referencing Game as a Clinical Intervention

To begin translating the research protocol into a therapeutic clinical intervention, we designed a clinical case study for Dave, a highly educated 67-year-old man who was an administrator responsible for managing multiple programs, teams of people, and a large operational budget (see Hengst et al., 2010). Dave was an excellent candidate to explore translating our protocols, in part because his mixed diagnosis of aphasia and amnesia aligned well with our research on collaborative referencing among communication partners managing aphasia (Hengst, 2003) and amnesia (Duff et al., 2006). Dave had experienced a series of left hemisphere strokes eight months prior to the study. His MRI results documented numerous brain lesions in the left temporal, parietal and occipital lobes; the left pons; and the genu of the left internal capsule. Neuropsychological testing (at five months post-onset) revealed: average intellectual functioning (*Wechsler Adult Intelligence Scale-III* Full Scale IQ = 107); a mild anomic aphasia (*Boston Naming Test* 53/60); moderate-severe deficits in executive functioning (*Wisconsin Card Sorting Task* 1 Category; 41 perseverative errors); and severe memory impairment (*Wechsler Memory Scale-III* General Memory Index=69) with incomplete retrograde amnesia spanning four years, impaired prospective memory, and difficulty carrying on conversations about current events. At the time of the study, Dave was medically stable, and he and his family were highly motivated to find creative and novel behavioral approaches to help him improve his everyday communication. Although Dave and his wife disagreed about whether his aphasia or amnesia symptoms were the most disruptive, they agreed he was struggling with staying on topic and coming up with the right words during conversations. Thus, we set out both to translate our research protocol into an intervention protocol and to design an intervention that would specifically target Dave's communication goals.

Our redesign, summarized in Table 9.1, maintained the general format of the collaborative referencing game. Guided by RCE (rich communicative environment) design principles, we worked to increase *meaningful complexity* during and between game play trials and across sessions; to encourage *voluntary participation* by all participants, especially Dave; and to *optimize experiential quality* of these sessions for Dave. Drawing on principles of *participatory design*, which involves users early and actively in designing a product or process (Spinuzzi, 2005), we began by inviting Dave and his wife to identify key treatment goals and to aid in identifying possible referencing targets. To reduce the likelihood that Dave would simply memorize a label for a specific photograph and to increase the likelihood the pair would interact collaboratively to identify and reference the images, we created two photocards taken from different perspectives and/or at different times of day for each of the 30 referencing targets (i.e., a total 60 photocards). During game play, we continued to encourage creative and open communication about the cards, but also built in opportunities for Dave to talk about the cards at the start and end of each session, and between game trials.

Beyond increasing the number and types of opportunities for Dave and Melissa (who served as the clinician game partner) to engage with these referencing targets over time, we also increased the number of people involved and specified different interactional roles for each person. To build continuity and support Dave's memory, each session began with a clinician moderator, Lori (a CSD graduate student), reviewing the purpose of the study, summarizing the pair's success during the previous session, and discussing any memory/word finding problems Dave reported during the past week. At the end of each session, Lori showed Dave and Melissa the twelve cards and asked them what label they had settled on for each card during

Table 9.1 Summary of changes made to redesign the collaborative referencing research protocol as a clinical intervention, and the Rich Communicative Environment (RCE) design principles motivating the changes.

	Original Research Protocol	Treatment Protocol	RCE Design principles
Referencing targets & cards	12 unknown targets researcher-selected tangram shapes	30 familiar targets selected with Dave & his wife, to address his everyday goals	Voluntariness Optimization
	12 cards, one card for each shape (e.g., see Figure 6.2)	60 complex photocards, 2 cards per referencing target (e.g., Figure 9.1)	Complexity
Referencing opportunities per protocol	12 cards/game-trial 6 trials/session 4 research sessions 288 Total CPS Note: 12 cards did not change across sessions	12 cards/game-trial 6 trials/session 10 treatment sessions 720 Total CPS Note: 6 of 12 cards changed each session	Complexity
Participants & their roles	1 client 1 familiar game-partner 1 researcher moderator	1 client 1 clinician game-partner 1 clinician-moderator	Complexity
	Client assigned as director all 6 trials*	Client & clinician alternated director roles each trial 1 researcher/consultant	Optimization
Communicative resources available during game (no change)	Communicate freely, and have fun! Don't look over the barrier at your partner's board!	Communicate freely, and have fun! Don't look over the barrier at your partner's board!	Voluntariness Optimization
Referencing opportunities pre/post game trials	(not designed for)	Beginning-of-session review of previous session & client's home communication	Complexity
		Between trial interactions about cards	Voluntariness
		End-of-session interview & discussion of referencing targets	Optimization

Note: In Hengst (2003), the first session replicated Clark's (1992) study by having one person (the one with aphasia) direct all six trials. In the following three sessions, partners alternated director and matcher roles. In Duff's (Duff et al., 2006) adaptation, the partner with amnesia directed all trials all sessions.

that session. These were recorded as the *agreed-upon target labels* (ATLs) that emerged during their game play that session. Broadly, our redesign aimed to optimize the quality of Dave's repeated engagement with the target cards and game play.

Overall, the clinical pilot was a success. Dave attended all 10 treatment sessions (average of 45 minutes per session). Dave and Melissa completed all six game trials each session, making a total of 720 card placements overall (12 photocards per trial x 6 trials per session x 10 sessions), and did so with 98.9-percent accuracy (712/720 correct). In addition, Dave and Melissa's pattern of referencing the photocards displayed the familiar patterns of building common ground across trials predicted by the *collaborative referencing model* (see Chapter 6). They developed specific referencing expressions (or labels) for all 30 targets, each of which became more specific and concise over time as they repeatedly referred to the target. For example, Table 9.2 shows the sequence of referencing labels used across six trials playing with a new photocard. Referencing became more specific and precise, shifting from descriptions, "a picture of someone" and "the fellow has a beard" in the first three trials to just the name "Oliver Sacks" (i.e., the neuropsychologist who authored many popular books) in the last three trials.

In addition to interactions tightly focused on placing cards as seen in Table 9.2, Dave and Melissa also engaged in a variety of sociocultural activities as they moved through the trials. For example, as they labeled and discussed target cards, Melissa and Dave discovered they both followed politics, had both stayed up late on election night in November 2004, and were both supporting an opponent to the incumbent president, George Bush. Their

Table 9.2 A chronological list (derived from the transcript) of referencing expressions used by Dave (D) and Melissa (M) as they identified and placed card #17 for the six game trials in the first session with this card. By the fourth trial *Oliver Sacks* was the consistent referencing expression for this card and their reported ATL.

Trial	Referencing Expression
Trial 1—	D: A picture of someone and you know he looks remarkably familiar.
	D: Fellow has a beard.
	M: Fellow with the beard.
	D: He's got a beard and glasses.
	M: Man with glasses.
Trial 2—	M: Man with glasses and the beard with hand on his chin.
	D: Man with glasses and beard.
Trial 3—	D: Guy with a beard.
	M: Guy with a beard . . . looking pensive.
Trial 4—	M: Oliver Sacks.
Trial 5—	D: Oliver Sacks.
	M: Oliver Sacks.
Trial 6—	M: Oliver Sacks.

political talk also changed across sessions. In early trials, this shared perspective was voiced tentatively during their labelling of a photo card showing George Bush:

D: The next one is George Bush.
M: You say that with a little bit of disdain.
D: Yes . . . a lot.

By the tenth session, Dave boldly voiced this shared perspective in labelling the card:

D: The second one is George Bush with his republican henchman.
M: [laugh]
D: No, did I say that?
M: I think that's a perfectly good label. George Bush and his republican henchman.

It is important to recall that one of Dave's goals was to get better at everyday conversations about current events, which led us to include photocards featuring major political figures and well-known authors.

Building Rich Communicative Environments in Clinical Spaces: Meaningful Activities Enhance Repeated Engagement

Sociocultural activities offer a situated framework for describing people's participation in *functional systems*. By designing interventions to build *rich communicative environments* (through complexity, voluntariness, and optimization), clinicians can marshal situated learning through clients' *repeated engagement* with meaningful activities and around clinical goals. Our guiding question for this section is: ***How can clinical activity display features of rich communicative environments while also being accountable to clinical goals?***

As seen throughout this book, functional systems are always shaped by multiple activities woven together in complex and dynamic ways as people work to accomplish multiple goals. In Chapter 1, we saw how even young children can manage communicative interactions in functional systems shaped by multiple activities. Paul, Nora, and Anna were able to juggle folding clothes, cleaning up a muddy spot on the rug, playing *Cindy Magic*, and being recorded for my research. Indeed, a hallmark of *Cindy Magic* was that game play was a dominant yet hybrid activity (e.g., the players working to manage folding the clothes within the game world rather than breaking frame). That clinical spaces and activities are complex is only tacitly acknowledged by strategies designed to limit and control such complexity. As we saw in Chapters 7 and 8, clinical practices are typically designed to limit communicative complexity in order to assess clients' independent (isolated) abilities, to transmit specific information to clients, to organize specific (often repetitive) drills, and to maintain clinician control so planned tasks are completed in the limited time of a session.

In contrast, building rich communicative environments requires clinicians to strategically recognize and align with multiple activities in the sociomaterial spaces of both the clinic and clients' everyday lives. Working to craft rich communicative environments in clinical spaces calls for accountability to both the core features of such environments (complexity, voluntariness, and optimization) and the clinical goals of intervention, and for making decisions about which activities will be *dominant* at any point in time.

For the treatment protocol, we identified friendly game play as the *dominant activity* because game play activities are widely recognized and play aligns powerfully with rich communicative environments and situated learning (Holzman, 2009; Vygotsky, 1978). Researchers have long argued that *play* is a universal human activity that people of all ages and all cultures engage in (Bateson, 1972; Huizinga, 1950; Pellegrini, 2011). Across species (including humans), Burghardt (2011) identifies five features that distinguish moments of play from other activities, features that align well with rich communicative environments:

1. Within the observed context, play is not otherwise functional; that is, play behaviors are not directed toward accomplishing other goals (e.g., play hunting does not result in catching food for diner).
2. Play is voluntary, spontaneous, pleasurable, and/or rewarding; that is, individuals engage in playful behaviors and activities for the fun of that engagement (e.g., not for extrinsic rewards).
3. Play differs from functional occurrences of similar behaviors; that is, play acting a role may be more exaggerated, enacted with "pretend" tools, or may developmentally precede the functional activities (such as when a 6-year-old siting in the driver's seat of a car is pretending to drive even though she can't reach the pedals or see over the dash).
4. Play involves repetitions with variations, not stereotypic or rote repetitions (which are more typically observed in individuals under stress); that is, play is creative and emergent.
5. Play is initiated in the absence of acute or chronic stress (e.g., safe spaces optimize opportunities for play).

Given the documented role of play in human development and learning, game play activities can offer clinicians powerful models for building rich communicative environments in clinical spaces.

Central to building rich communicative environments in clinical spaces is selecting a dominant activity (or set of activities) and designing interventions around such activities. This includes:

1. designing interventions around *dominant activities* that are complex, voluntary, and optimize experiential quality for specific clients;
2. embedding clinical goals meaningfully within a dominant activity; and then
3. staying fully accountable to the dominant activity and relying on the communicative practices typical of that activity.

In other words, if the dominant activity is playing a game, then a prime directive for the clinician is to *play the game*. However, in my experience, a challenge for clinicians is to simply trust the game, to resist sacrificing the power of game play, for example, by re-aligning around a clinician-directed drill as the dominant activity and treating game play merely as a reward.

When clinicians strategically embed clinical goals into meaningful activities aligned with rich communicative environments, repetition-by-drill is largely replaced by *repeated engagement* (Chapter 6)—emergent and voluntary use and reuse of target language amidst those activities. Unforced repetition is actually pervasive in everyday communicative interactions. For example, Deborah Tannen (2007) has analyzed how dense conversational repetitions create and sustain people's interactional involvement with one another, and our analysis of everyday interactions of individuals with CP (Chapter 5; Hengst et al., 2016) found conversational repetition was the most common interactional discourse resource (IDR). Nevertheless, if clinicians don't trust the game (the dominant activity) to generate repeated engagement with clinical targets (a clinical goal), then they may shift or slip into the traditional clinical stance. Because of these challenges, we designed our pilot study to address two key questions: Could we use the collaborative referencing game to marshal repeated engagement around more targets over more sessions, and could the clinician sustain the role of game and communication partner despite her clinical status in this space?

Building Rich Communicative Environments With Dave and Fostering Repeated Engagement Through Conversational Repetition

The *dominant activity* of the collaborative referencing game as a clinical intervention was friendly game play. Dave's clinical goals of recognizing and recalling names of people, places, and events in everyday conversation were *embedded* within the design of the game play activity. Clinically, this embedding was first accomplished through participatory design. Before the sessions began, we worked with Dave to identify meaningful referencing targets and develop personalized (not generic) photocards for game play. During sessions, Melissa worked to prioritize the dominant activity by engaging as a friendly game partner during the six trials of each session, and to take advantage of friendly game play for Dave and Melissa to talk freely with one another as they worked to identify and place cards. The dominant activity, friendly game play, was selected as a way to build a rich communicative environment in this clinical space. The game invited Dave's *repeated engagement* with target references embedded in the cards and also engaged Dave and Melissa in building *common ground* over time.

Broadly, our analysis of the sessions concluded the intervention was successful because we found clear evidence of Dave's voluntary and consistent participation (e.g., attending all sessions), of Dave and Melissa's successful pattern of collaborative referencing (as predicted by the collaborative referencing model), and of the wide array of everyday communicative interactions (e.g., telling stories, joking, talking about politics) that arose around the game.

Designing the collaborative referencing intervention as friendly game play primed Melissa and Dave to engage in *conversational repetition* around their emerging labels for the referencing targets depicted by the photocards. As researchers, we discussed the potential therapeutic value of conversational repetition with Dave during the informed consent process for the research study. Lori (the clinician moderator) also encouraged the matchers (Dave and Melissa) to confirm the cards by repeating the referencing labels used by the director. We also embedded conversational repetition as a clinical goal into the design of the game through a point system. During game play, the pair was assigned up to three points for each of 12 cards, for a total of 36 possible points at the end of each game trial. One point was given for each card correctly placed on the matcher's board (12 possible points per trial), a second point for the director's use of the pair's *agreed-upon target label* (ATL) to reference the card, and a third point if the matcher conversationally repeated the director's referencing label when confirming the card (e.g., D: "Barack Obama is next" M: "Okay, Barack Obama, got it").

Lori monitored the points and gave feedback on their correct card placements at the end of each trial. Summary feedback on the full points earned (e.g., the director's use of ATL's and the matcher's use of conversational repetition) was calculated from the video after each session and summarized for the pair at the beginning of the next session. Given that Melissa and Dave were the only people in the clinic room during game trials, any prompting to repeat labels during game play came directly from the pair (e.g., "What did you call it?" or "You have to say it for us to get full points"). One of our motivations for focusing on immediate repetition and stabilized labels was that both could easily be tracked by clinicians.

To analyze the success of the collaborative referencing game in marshalling conversational repetition around the target cards, we identified all *referencing expressions* used by Dave and Melissa during the *card-placement-sequence* (CPS) for each card, comparing them to the reported ATL for that session and to other previously used referencing expressions during that CPS (see Hengst et al., 2010). ATLs represented highly stable long-term repetitions, while the conversational repetition within a specific CPS represented immediate

repetitions. We also tracked non-agreed upon target labels (NATLs), potential labels that were offered but not collaboratively sustained. Briefly, this let
us count the total number of referencing expressions used and code each
expression as one of the following:

1. ATL (initial use in CPS of a referencing expression matching the ATL);
2. NATL (initial use in CPS of a referencing expression different from the
    ATL);
3. R-ATL (an immediate conversational repetition of the ATL);
4. R-NATL (an immediate conversational repetition of a specific NATL).

Our analysis confirmed that the dominant activity, the collaborative referencing game, was sustained as an activity frame and that the clinical goal of
repeated engagement in referencing expressions around the photocards was
highly successful.

For example, Dave and Melissa used more referencing expressions than
could be predicted by the game design itself. Specifically, the game design
promoted 144 referencing expressions per session, 2 referencing expressions
(director and matcher) per CPS times 12 CPS per trial times 6 trials per session. However, Dave and Melissa exceeded this number on all sessions, with
an overall average of 202.2 referencing expressions per session (range 196 to
222). Analysis also confirmed that Dave and Melissa were collaborating to
develop and use consistent, specific, and meaningful labels. On average, the
majority (153.2, or 76 percent) of referencing expressions per session were
coded as first or repeated productions of the ATL (77.5 ATL, 75.7 R-ATL),
whereas only 49 (24 percent) per session were coded as NATL (36.4 NALT,
12.6 R-NALT).

Across sessions referencing expressions coded as (R-)NATL declined
while references coded as (R-)ATL increased. This pattern can be seen in
the *Oliver Sacks* example that was shown in Table 9.2. Across the six trials,
Dave and Melissa referenced the card directly 13 times, 6 of which were
immediate conversational repetitions. However, the majority of references
(9/13) were used in early trials (1, 2, 3) and were NATLs (e.g., *Fellow with
the beard*), which they repeated conversationally. However, by the last three
trials (4, 5, 6) they had settled on *Oliver Sacks* as their ATL, and their use of
referencing labels and immediate conversational repetition was strikingly less
(e.g., only 4 referencing expressions, and only 1 an immediate repetition).
Although this pattern generally held for all cards, Dave and Melissa consistently produced more referencing expressions and drew on more conversational repetition for targets they struggled to co-identify.

To illustrate what those struggles looked like (and further illustrate the
coding), Table 9.3 shows the referencing expressions used during the first
session with Card #11, along with the codes assigned to each expression.
Dave and Melissa did not settle on a stable referencing expression during

Table 9.3 Chronological listing (derived from the transcript) of referencing expressions used by Dave (D) and Melissa (M) for Card #11 during all six trials of the first treatment session with this card. The last column lists how each reference was coded (ATL, NATL, R-ATL, or R-NATL). Dave and Melissa reported two agreed upon target labels (ATLs) for this card this session was: *University and Neil . . . two cars.* The bolding here identities places where Melissa and Dave display more repetitions of referencing expressions used during earlier sessions, a kind of repetition we did not code in our analysis.

Trial	Referencing Expression	Code
Trial 1—	D: An intersection.	NATL
	D: An intersection with a yellow car.	R-NATL
	M: City?	NATL
	D: City	R-NATL
	M: It doesn't look like a parking lot.	NATL
	D: No, no parking lot.	R-NATL
	M: A **big** five story **building on the left**.	NATL
	M: University and Neil?	ATL
	M: It looks like downtown.	NATL
	M: **Esquire?**	NATL
	M: **Esquire.**	R-NATL
	M: University.	R-ATL
	M: I think it's Neil.	R-ATL
	M: University and Neil	R-ATL
Trial 2—	M: Picture of the intersection.	NATL
	M: University and I think it's Neil Street.	ATL
	M: With **the big building on the left**.	NATL
	D: Two cars in the picture?	ATL
Trial 3—	D: A street scene probably Urbana:: . . . Two cars visible.	ATL
	M: University and Neil . . . Down by **Esquire**.	ATL
Trial 4—	M: Intersection of University and Neil.	ATL
	D: Two cars in the road?	ATL
Trial 5—	D: Street scene in Champaign . . . with two cars visible.	ATL
	M: University and Neil.	ATL
Trial 6—	M: University and Neil . . . with **the big building on the left**.	ATL

Source: Hengst et al., 2010.

this session, and in fact reported two different ATLs (*University and Neil . . . two cars*) during the final interview. Across the six trials they produced 25 different referencing expressions, with over half (14/25) used during the first trial alone. Fascinatingly, in later trials, Melissa and Dave often confirmed each other's referencing expressions with a more distant kind of repetition, recycling candidate labels from earlier trials. In Table 9.3, I have bolded these replays, which pointed to a building in the picture and a possible name for it. The focus of our coding on immediate conversational repetition and ATLs (to align with clinical observation) did not capture this kind of distant repetition of NATLs, but, of course, more dispersed patterns of repetition can be tracked across interactions.

This analysis displays that the translation of the collaborative referencing protocol for clinical intervention was successful in aligning the dominant activity of the game with the clinical goal of promoting conversational repetition of referencing expressions for clinical targets. Discourse analysis of the full sessions documented the ways immediate repetitions were anchored in dispersed and diverse chains of interactions that Dave and Melissa had with each other and the researchers across trials and sessions as they discussed specific cards. Exploring such chains offers further evidence that, as we discuss in the next section, game-centered design aligns with the core criteria for rich communicative environments (complexity, voluntariness, and optimization).

Designing and Using Affinity Spaces in Clinical Settings

In Chapter 3 we introduced Lave and Wenger's (1991) concept of *legitimate peripheral participation*, which describes learning as people's changing patterns of participation as they repeatedly engage with specific sociomaterial spaces and functional systems. Chapter 6 highlighted ways that people shift their patterns of participation to manage multiple activities, as when Mary and Rob layered their own personal goals (e.g., practicing language, managing social relationships) onto the research activity (e.g., the barrier task; Hengst, 2006). Here I introduce Gee's (2003) concept of *affinity spaces* that support people's voluntary participation in interest-focused activities to explore the question: *How can the concept of affinity spaces help clinicians optimize clients' participation in situated learning?*

As a discourse analyst and educator, James Gee became interested in how playing computer games could keep children, youth, and adults engaged in the challenging task of learning complex computer games (e.g., *Portal 2*) or mastering online game worlds (e.g., *World of Warcraft*). Studying the world of gamers and game play, Gee (2003) concluded that well-designed gaming platforms displayed an array of powerful situated learning principles, including: *adaptable and flexible learning systems*, where players can succeed/win in multiple ways; *meaningful "just-in-time" supports within the game; encouragement of problem solving and mastery*, as "facts" and "skills" are learned as meaningful tools to solve problems during repeated play; *immersive and playful activity*, as "novel" and augmented realities motivate learning how to learn and persistence and build on players' interests; and a *collaborative ethos*, encouraging players to utilize multiple media, tools and input from other players with no penalties.

As Gee and his colleagues (Gee, 2003, 2005; Gee & Hayes, 2010) studied videogame play and players, they realized that learning was not only supported during play by well-designed gaming platforms, but also by sociomaterial spaces where players engaged with one another and game designers outside of game play (e.g., fan sites). Gee described these spaces as *affinity spaces*, highlighting that people were drawn to them as a means of learning more about, and engaging with others around, their common interests in the game.

Driven by the common interests that motivate people to seek out and create opportunities to engage with one another around interest-focused activities, affinity spaces are not unique to video gaming. Using Gee's broad definition, we can identify many examples of *affinity spaces*, including formal clubs and informal groups that meet face-to-face or online. For example, you may know of groups of people who come together around specific hobbies (e.g., reading books, knitting), around specific sports teams or music groups (e.g., fan clubs), and even professional organizations (e.g., ASHA). Such interest-focused groups, or clubs, have long been recognized as powerful sites for (and models of) situated learning (Smith, 1986).

Affinity spaces also highlight how dispersed interest-focused activities are often embedded in activities designed to address other goals. For example, when I take my daily walk (for exercise and health), I often take binoculars with me and plan a route that lets me engage in birdwatching. The affinity spaces for birdwatching range from incidental opportunities like my walks to routine family activities (e.g., family members looking up birds in field guides and organizing recreational opportunities to view birds). There are also community affinity spaces like the *National Audubon Society* and the *Cornell Lab of Ornithology* (where members get newsletters and other materials as well as specialized learning opportunities and events) and monetized enterprises like the *World Series of Birding* (WSB; http://worldseriesofbirding.org/) or guided ecotourism (which draw in a wide range of participants). These affinity spaces structure networks of sociocultural activities with diverse motives, complex participation structures, and varied learning opportunities (Prior & Schaffner, 2011).

Affinity spaces have strong potentials to function as rich communicative environments that support situated learning as people pursue their own interests.[1] However, all affinity spaces are not equal. In their research, Gee and his colleagues (Gee, 2003, 2004; Gee & Hayes, 2010) identified over a dozen key characteristics of highly engaging affinity spaces that support people's developing mastery of online game worlds.

Highly engaging affinity spaces are *complex spaces* that support multiple and diverse interest-focused activities, encourage people at all skill and knowledge levels to participate, and expect participants to contribute to one another's learning as well as to the ongoing design and development of activities and artifacts in these spaces. Highly engaging affinity spaces are *voluntary spaces* that support multiple ways to participate, to attain status in the emerging communities, and to develop different types of expertise. People choose how and when to participate. Leadership roles are porous as people with different expertise may step forward as needed to help accomplish goals. Leaders serve more as resources supporting people's participation rather than directors ordering people around and enforcing rigid hierarchies. Highly engaging affinity spaces are tuned to *experiential quality*. People are encouraged to pursue their interests by drawing on and developing distributed knowledge and dispersed networks of people, resources, and practices that mediate and enrich their individual participation. In short, a promising strategy for building rich communicative environments is to reconceptualize clinical spaces as affinity spaces designed to connect clients' successful participation in clinical activities to the rich communicative environments of their everyday worlds.

Affinity Spaces of the Collaborative Referencing Game

Thinking of the clinical space as an affinity space supporting client interests offers an opportunity to marshal communicative interactions in support of client (and clinician) learning. Linked to RCE principles of voluntariness and optimization, interest-focused design requires clinicians to identify the interests that can bridge client goals to clinical activities. In our pilot study we designed the *collaborative referencing game* as an affinity space supporting Dave's everyday interests in navigating the city independently and engaging in talk about current events.

Consistent with friendly game play as the dominant activity, the pilot intervention encouraged Dave and Melissa to socialize around game play both during and beyond the six game play trials scheduled each session, and to draw on one another and the research team as resources in learning about the photocards and getting better at referencing the 30 targets. Critically, the researcher-clinicians used the friendly socializing associated with the dominant activity to situate game play and the specific people, locations, and events pictured on the photocards as emerging common interests for this team. For example, in her role as game-partner, Melissa routinely had conversations with Dave during game trials: they discussed what was confusing about specific photocards, told stories about the people or places pictured, strategized together about game play, and celebrated their successes with specific cards and trials. In her role as clinician-moderator, Lori was alert for opportunities during socializing between trials to participate as a resource about game rules as well as to provide background and clarifying details about specific photocards. For example, she clarified that showing each other the cards was fine (when Dave was concerned it might be cheating), referred to her master sheet to identify specific locations and street names (when Dave and Melissa asked her), and offered to ask me (as lead researcher) when she didn't know an answer to their questions.

As illustrated earlier in Table 9.3, the most extended conversations often focused on cards Dave and Melissa found difficult to identify during game trials. During the ATL interview at the end of the second session with card

#11 (the target in Table 9.3), Dave initiated a discussion about where this photo was taken, reporting that he had switched to referring to it by the name of the building (a historic landmark) in the photo (*Corner with the Inman Hotel*). When Melissa and Lori continued discussing which streets were actually pictured (and what the street names were), Dave questioned if his label was okay for the game (*You don't like Inman Hotel?*), and Julie responded that would be a fine label. Lori, while checking her master list, offered the correct street names *University and Walnut*, assuring Melissa and Dave that she was sure that *Walnut* was the correct street name because she checked it out that morning when she took that street to work. Traditional clinical approaches view conversational interactions as important for building rapport with clients and managing sessions, or as off-task disruptions and distractions. However, seeing the clinic as an affinity space encourages us to use informal conversational interactions within and across sessions as a means of building common ground and supporting engagement with dominant activities (in this case the barrier task game).

Finally, the notion of affinity spaces offers another way of understanding the relation of clinical interactions to clients' everyday interactions at home, work and in the community. As they collaboratively identified images and locations in the photocards, the conversational interactions Dave, Melissa, and Lori had around game play mirrored the family's goal of improving Dave's abilities to describe where he was in the city and to talk about current affairs. Across sessions (in the game and around it), Dave and Melissa also built common ground around shared interests, infusing affect and identity into the task, and blending other figured worlds (e.g., that of current political affairs) into their interactions. Informally during the intervention, Dave's wife reported that he was displaying increased "communication confidence" (e.g., initiating more conversations at home). The resonances between clinical and everyday interactions (not only in content, but also in patterns of distributed communication) were built into the design, an RCE practice we will turn to next.

Designing for Interactional Correlates of Clinical Techniques

In this chapter, we have detailed the deep connections of the collaborative referencing game (as research protocol and clinical intervention) with everyday sociocultural activities, functional systems, and figured worlds of game play. Next, we explore how the communicative resources associated with particular activities can serve as *interactional correlates* that meaningfully extend what are typically isolated clinical techniques. By design, traditional clinical drills are not aligned with rich communicative environments: they aim to limit complexity, to be directive and rigid interactionally, and to not be optimized for clients' engagement. There may be reasons to make drill the dominant activity in some clinical interactions; however, the literature on rich communicative environments suggests that there is value in identifying rich everyday activities (like games) that can be linked to clinical goals through communicative resources that align the two. Thus, we next want to ask: ***How can clinical activities leverage interactional correlates to support clients' voluntary use of communicative resources?***

Throughout the book, we have sampled a wide range of interactional resources found in everyday communicative interactions. As we saw in Chapters 1 and 2, different patterns of talk index different activities, social roles, and identities. For example, the way we ask for help or permission will differ dramatically if we are asking a friend for a ride to work, a teacher for an appointment, or a loan officer at a bank for a mortgage. Everyday communicative resources are often recruited and reshaped for specialized purposes. For example, poets didn't create completely new patterns of sound and lexical repetition, but rather honed and amplified everyday communicative resources (patterns of repetition found in all kinds of talk) for poetic purposes (see Tannen, 2007). In a similar fashion, the specialized techniques clinicians have developed to support successful communication and learning with clients also have their roots in diverse resources of everyday interactions.

The clinical literature describes many techniques or prompts that clinicians can use, for example, to support a client's word retrieval and naming (e.g., phonemic or semantic cues), to direct and sustain a client's attention to the target task (e.g., alerting and orienting signals), or to support a client's discourse comprehension (e.g., contextual cues and priming), to name a few. Clinicians often develop *cuing hierarchies*—a hierarchical series of cues providing progressively more support—for specific clients and tasks. For example, when cuing a client with aphasia in naming specific items, the clinician might first describe the function (*you use this to go places*), followed by a phonemic cue (*it starts with "bi-"*), then a written cue or a sentence completion prompt (*I like to ride my ___*), and finally directed repetition (*bicycle—say bicycle*) (e.g., Patterson, 2001). In traditional clinical approaches, these prompts or cues are deficit-specific and clinician-directed, which limits how flexibly they can be used to support everyday communicative interactions outside of clinical spaces.

In contrast, outside of clinical spaces reminders and prompts are more often directed at getting things done (e.g., remembering who was at the party, what your friend's new married name is, or how many tablespoons equal a cup) rather than evaluating and directing specific production patterns. The challenge then for clinicians is to find ways to design activity-appropriate cues that also work to prime the client's success.

For example, in Chapter 7 we noted how didactic models might push clinicians and teachers to turn rich and engaging storybook reading into highly directive metalinguistic drill about rhyming sounds: ("What's the last sound in Fred?") and phonemes ("Let's count the sounds in Fred") (e.g., Ukrainetz, 2006). An interactional correlates approach would instead aim to keep the richness of the reading but still enhance attention to sound patterns. In other words, we need to ask if there are ways to call attention to rhyming patterns that align with the rich cultural practices of storybook reading. For example, rhyming patterns in the story could be animated to emphasize rhythmic cadence and rhyming patterns (e.g., This is a boy named **Fred**. He hates to go to **bed**. He hides out in a **shed**.). Or the clinician could share reader responses by *savoring* (Tannen, 2007) the repetition with variation (e.g., "Wow, it is fun to read rhymes: Fred, bed, shed!") or by engaging in creative verbal play ("Fred, bed, shed! That sticks in my head!"). All of these might (or might not) prime the student to animate the reading, share their responses to rhymes, or engage in further verbal play ("You have a shed in your head!?").

Another example emerged when I was working as a clinical instructor. I designed and ran a communication group for young adults with developmental pragmatic communication disorders who were transitioning from home to more independent living. The original group included nine people: four clients, four graduate student clinicians (each assigned to one client), and me. All four clients were in their early 20s, had received special educational services through the public schools, and at the time were receiving disability and/or vocational support services (e.g., SSDI; Vocational Rehab). Each week the clients attended a group session (with all 9 of us) and an individual session with their graduate clinician. The group sessions were designed as affinity spaces around the clients' common interests or goals (e.g., reading people's facial expressions, ordering fast food and take out, playing board and card games, and hosting parties). All of the clients had expressed an interest in improving their social skills, specifically in getting better at "reading" people's moods and intentions.

To work on *reading people*, during the first group session we watched a collection of videos, including clips from television shows, commercials, and videos made by the graduate clinicians interacting with their friends. However, we quickly realized the clients had limited practices for *talking about* people, their looks and actions, their histories and social networks, or their intentions, feelings and expectations. As we went around the group taking turns noting things we observed, the four clients commented almost exclusively on "eye gaze" (e.g., *she's not looking at him, so she's not listening*). Their observations were probably a by-product of lots of previous (often empirically questionable) instruction on "correct" non-verbal behaviors.

Based on that activity and our observations, our group goal switched from "reading" people to "talking about" people. We identified an interactional correlate, *everyday gossiping*, that tapped into diverse everyday communicative practices for talking about people. Although gossiping is often used in its negative sense, anthropologists have noted the centrality of gossiping (basically, talking about people, including story swapping) both in everyday social settings (Besnier, 2007) and in scientific and technical settings (e.g., Knorr Cetina, 1999, discussing how technical gossip and gossip circles power the work of scientific teams).

Let's consider another example of an interactional correlate. A specialized clinical technique to support naming, oral production, and memory is the use of exaggerated or musical-like prosody. This technique is a core feature of Melodic Intonation Therapy (MIT), which involves the clinician directing the client to repeat short phrases with exaggerated and simplified pitch changes. Studies of everyday communicative interactions identify a number of possible interactional correlates where exaggerated prosody is a communicative resource typical of different registers used in variety of situations for a variety of goals. For example, adults and older children routinely shift to a sing-song prosody and simple linguistic forms when speaking to younger children (often called *motherese*), care workers will use a similar register when speaking to residents in an extended care facility (e.g., *elderspeak*), children will use it for teasing and taunting others, and animal-lovers will routinely shift to using *pet register* when speaking endearingly to and about pets (theirs and others).

Indeed, in her study of Animal Assisted Therapy (AAT) in rehab settings, Martha Sherrill (2018) found that during AAT sessions all of the participants (patients, doctors, therapists, and family visitors) and many people just passing by the AAT sessions used pet register (with no direction to do so). Pet register is an everyday interactional correlate of clinical techniques using exaggerated prosody. However, unlike MIT, interactively engaging with pets in social settings has strong potential to build a rich communicative environment where people tell stories, play multiple roles, and (as long as the client likes pets) have fun. Identifying interactional correlates offers clinicians ways to achieve clinical goals within the context of rich communicative environments marked by complexity, voluntariness and optimization.

Interactional Correlates and the Collaborative Referencing Game

Earlier in this chapter, discussing the blend of clinical and everyday activities in the collaborative referencing game, I analyzed how the process of *collaborative referencing*, without direct instruction or elicitation from the clinician, led pairs to repeated engagement with their own and each other's labels for the cards (see also Hengst et al., 2010). For example, look at the dense patterns of lexical repetition in Table 9.3. This conversational repetition during game play is an everyday *interactional correlate* of the drill-based repetition typical of clinical tasks. As noted earlier, conversational repetition is a pervasive and remarkably dense feature of everyday talk (Chapter 5; Tannen, 2007; Hengst et al., 2016). Interactional correlates can work as clinical interventions if they are designed into the dominant activity of the clinical interaction. In the barrier task game intervention for Dave, he was repeating target references related to names of places in the town and people or activities relevant to current affairs that he wanted to be able to use in talk with friends, family, and co-workers. However, unlike clinical drills that insist on rigid adherence to the drill activity alone, this conversational repetition happened amidst complex and emergent communicative interactions. Friendly game play invited casual conversations, friendly competition, teasing and taunting, celebrations over wins, storytelling, and side talk.

In our analysis focusing on the diverse ways Dave and Melissa voiced different identities and roles (Hengst, Duff, & Prior, 2008), we noted another communicative resource that was striking in the interactions, uses of dialogic voicing as a communicative resource to manage both task-focused and non-task interactions in these clinical sessions. Dave and Melissa both drew on a wide range of typified social voices that indexed their professional expertise, their family identities, and their shared interests and experiences. In constructed dialogue (as Tannen, 2007, refers to what is often called reported speech), they also re-voiced others' words and nonverbally re-animated others' acts throughout the clinical interactions as they replayed discussions around target cards, repeated each other's card labels, and generally recycled words, actions, and tones of each other's multimodal productions across the sessions.

Designing an intervention around core features of RCE (complexity, voluntariness, and experiential optimization) supported Dave's engagement with multiple interactional correlates. He not only engaged in rich, pervasive, and situated conversational repetition, but also used a wide variety of other communicative resources (other IDRs like conversational narrative, verbal play, constructed dialogue, and social voices/registers) In terms of Gee's (2011a) building tasks (see Chapter 5), the interactions we identified in these sessions involved the whole gamut of building tasks achieved in interaction: *significance, activities, identities, relationships, politics connections,* and *sign systems and knowledge.*

Note on Methods: Participatory Design for Rich Communicative Environments

To design interventions around the three key markers of RCEs (complexity, voluntariness, and optimization), clinicians need to move deliberately away from reliance on the traditional clinical roles grounded in IRE discourse, from the controlled, detached clinical stance grounded in practices of assessment (Chapter 7). The protocol we developed for the MDEP (see Table 8.1) illustrates how to design and monitor communicative practices that stay accountable to dominant activities for RCE. In many respects, once a clinician shifts communicative stance, the communicative practices needed are ones clinicians are likely to be adept at as everyday communicators (e.g., swapping stories, making small talk, playing a game). The larger challenge for building RCEs in institutional settings is how to design for voluntariness and optimization. Fortunately, participatory design theory and research offers a toolkit designed precisely to shift from top-down design to involving users actively in defining problems and potential solutions (central for voluntariness) and to building user needs, preferences, and interests into new tools and practices (central for optimization).

Spinuzzi (2005) provides an excellent introduction to the theory and methods of participatory design. Although he focuses on the work of technical communicators, his articulation of a framework for participatory design is very consistent with SDA, and we can easily adapt it to support the development and implementation of rich communicative interventions. Central to the framework is the basic principle that "design is research" (p. 164), whether the design is for a tool, a cultural practice, or the organization of a workplace. Participatory design begins with assembling a *design team*, the interested parties working together to design for a specific purpose. Unlike classical design, the team must include end users from the start. Key principles for participatory design include improving the quality of life of those users (in our case clients), supporting collaborative design (e.g., developing common language among the team), and using an iterative (or cyclical) process of assessing, adjusting, and refining the design.

For clinical work, a team would likely include the clinician-researcher, the client-participant, and possibly the client's family, friends, and co-workers. The purpose would focus on the client's goals (e.g., *to explore ways to use photography to communicate with friends and family*). Assessing client needs and everyday contexts would draw heavily on SDA and ethnographic methods (e.g., observations, collection of documents, and interviews to better understand relevant histories and the organization of functional systems); however, critically the whole team (e.g., client and clinician) would pull together data and assess progress. Spinuzzi summarizes three phases of participatory design: 1) initial exploratory phase; 2) discovery processes; and 3) prototyping (sketching, trying out, and iteratively refining the design). Methodologically, participatory design requires continual participation of users throughout the process and recursive cycling through the three stages. For example, prototyping may lead back to re-defining the goals and team (tasks of the initial exploratory phase) or back to discovery processes to better understand communicative practices, social identities, typical tools, and so on.

Chapter 5 offered an example of participatory design for CSD. As I noted early in that chapter, the research with Jessie and his personal assistant was part of a project to develop novel Augmentative and Assistive Communication (AAC) technologies for face-to-face interactions by understanding the everyday communicative environments of young adults on campus (current or former students) who self-identified as potential AAC users. We also talked with Jessie about his experiences with AAC devices and the needs he perceived in his everyday interactions. Jessie and other participants were recruited in short as *co-researchers* and were also involved in sessions where we prototyped particular AAC designs. Methods for ethnographic thick description in case studies (discussed in Chapter 3) and SDA (detailed throughout this book) were central to that AAC participatory design project. The same methods can helps us reconceive relations between research and clinical practice. To design RCEs for clinical practice, we need to see each client as a case for participatory design and to partner with them to optimize development and (re)build communicative lives.

Summary: Designing Interventions Around Rich Communicative Environments

This chapter highlights the potential of rich communicative environments to marshal situated learning in support of the ongoing (re)organization of flexible emergent communicative practices for individuals managing communication disorders. Drawing on neuroscience research on enriched environments for lab animals, this notion of rich communicative environments can be defined broadly around three characteristics: environmental complexity (not overly structured or random) that creates meaningful connections; voluntariness of participation (not coercive, limited, or highly directed); and optimization of quality for specific individuals and over time (not static, one-size fits all).

Drawing on these design principles, clinicians can structure interventions around rich communicative environments by selecting *dominant activities* that meaningful engage clients, by building *affinity spaces* that support dispersed chains of interaction around clients' interests, and by identifying and using *interactional correlates* of clinical techniques that emerge in everyday interactions. The following questions guided our discussion of these approaches to clinical intervention:

- *How can clinical activity display features of rich communicative environments while also being accountable to clinical goals?*
- *How can the concept of affinity spaces help clinicians optimize clients' participation in situated learning?*
- *How can clinical activities leverage interactional correlates to support clients' voluntary use of communicative resources?*

Taking up this perspective involves changing some engrained notions around learning. For example, everyday games are often discounted as sites of learning. Gee (2005) noted that, when designed well, games and game play trigger deep learning and engage players in having fun (p. 15). Games are also often thought of as linguistically simplistic spaces. Interested in the potential of massive, multiplayer online games like *World of Warcraft (WoW)* to support learning English as a second language, Thorne, Fischer, and Lu (2012) identified both in-game texts and websites that functioned as affinity spaces for game players and then analyzed small corpora (about 20,000 words) from the games and the websites to determine their lexical and syntactic complexity. In both corpora, they did find high percentages of syntactically and lexically simple, everyday sentences but also high percentages of syntactically complex sentences with considerable technical vocabulary. In summarizing their findings, they noted, for example:

> the most popular WoW-related external websites are relatively rich in lexical sophistication and diversity, include multiple genres—from informational and expository prose to interactive "I-you" and conversational text types, and illustrate a high proportion of both complex syntactic structures as well as interactive and interpersonally engaged discourse.
> (Thorne et al., 2012, p. 297)

In interviews with regular players of *World of Warcraft*, they also found strong evidence of high levels of meaningful engagement with the game, including deep immersion over time (e.g., multiple hours a day and multiple days a week over years of play). In short, they concluded that the game had both linguistic features and affective engagement that would make it a rich environment for language learning.

As sites of learning, everyday sociocultural activities (along with rich interest-driven affinity spaces) often display marked complexity, voluntariness, and optimization of experiential quality. It is worth noting that it is precisely in such activities that people learn communicative practices typical of their cultures and develop their enduring identities. It is no surprise then that such spaces can offer powerful interactional correlates for typical clinical targets (e.g., lexical repetition, interactional exchanges, animated prosody).

Reflective Observations

1. *Designing dominant activities to support clinical/learning goals.* Clinicians new to designing activity-focused interventions find it difficult to trust in the power of play or other everyday activities, in part because markers of professional clinical practice are not explicit and evident. For this reflective observation, work with a partner to select a *dominant activity* that aligns with rich communicative environments and to select *learning (clinical) goals* to embed into the activity (e.g., you might want to develop your own version of the collaborative referencing game). Set

up several activity sessions and record them. Use the following questions to summarize your sessions and reflect on what you learned.

   a.   Describe the dominant activity and how you embedded the learning goals.

   b.   Across sessions, did the dominant activity shift? If so, how and when did these shifts occur?

   c.   Did you improve on the embedded learning goals?

2.   *Designing and accessing affinity spaces*. Select an interest of yours to focus on and think about the different types of affinity spaces you engage with related to that interest. For the next week, keep field notes about your participation in these spaces. Use the following questions to summarize your experiences.

   a.   What common interest(s) link these spaces?

   b.   Who was participating in the affinity spaces? What roles did they take and what role did you take?

   c.   What did you learn about, and/or help other learn about or accomplish?

   d.   How might you tap into these affinity spaces to support clinical goals for a client with similar interests?

3.   *Designing for interactional correlates*. Select an activity to observe, such as attending a sporting event or a concert. Take field notes about the communicative environment of this space, paying special attention to these questions:

   a.   How do people "cue" each other in this social space, that is, when and how do they give each other reminders, prompt recall of people/events/plans, and guide people to decisions?

   b.   How are these social cuing techniques similar to, of different from cuing hierarchies used in clinical assessment or treatment tasks?

   c.   Finally, based on your notes, provide a detailed example and then compare it with those of others in your class or research group or with examples in the literature.

Suggested Readings

SDA can be used to structure rich communicative environments, to organize clinical activities as affinity spaces for everyday goals, and generally to align clinical activity with the everyday worlds of clients and their friends and family. Here are three articles that illustrate the varied ways these approaches can be applied to different clinical settings and goals.

1.   "Reading experiences and use of supports by people with chronic aphasia" (Knollman-Porter, Wallace, Hux, Brown, & Long, 2015). Kelly

Knollman-Porter and her colleagues interview people with aphasia about, and observe them engaged in, their everyday reading experiences, and discuss implications for supporting functional reading activities.

2. "Severe speech sound disorders: An integrated multimodal intervention" (King, Hengst, & DeThorne, 2013). In this article Amie King, Julie A. Hengst, and Laura DeThorne describe an activity-based treatment approach, the *Integrated Multimodal Intervention* (IMI) intervention, designed for children with severe speech-sound disorders (SSD), and present results from a multiple-probe single-case study examining the effects of IMI for three boys (ages 4–8) with moderate-severe SSD, all of whom used speech-generating AAC devices.

3. "'But-he'll fall!': Children with autism, interspecies intersubjectivity, and the problem of 'being social'" (Solomon, 2015). Olga Solomon complicates the story that ASD is an impairment of sociality and intersubjectivity through her analysis of interactions involving animals, a psychological interview in a mental health clinic, and an animal-assisted activity in a child's neighborhood.

Note

1. One major educational initiative built around this perspective is the *Connected Learning Research Network* (https://clrn.dmlhub.net/), an interdisciplinary network of researchers aiming to understand and support *connected learning*—learning that is social, interest-driven, and oriented towards expanding educational opportunity. The *Network* aims in particular to build new connected learning environments that support educational equity.

Postscript
Clinical, Research, and Disciplinary Implications

In the preface, I noted that communicative interactions are at the heart of all aspects of CSD. Communicative interactions are what we aim to assess, what we aim to impact through therapy, and how we conduct both assessment and therapy. This book has offered a range of conceptual and methodological tools developed around *situated discourse analysis* (SDA) for students and professionals in CSD. Drawing on theory and research from fields like sociolinguistics, anthropology, applied linguistics, and cultural psychology as well as CSD, the book began by reviewing ways of understanding sociocultural activities, forms of participation, and communicative resources in everyday settings. We then shifted to applying those tools to interactions that include individuals with communicative disorders. Finally, after exploring how SDA illuminates the restrictive nature of traditional clinical practices in CSD, we concluded by exploring how SDA can be marshalled to redesign clinical approaches to assessment, the typical clinical stance, and clinical interventions through rich communicative environments.

In this postscript, I conclude by highlighting important implications of this book for 1) how SDA should inform the brain-behavior research that CSD looks to as a key source of evidence; 2) how SDA would recommend reimagining disciplinary identity and university curricula in CSD; and 3) how SDA perspectives argue for a fundamental set of transformations in our clinical practice.

First, although neuroscience research has been a growing source of evidence for CSD practice, SDA argues for a different approach to designing and interpreting brain-behavior research. Reading this literature from an SDA perspective, it is clear that increasingly sophisticated tools for understanding the processes of the brain are routinely being correlated with limited and problematic models of communicative behavior, often grounded more in everyday folk theories of communication than in situated research on actual communicative practices. Experimental studies typically isolate language (sometimes even making up artificial proxies), ignoring what we know about how everyday language practices are situated, embodied, multimodal, and nested in multiple sociocultural activities. SDA offers tools for attending to the actual processes of communication that can provide new specifications of behavior.

For example, the SDA approaches that led to my redesign of barrier task protocols (as detailed in Chapters 6 and 9) contrast sharply with the theoretical framing and research designs of experimental semiotics (ES). Drawing on earlier barrier task protocols for studying language behaviors, ES (Galantucci, 2009; Galantucci & Garrod, 2011; Roberts & Galantucci, 2016) has devised a variety of experimental tasks in which two or more people engage in some kind of semiotic game (using non-conventional graphical signs) to achieve a goal (e.g., to match boards where one participant has a model that the other is working to match). Rather than enhancing participants' ability to use their full arrays of semiotic resources, ES designs have worked to intensify participants' isolation and strictly limit communicative resources. Participants are asked to communicate with non-conventional semiotic resources and are normally physically separated (i.e., in different rooms communicating only via texts, typically on screens, synchronously or asynchronously). In fact, ES has claimed these controls allow researchers to trace the emergence of novel forms of communication, giving researchers access to "the complete history of the emergence of a communication system" (Galantucci, 2009, p. 395).

SDA perspectives cast doubt on such claims of novelty for the communicative practices displayed across ES designs. For example, one of the communication systems (using visual inscriptions to represent objects) is a long-standing, cultural practice that ES participants recruit in the highly controlled and limited communicative environments of ES protocols. Sample drawings from several studies in this line (see Galantucci & Garrod, 2011, Figures 5–9) are recognizable, even if their specific uses in the context of a particular interaction are not. The use of metonymic images, like a stethoscope representing a doctor in Figure 5 from Theisen, Oberlander, and Kirby (2010), is actually a very typical semiotic practice (see Kress & Van Leeuwen, 1996). In another semiotic game protocol (de Ruiter et al., 2010; Galantucci & Garrod, 2011), participants' communication is limited to online movements of cursors or objects in grids. Participants use the few semiotic resources available: cursor movement pathways, timing (e.g., pausing the cursor over a square), and wiggles (back-and-forth cursor movements between squares that can signal how a geometric shape is oriented). However, such movements are not novel communication systems that have no history. Situated research in various environments (e.g., Goodwin, 2003b; Mondada & Svinhufvud, 2016; Prior, 2010; Roth, 2003) have documented people's routine use of these kinds of gestures over paper, whiteboard, and screens, including studies (Corrie & Story, 2007; Prior, 2010) that capture participants using cursors to gesture on screens. In short, ES designs and interpretations, as is typical across a wide range of brain-behavior studies, are not grounded in research on people's situated communicative activities, forms of participation, and communicative resources. As illustrated in the studies reported in this book (e.g., Duff et al., 2006), grounding research designs in SDA can result in novel findings with important theoretical implications and enhanced ecological validity.

Second, this book argues that CSD should adopt a transdisciplinary stance that recognizes the value of SDA and the disciplines that have developed it and that CSD should reform its curricula so that clinicians and researchers can draw on well-grounded empirical work on communicative practices. As I have noted, communicative interactions are central to everything we do in CSD, but the field and typical undergraduate and graduate curricula have paid little to no attention to SDA theories and research or the multidisciplinary fields that have developed them. It is as if we offered courses on aphasia that ignored neuroscientific evidence on functional specialization of hemispheres or courses on voice that ignored the structural, functional and acoustic nature of the human vocal tract. Whether to support clinical or research missions, this glaring gap in our curricula should be rectified.

A transdisciplinary orientation is central to this disciplinary reorientation. Transdisciplinarity (e.g., Jörg, 2011; Hirsch Hadorn et al., 2008) calls for bringing together the multiple disciplines relevant to solving real-world problems. It includes working (as in participatory design research discussed in Chapter 9) with the users (our clients and their families and communities) at every stage of the research and design process. Given the centrality of communication to the fundamental missions of CSD, SDA certainly points to a very relevant group of disciplines. Our disciplinary boundaries should be redrawn to embrace SDA theory and research and our curricula should include these resources to support case-based clinical evidence and reasoning. This book is intended as a small step in this wider educational reform and offers a map for key concepts and methods that should be core knowledge for students in CSD.

Third and finally, SDA argues for significant transformations in clinical practice. Part 3 of the book noted limits of basing clinical work on dominant models drawn from school practices of instruction and assessment. For diagnostic assessment, I have argued for the value of embracing distributed communication rather than imagining isolated language production as the fundamental basis for communicative competence. For clinical intervention, I have suggested working with clients to build rich communicative environments in clinical settings and for enhancing connections between clinical and everyday activities (e.g., designing for interactional correlates). Here I want to highlight some core grounds for this approach to clinical practice.

This approach assumes we do not meet and should not treat the "average client." As Todd Rose notes in *The End of Average* (Rose, 2015), much research in education and health has overemphasized the statistics of *central tendency* (means, medians), often on a single dimension, rather than attending to multi-dimensional *variability*. Such studies become the basis for evidence-based practices aimed at the mean (average) individual. However, almost no one fits the mean (especially if you are interested in the multiple characteristics of a person). Rose argues it is time to take seriously the science of the individual and to reckon with variability.

When we encounter clients, we work with individuals with quite varied and complex features who participate in remarkably diverse sociocultural worlds. Thus, our clinical practice should fundamentally be reimagined as a specialized form of case-based (participatory design) research, where the clinician seeks to understand the client they encounter and to partner with the client in crafting interventions for that person rather than relying mainly on off-the-shelf tools designed to treat an idealized statistical mean. SDA provides a rich toolkit of concepts and methods to guide such case-based design research focused on clients and their practices.

For case-based clinical inquiry, it is also critical to realize people do not use a generic language in everyday environments. Instead, as we have seen, people engage in complexly situated, multimodal communication in mobile functional systems aligned with varied sociocultural activities. No dictionary and grammar book, however sophisticated, can describe the diverse communicative resources clients need to use in the evolving practices they are engaged in. Thus, clinicians need to conduct their own research or access SDA literature about related contexts that can inform their understandings of the everyday communicative practices their clients need to develop and use.

Chapter 9 points to the often underestimated richness of everyday sociocultural activities and recommends clinicians be alert to the power of such activities to impact situated learning in clinical settings and the potential to leverage everyday rich environments to support clients' reorganization of their distributed communicative competences. The epigraph to Part 3 is taken from Diane Ackerman's (2011) account of how she helped reorganize everyday home activities to support her husband's recovery from aphasia.

In a review of her book (Hengst, 2018), I noted that a key to that home program was providing ongoing opportunities for Paul to be engaged in meaningful conversations throughout the day. At one point, Diane heard Liz (a home assistant she had hired specifically to create a richer, more complex communicative environment for Paul) casually ask Paul if he had pet names for his wife. Crestfallen, he replied: "Used to have . . . hundreds," he said with infinite sadness. "Now I can't think of one." (Ackerman, 2011, p. 249). So, Diane challenged Paul to make up new names for her, and he responded by greeting her every morning for one hundred days with a new imaginative nickname—*Celandine Hunter* (celandine is a yellow-flowering poppy that has been used as an herbal medicine); *Swallow Haven*; *Spy Elf of the Morning Hallelujahs*; and 97 more. This playful activity of devising a new repertoire of romantic nicknames became the title for Ackerman's book, *One Hundred Names for Love*. This creative use of novel pet names for Diane served as an everyday *interactional correlate* (as discussed in Chapter 9) for naming drills that focus on identifying synonyms and related semantic features. At the same time, it helped achieve what no drill could, reweaving the texture of Diane and Paul's ongoing relationship.

Finally, SDA makes it clear that clinical practice should recognize communicative diversity and its relationship to the ways we imagine client identities and practices. Much traditional clinical practice continues to be oriented to idealized identities in uniform language communities. In contrast with that idealized world, SDA suggests interactions are more likely to be *contact zones* where differences are negotiated. Reflecting on the implications of contact zones for sociolinguistics, Goebel (2019) observes:

> Sociolinguists have been studying human contact for more than half a century and during this time understanding of what constitutes contact has changed from contact between different ethnic groups, religious groups, and nationalities, to also include contact between those of different genders, generation, education, socioeconomic background, or in sum contact between those with different trajectories of socialization. Taken together with the observation that increased human mobility and connectivity is now the default human condition, sociolinguists have increasingly argued that we need to start with the assumption that those involved in interaction typically share few semiotic resources. One implication of this change in our starting assumptions about human contact is that it enables us to focus our work on the question of how people in these contact settings go about organizing and managing social life.
>
> (p. 347)

SDA again offers a rich toolkit for understanding and respecting how our clients and their families and communities go about organizing and managing their everyday community interactions.

In conclusion, I believe deeply that clinical practice must evolve to engage with clients in their everyday contact zones and to embrace neurodiverse developmental pathways. As a professional in CSD, I have had too many agonizing conversations with parents who read school and clinical assessments of their children and find not the complex child they know and love, but instead a catalogue of deficits, some of which seem little more than projections of prejudice. We have learned in the case of many sensory and physical differences that accepting difference and working on building sociocultural worlds that accommodate that difference can realize rather than waste human potential. Learning to accept communicative difference and build communicative practices and environments that accommodate such differences should be an area where CSD becomes a leader.

References

Ackerman, D. (2004). *An alchemy of mind: The marvel and mystery of the brain*. New York: Scribner.

Ackerman, D. (2011). *One hundred names for love: A stroke, a marriage, and the language of healing*. New York: W.W. Norton and Company.

Agha, A. (2007). *Language and social relations*. Cambridge, UK: Cambridge University Press.

Alač, M., & Hutchins, E. (2004). I see what you are saying: Action as cognition in fMRI brain mapping practice. *Journal of Cognition and Culture, 4*(3–4), 629–661.

Alexander, K., Miller, P. J., & Hengst, J. A. (2002). Young children's emotional attachment to stories. *Social Development, 10*(3), 374–398. doi:10.1111/1467-9507.00171

ASHA. (2016). *Scope of practice in speech-language pathology* [Scope of Practice]. Retrieved from www.asha.org/policy

Azios, J. H., Damico, J. S., & Roussel, N. (2018). Communicative accessibility in aphasia: An investigation of the interactional context of long-term care facilities. *American Journal of Speech-Language Pathology, 27*, 1474–1490.

Bagatell, N. (2010). From cure to community: Transforming notions of autism. *Ethos, 38*(1), 33–55.

Basso, K. (1996). Stalking with stories. In K. Basso (Ed.), *Wisdom sits in places: Landscapes and language among the Western Apache* (pp. 37–70). Albuquerque, NM: University of New Mexico Press.

Bateson, G. (1972). *Steps to an ecology of mind: The new information sciences can lead to a new understanding of man*. New York: Ballantine Books.

Bauman, R. (1986). *Story, performance, and event: Contextual studies of oral narrative*. Cambridge, UK: Cambridge University Press.

Besnier, N. (2007). *Gossip and the everyday production of politics*. Honolulu, HI: University of Hawai'i Press.

Blommaert, J. (2010). *The sociolinguistics of globalization*. Cambridge, UK: Cambridge University Press.

Bloome, D., Puro, P., & Theodorou, E. (1989). Procedural display and classroom lessons. *Curriculum Inquiry, 19*(3), 265–291.

Bruner, J. (1990). *Acts of meaning*. Cambridge, MA: Harvard University Press.

Bucholtz, M., & Hall, K. (2005). Identity and interaction: A sociocultural linguistic approach. *Discourse Studies, 7*, 585–614.

Burghardt, G. M. (2011). Defining and recognizing play. In A. D. Pellegrini (Ed.), *The Oxford handbook of the development of play* (pp. 9–18). New York: Oxford University Press.

Cain, C. (1991). Personal stories: Identity acquisition and self-understanding in Alcoholics Anonymous. *Ethos, 19*, 210–253.

Campbell, D. T. (1988). *Methodology and epistemology for social science: Selected papers.* Chicago: University of Chicago Press.

Campbell, D. T. (1996). Can we overcome worldview incommensurability/relativity in trying to understand the other? In R. Jessor, A. Colby, & R. A. Shweder (Eds.), *Ethnography and human development: Context and meaning in social inquiry* (pp. 153–174). Chicago: University of Chicago Press.

Caty, M.-E., Kinsella, E. A., & Doyle, P. C. (2015). Reflective practice in speech-language pathology: A scoping review. *International Journal of Speech-Language Pathology, 17*(4), 411–420. doi:10.3109/17549507.2014.979870

Cicourel, A. V. (1964). *Method and measurement in sociology.* London: The Free Press of Glencoe.

Cicourel, A. V. (1992). The interpenetration of communicative contexts. In A. Duranti & C. Goodwin (Eds.), *Rethinking context: Language as an interactive phenomenon* (pp. 291–310). Cambridge, UK: Cambridge University Press.

Clark, H. H. (1992). *Arenas of language use.* Chicago: University of Chicago Press.

Clark, H. H., & Wilkes-Gibbs, D. (1986). Referring as a collaborative process. *Cognition, 22*, 1–39.

Cole, M. (1996). *Cultural psychology: A once and future discipline.* Cambridge, MA: Harvard University Press.

Corrie, B., & Story, M.-A. (2007). Toward understanding the importance of gesture in distributed scientific collaboration. *Knowledge and Information Systems, 13*, 743–771.

Costandi, M. (2016). *Neuroplasticity.* Cambridge, MA: MIT Press.

Damasio, A. R. (1994). *Decartes' error: Emotion, reason, and the human brain.* New York: Putnam.

Damico, J. S., Oelschlaeger, M., & Simmons-Mackie, N. (1999). Qualitative methods in aphasia research: Conversational analysis. *Aphasiology, 13*(9), 667–679.

Damico, J. S., Simmons-Mackie, N., & Hawley, H. (2005). Language and power. In M. J. Ball (Ed.), *Clinical sociolinguistics* (pp. 63–73). Malden, MA: Blackwell.

Davis, A. (2014). *Aphasia and related cognitive-communication disorders.* Boston: Pearson.

Davis, B. H. (Ed.). (2005). *Alzheimer talk, text and context: Enhancing communication.* Houndmills, UK: Palgrave Macmillan.

Dean, M., Adams, G. F., & Kasari, C. (2013). How narrative difficulties build peer rejection: A discourse analysis of a girl with autism and her female peers. *Discourse Studies, 15*(2), 147–166.

De Fina, A. (2012). Family interaction and engagement with the heritage language: A case study. *Multilingual Journal of Cross-Cultural and Interlanguage Communication, 31*(4), 349–379. doi:10.1515/multi-2012-0017

Denes, P. B., & Pinson, E. N. (1993). *The speech chain: The physics and biology of spoken language.* New York: W. H. Freeman & Company.

de Ruiter, J. P., Noordzij, M. L., Newman-Norlund, S., Newman-Norlund, R., Hagoort, P., Levinson, S. C., & Toni, I. (2010). Exploring the cognitive infrastructure of communication. *Interaction Studies, 11*, 51–77.

Dorner, L. M., Orellana, M. F., & Jiménez, R. (2008). "It's one of those things that you do to help the family": Language brokering and the development of immigrant adolescents. *Journal of Adolescent Research, 23*(5), 515–543.

Doron, K. W., Bassett, D. S., & Gazzaniga, M. S. (2012). Dynamic network structure of interhemispheric coordination. *PNAS Early Edition, published October 29, 2012, ahead of print.* https://doi.org/10.1073/pnas.1216402109

Duff, M. C., Hengst, J. A., Tranel, D., & Cohen, N. J. (2006). Development of shared information in communication despite hippocampal amnesia. *Nature Neuroscience, 9*(1), 140–146.

Duff, M. C., Hengst, J. A., Tranel, D., & Cohen, N. J. (2008). Collaborative discourse facilitates efficient communication and new learning in amnesia. *Brain and Language, 106*, 41–54.

Duranti, A. (1992). Language in context and language as context: The Samoan respect vocabulary. In A. Duranti & C. Goodwin (Eds.), *Rethinking context: Language as an interactive phenomenon* (pp. 77–100). Cambridge, UK: Cambridge University Press.

Dyson, A. H., & Genishi, C. (2005). *On the case: Approaches to language and literacy research.* New York: Teachers College Press.

Federal Housing Administration. (1938). *Underwriting manual: Underwriting and valuation procedures under Title II of the National Housing Act.* (HA Form No. 2049; Revised Feb. 1938). Washington, DC: U.S. Government Printing Office.

Ford, C. E., & Thompson, S. A. (1996). Interactional units in conversation: Syntactic, intonational, and pragmatic resources for the management of turns. In E. Ochs, E. A. Schegloff, & S. A. Thompson (Eds.), *Interaction and grammar* (pp. 134–184). Cambridge, UK: Cambridge University Press.

Foucault, M. (1972). *The archaeology of knowledge and the discourse on language.* New York: Pantheon Books.

Galantucci, B. (2009). Experimental semiotics: A new approach for studying communication as a form of joint action. *Topics in Cognitive Science, 1*, 393–410.

Galantucci, B., & Garrod, S. (2011). Experimental semiotics: A review. *Frontiers in Human Neuroscience, 5*, Article 11. doi:10.3389/fnhum.2011.00011

Gazzaniga, M. S. (1967). The split brain in man. *Scientific American, 217*(2), 24–29. doi: 10.1038/scientificamerican0867-24

Gee, J. P. (2003). *What video games have to teach us about learning and literacy.* New York: Palgrave Macmillan.

Gee, J. P. (2004). *Situated language and learning: A critique of traditional schooling.* New York: Routledge.

Gee, J. P. (2005). Semiotic social spaces and affinity spaces: From the age of mythology to today's schools. In D. Barton & K. Tusting (Eds.), *Beyond communities of practice: Language, power and social context* (pp. 214–232). Cambridge, UK: Cambridge University Press.

Gee, J. P. (2011a). *An introduction to discourse analysis: Theory and method* (3rd ed.). New York: Routledge.

Gee, J. P. (2011b). *How to do discourse analysis: A toolkit.* New York: Routledge.

Gee, J. P., & Hayes, E. R. (2010). *Women and gaming: The Sims and 21st century learning.* New York: Palgrave Macmillan.

Geertz, C. (1973). *The interpretation of cultures: Selected essays.* New York: Basic Books.

Geertz, C. (1996). Afterword. In S. Feld & K. H. Basso (Eds.), *Senses of place* (pp. 259–262). Santa Fe, NM: School of American Research Press.

Goebel, Z. (2019). Contact discourse. *Language in Society, 48*, 331–351.

Goffman, E. (1961). *Encounters: Two studies in the sociology of interaction.* Indianapolis: The Bobbs-Merrill Company, Inc.

Goffman, E. (1981). *Forms of talk*. Philadelphia: University of Pennsylvania Press.

Göncü, A. (1999). *Children's engagement in the world*. New York: Cambridge University Press.

Goodglass, H., & Kaplan, E. (1983). *The assessment of aphasia and related disorders* (2nd ed.). Philadelphia: Lea & Febiger.

Goodwin, C. (1981). *Conversational organization: Interaction between speakers and hearers*. New York: Academic Press.

Goodwin, C. (2003a). Conversational frameworks for the accomplishment of meaning in aphasia. In C. Goodwin (Ed.), *Conversation and brain damage* (pp. 90–116). New York: Oxford University Press.

Goodwin, C. (2003b). Pointing as situated practice. In S. Kita (Ed.), *Pointing: Where language, culture and cognition meet* (pp. 217–247). Mahwah, NJ: Lawrence Erlbaum Associates.

Goodwin, C., & Duranti, A. (1992). Rethinking context: An introduction. In A. Duranti & C. Goodwin (Eds.), *Rethinking context: Language as an interactive phenomenon* (pp. 1–42). Cambridge, UK: Cambridge University Press.

Goodwin, C., & Goodwin, M. H. (1996). Seeing as a situated activity: Formulating planes. In Y. Engeström & D. Middleton (Eds.), *Cognition and communication at work* (pp. 61–95). Cambridge, UK: Cambridge University Press.

Goodwin, M. H., & Alim, H. S. (2010). "Whatever (neck roll, eye roll, teeth suck)": The situated coproduction of social categories and identities through stance taking and transmodal stylization. *Journal of Linguistic Anthropology, 20*(1), 179–194.

Goody, E. N. (1995). Introduction: Some implications of a social origin of intelligence. In E. N. Goody (Ed.), *Social intelligence and interaction: Expressions and implications of the social bias in human intelligence* (pp. 1–36). Cambridge, UK: Cambridge University Press.

Gould, S. J. (1996). *Full house: The spread of excellence from Plato to Darwin*. New York: Three Rivers Press.

Green, J., Franquiz, M., & Dixon, C. (1997). The myth of the objective transcript: Transcribing as a situated act. *TESOL Quarterly, 31*(1), 172–176.

Greenough, W. T. (1976). Enduring brain effects of differential experience and training. In M. R. Rosenzweig & E. L. Bennett (Eds.), *Neural mechanisms of learning and memory* (pp. 255–278). Cambridge, MA: MIT Press.

Hamilton, H. (1994). *Conversations with an Alzheimer's patient: An interactional sociolinguistic study*. Cambridge, UK: Cambridge University Press.

Hanks, W. F. (1990). *Referential practice: Language and lived space among the Maya*. Chicago: University of Chicago Press.

Hanks, W. F. (1996). *Language and communicative practices*. Boulder, CO: Westview Press.

Hart, B., & Risley, T. R. (1995). *Meaningful differences in the everyday experience of young American children*. Baltimore, MD: Brookes.

Haviland, J. B. (2011). Musical spaces. In J. Streeck, C. Goodwin, & C. LeBaron (Eds.), *Embodied interaction: Language and body in the material world* (pp. 289–304). Cambridge, UK: Cambridge University Press.

Heath, C., Hindmarsh, J., & Luff, P. (2003). *Video in qualitative research: Analyzing social interaction in everyday life*. Los Angeles: Sage Publications.

Hebb, D. O. (1949). *The organization of behavior: A neuropsychological theory*. New York: Wiley.

Helm-Estabrooks, N., & Albert, M. L. (1991). *Manual of aphasia therapy*. Austin, TX: Pro-Ed.

Hengst, J. A. (2001). *Collaborating on reference: A study of discourse and aphasia* (Doctor of Philosophy). University of Illinois at Urbana-Champaign, Urbana, IL.

Hengst, J. A. (2003). Collaborative referencing between individuals with aphasia and routine communication partners. *Journal of Speech, Language, and Hearing Research, 46*, 831–848.

Hengst, J. A. (2006). "That mea::n dog": Linguistic mischief and verbal play as a communicative resource in aphasia. *Aphasiology, 20*(2/3/4), 312–326.

Hengst, J. A. (2010). Semiotic remediation, conversational narratives and aphasia. In P. A. Prior & J. A. Hengst (Eds.), *Exploring semiotic remediation as discourse practice* (pp. 107–138). Houndmills, UK: Palgrave Macmillan.

Hengst, J. A. (2015). Distributed communication: Implications of Cultural-Historical Activity Theory (CHAT) for communication disorders. *Journal of Communication Disorders, 57*, 16–28.

Hengst, J. A. (2018). Bringing therapy home: Book review. *Journal of Humanities and Rehabilitation.* Retrieved April 30, 2018, from www.journalofhumanitiesinrehabilitation.org

Hengst, J. A., Devanga, S., & Mosier, H. (2015). Thin versus thick description: Analyzing representations of people and their life worlds in the literature of communication sciences and disorders. *American Journal of Speech-Language Pathology, 24*, S838–S853.

Hengst, J. A., & Duff, M. C. (2007). Clinicians as communication partners: Developing a mediated discourse elicitation protocol. *Topics in Language Disorders, 27*(1), 37–49.

Hengst, J. A., Duff, M. C., & Dettmer, A. (2010). Rethinking repetition in therapy: Repeated engagement as the social ground of learning. *Aphasiology, 24*, 887–901.

Hengst, J. A., Duff, M. C., & Jones, T. A. (2019, March). Enriching communicative environments: Leveraging advances in neuroplasticity for improving outcomes in neurogenic communication disorders. *American Journal of Speech-Language Pathology, 28*, 216–229. doi:10.1044/2018_AJSLP-17-0157

Hengst, J. A., Duff, M. C., & Prior, P. A. (2008). Multiple voices in clinical discourse and as clinical intervention. *International Journal of Language & Communication Disorders, 43*, 58–68.

Hengst, J. A., Frame, S. R., Neuman-Stritzel, T., & Gannaway, R. (2005). Using others' words: Conversational use of reported speech by individuals with aphasia and their communication partners. *Journal of Speech, Language, and Hearing Research, 48*, 137–156.

Hengst, J. A., McCartin, M., Valentino, H., Devanga, S., & Sherrill, M. H. (2016). Mapping communicative activity: A CHAT approach to design of pseudo-intelligent mediators for Augmentative and Alternative Communication (AAC). *Outlines Critical Practice Studies, 17*(1), 5–38. Retrieved from www.outlines.dk

Hengst, J. A., & Miller, P. J. (1999). The heterogeneity of discourse genres: Implications for development. *World Englishes, 18*(3), 325–341.

Hengst, J. A., & Prior, P. A. (1998). *Playing with voices: Heterogeneous socialization into language in the wild.* Paper presented at the Modern Language Association Convention, San Francisco, CA.

Herndl, C., Fennell, B., & Miller, C. (1991). Understanding failures in organizational discourse: The accident at Three Mile Island and the shuttle challenger disaster. In C. Bazerman & J. Paradis (Eds.), *Textual dynamics of the professions: Historical and contemporary studies of writing in professional communities* (pp. 379–305). Madison, WI: University of Wisconsin Press.

Higginbotham, D. J., & Wilkins, D. P. (1999). Slipping through the timestream: Social issues of time and timing in augmented interactions. In D. Kovarsky, J. F. Duchan, & M. Maxwell (Eds.), *Constructing (in)competence: Disabling evaluations in clinical and social interaction* (pp. 49–82). Mahwah, NJ: Lawrence Erlbaum Associates.

Hikida, M., & Lee, J. (2018). Positioning readers in one-on-one conferences. *Literacy Research: Theory, Method, and Practice, 20,* 1–15. doi:10.1177/2381336918786887

Hirsch Hadorn, G., Hoffmann-Riem, H., Biber-Klemm, S., Grossenbacher-Mansuy, W., Joye, D., Pohl, C., . . . Zemp, E. (Eds.). (2008). *Handbook of transdisciplinary research.* Dordrecht, NL: Springer.

Holland, A. L. (1998). Why can't clinicians talk to aphasic adults? *Aphasiology, 12,* 844–847.

Holland, D., Lachicotte, W., Jr., Skinner, D., & Cain, C. (1998). *Identity and agency in cultural worlds.* Cambridge, MA: Harvard University Press.

Holzman, L. (2009). *Vygotsky at work and play.* London: Routledge.

Horton, S. (2006). A framework for description and analysis of therapy for language impairment in aphasia. *Aphasiology, 20*(6), 528–564.

Huizinga, J. (1950). *Homo ludens: A study of the play element in culture.* Boston: Beacon Press.

Hutchins, E. (1995). *Cognition in the wild.* Cambridge, MA: MIT Press.

Hymes, D. (1974). *Foundations in sociolinguistics: An ethnographic approach.* Philadelphia: University of Pennsylvania Press.

Hymes, D. (1975). Breakthrough into performance. In D. Ben-Amos & K. S. Goldstein (Eds.), *Folklore: Performance and communication* (pp. 11–74). The Hague: Mouton.

Hymes, D. (1981). *"In vain I tried to tell you": Essays in Native American ethnopoetics.* Philadelphia: University of Pennsylvania Press.

Irvine, J. (1996). Shadow conversations: The indeterminacy of participant roles. In M. Silverstein & G. Urban (Eds.), *Natural histories of discourse* (pp. 131–159). Chicago: University of Chicago Press.

Jakobson, R. (1990). *On language* (L. Waugh & M. Monville-Burston, Eds.). Cambridge, MA: Harvard University Press.

Jörg, T. (2011). *New thinking in complexity for the social sciences and humanities: A generative, transdisciplinary approach.* Dordrecht, NL: Springer. doi:10.1007/978-94-007-1303-1_4

Kagen, A. (1998). Supported conversation for adults with aphasia: Methods and resources for training conversational partners. *Aphasiology, 12,* 816–830.

Keating, E., & Mirus, G. (2003). Examining interactions across language modalities: Deaf children and hearing peers at school. *Anthropology and Education Quarterly, 34*(2), 115–135.

King, A. M., Hengst, J. A., & DeThorne, L. S. (2013). Severe speech sound disorders: An integrated multimodal intervention. *Language, Speech, and Hearing Services in Schools, 44,* 195–210.

Knollman-Porter, K., Wallace, S. E., Hux, K., Brown, J., & Long, C. (2015). Reading experiences and use of supports by people with chronic aphasia. *Aphasiology, 29*(12), 1448–1472. doi:10.1080/02687038.2015.1041093

Knorr Cetina, K. (1999). *Epistemic cultures: How the sciences make knowledge.* Cambridge, MA: Harvard University Press.

Kovarsky, D., Kimbarow, M., & Kastner, D. (1999). The construction of incompetence during group therapy with traumatically brain injured adults. In D. Kovarsky, J. F. Duchan, & M. Maxwell (Eds.), *Constructing (in)competence: Disabling evaluations in clinical and social interaction* (pp. 291–312). Mahwah, NJ: Lawrence Erlbaum Associates.

Kress, G., & Van Leeuwen, T. (1996). *Reading images: The grammar of visual design.* London: Routledge.

Kroskrity, P. V. (2004). Language ideologies. In A. Duranti (Ed.), *A companion to linguistic anthropology* (online ed., pp. 496–517). Malden, MA: Blackwell Publishing, Ltd.

Laakso, M. (2003). Collaborative construction of repair in aphasic conversation. In C. Goodwin (Ed.), *Conversation and brain damage* (pp. 163–188). Oxford: Oxford University Press.

Labov, W., & Fanshel, D. (1977). *Therapeutic discourse: Psychotherapy as conversation.* New York: Academic Press.

Lakoff, G., & Johnson, M. (1980). *Metaphors we live by.* Chicago: University of Chicago Press.

Lave, J., & Wenger, E. (1991). *Situated learning: Legitimate peripheral participation.* Cambridge, UK: Cambridge University Press.

Leahy, M. M. (2004). Therapy talk: Analyzing therapeutic discourse. *Language, Speech, and Hearing Services in Schools, 35,* 70–81.

Leander, K., & Prior, P. A. (2004). Speaking and writing: How talk and text interact. In C. Bazerman & P. A. Prior (Eds.), *What writing does and how it does it: An introduction to analysis of texts and textual practices* (pp. 201–238). Mahwah, NJ: Lawrence Erlbaum Associates.

Lemke J. L. (2000). Across the scales of time: Artifacts, activities, and meanings in ecosocial systems. *Mind, Culture, and Activity, 7*(4), 273–290.

Leontyev, A. N. (1981). *Problems of the development of the mind.* Moscow, USSR: Progress Publishers.

Lesser, R., & Perkins, L. (1999). *Cognitive neuropsychology and conversation analysis in aphasia: An introductory casebook.* London: Whurr Publishers.

Luria, A. R. (1963). *Restoration of function after brain injury.* New York, NY: The Macmillan Company.

Luria, A. R. (1968). *The mind of a mnemonist: A little book about a vast memory.* New York, NY: Basic Books.

Luria, A. R. (1972). *The man with a shattered world: The history of a brain wound.* New York, NY: Basic Books.

Manns, J. (2004). JFK, LBJ, and HM: The famous memories of a famous amnesic. *Hippocampus, 14,* 411–412.

Marcus, G. E. (1998). *Ethnography through thick and thin.* Princeton, NJ: Princeton University Press.

Maynard, D., & Marlaire, C. L. (1992). Good reasons for bad testing performance: The interactional substrate of educational exams. *Qualitative Sociology, 15*(2), 177–202.

McDermott, R. P. (1993). The acquisition of a child by a learning disability. In S. Chaiklin & J. Lave (Eds.), *Understanding practice: Perspectives on activity and context* (pp. 64–103). Cambridge, UK: Cambridge University Press.

McQuillan, J., & Tse, L. (1995). Child language brokering in linguistic minority communities: Effects on cultural interaction, cognition, and literacy. *Language and Education, 9*(3), 195–215.

Mehan, H. (1979). *Learning lessons.* Cambridge, MA: Harvard University Press.

Mehan, H. (1993). Beneath the skin and between the ears: A case study in the politics of representation. In S. Chaiklin & J. Lave (Eds.), *Understanding practice: Perspectives on activity and context* (pp. 241–268). Cambridge, UK: Cambridge University Press.

Mialet, H. (2012). *Hawking incorporated: Stephen Hawking and the anthropology of the knowing subject.* Chicago: University of Chicago Press.

Miller, E. L. (2019). Negotiating communicative access in practice: A study of a memoir group for people with aphasia. *Written Communication, Pre-Print,* 1–35.

Miller, P. J. (1986). Teasing as language socialization and verbal play in a white working-class community. In B. Schieffelin & E. Ochs (Eds.), *Language and socialization across cultures* (pp. 199–212). Cambridge, UK: Cambridge University Press.

Miller, P. J., Fung, H., & Koven, M. (2007). Narrative reverberations: How participation in narrative practices co-creates persons and cultures. In S. Kitayama & D. Cohen (Eds.), *The handbook of cultural psychology* (pp. 595–614). New York: Guilford Press.

Miller, P. J., Hengst, J. A., & Wang, S. H. (2003). Ethnographic methods: Applications from developmental cultural psychology. In P. Camic, J. Rhodes, & L. Yardley (Eds.), *Qualitative research in psychology: Expanding perspectives in methodology and design* (pp. 219–242). Washington, DC: American Psychological Association.

Minick, N. (1993). Teacher's directives: The social construction of "literal meanings" and "real worlds" in classroom discourse. In S. Chaiklin & J. Lave (Eds.), *Understanding practice: Perspectives on activity and context* (pp. 343–376). Cambridge, UK: Cambridge University Press.

Mirabelli, T. (2004). Learning to serve: The language and literacy of food service workers. In J. Mahiri (Ed.), *What they don't learn in school: Literacy in the lives of urban youth* (pp. 143–162). New York: Peter Lang.

Mondada, L., & Svinhufvud, K. (2016). Writing-in-interaction: Studying writing as a multimodal phenomenon in social interaction. *Language and Dialogue, 6,* 1–53.

Mortensen, C. R., & Cialdini, R. B. (2010). Full-cycle social psychology for theory and application. *Social and Personality Psychology Compass, 4*(1), 53–63. doi:10.1111/j.1751-9004.2009.00239.x

Nguyen, M., Vanderwal, T., & Hasson, U. (2019). Shared understanding of narratives is correlated with shared neural responses. *NeuroImage, 184,* 161–170.

Nicolopoulou, A., & Cole, M. (1993). Generation and transmission of shared knowledge in the culture of collaborative learning: The Fifth Dimension, its play-world, and its institutional contexts. In E. Forman, N. Minick, & C. A. Stone (Eds.), *Contexts for learning: Sociocultural dynamics in children's development* (pp. 283–314). New York: Oxford University Press.

Nold, G. M. J. (2005). Alzheimer's speakers and two languages. In B. H. Davis (Ed.), *Alzheimer talk, text and context: Enhancing communication* (pp. 102–127). Houndmills, UK: Palgrave Macmillan.

Nordquist, B. (2017). *Literacy and mobility: Complexity, uncertainty, and agency at the nexus of high school and college.* New York: Routledge.

Nordquist, B. (2018). *Writing across the city: Translingual/transmodal composing on the 7 train.* Paper presented at the Center for Writing Studies Symposium, University of Illinois at Urbana-Champaign, Urbana, IL.

Ochs, E. (1979). Transcription as theory. In E. Ochs & B. B. Schiefflen (Eds.), *Developmental pragmatics* (pp. 43–72). New York: Academic Press.

Ochs, E., & Capps, L. (2001). *Living narrative: Creating lives in everyday storytelling.* Cambridge, MA: Harvard University Press.

Ochs, E., Gonzales, P., & Jacoby, S. (1994). "When I come down I'm in the domain state": Grammar and the graphic representation in the interpretive activity of physics.

In E. Ochs, E. A. Schegloff, & S. A. Thompson (Eds.), *Interaction and grammar* (pp. 328–369). Cambridge, UK: Cambridge University Press.

Ochs, E., Taylor, C., Rudolph, D., & Smith, R. (1992). Storytelling as a theory-building activity. *Discourse Processes, 15*(1), 37–72. doi:10.1080/01638539209544801

Oxford English Dictionary. (2019). (Online Reference Collection, Ed.). Oxford: Oxford University Press.

Orange, J. B. (2001). Family caregivers, communication, and Alzheimer's disease. In M. L. Hummert & J. F. Nussbaum (Eds.), *Aging, communication, and health: Linking research and practice for successful aging* (pp. 225–248). Mahwah, NJ: Lawrence Erlbaum Associates.

Orange, J. B., Lubinski, R. B., & Higginbotham, D. J. (1996). Conversational repair by individuals with dementia of the Alzheimer's type. *Journal of Speech and Hearing Research, 39*, 881–895.

Patterson, J. (2001). The effectiveness of cueing hierarchies as a treatment for word retrieval impairment. *Perspectives on Neurophysiology and Neurogenic Speech and Language Disorders, 11*(2), 11–18.

Pellegrini, A. D. (Ed.). (2011). *The Oxford handbook of the development of play.* New York: Oxford University Press.

Perry, K. H. (2009). Genres, contexts, and literacy practices: Literacy brokering among Sudanese refugee families. *Reading Research Quarterly, 44*(3), 256–276.

Pizer, G., Walters, K., & Meier, R. P. (2013). "We communicated that way for a reason": Language practices and language ideologies among hearing adults whose parents are deaf. *Journal of Deaf Studies and Deaf Education, 18*(1), 75–92.

Prior, P. A. (2001). Voices in text, mind, and society: Sociohistoric accounts of discourse acquisition and use. *Journal of Second Language Writing, 10*, 55–81.

Prior, P. A. (2010). Remaking IO: Semiotic remediation in the design process. In P. A. Prior & J. A. Hengst (Eds.), *Exploring semiotic remediation as discourse practice* (pp. 206–234). Houndmills, UK: Palgrave Macmillan.

Prior, P. A., Hengst, J. A., Roozen, K., & Shipka, J. (2006). "I'll be the sun": From reported speech to semiotic remediation practices. *Text & Talk, 26*(6), 733–766.

Prior, P. A., & Schaffner, S. (2011). Bird identification as a family of activities: Motives, mediating artifacts, and laminated assemblages. *Ethos: Journal of the Society for Psychological Anthropology, 39*, 51–70.

Ramanathan-Abbott, V. (1994). Interactional differences in Alzheimer's discourse: An examination of AD speech across two audiences. *Language in Society, 23*, 31–58.

Ramanathan-Abbott, V. (1997). *Alzheimer discourse: Some sociolinguistic dimensions.* Mahwah, NJ: Lawrence Erlbaum Associates.

Reddy, M. (1979). The conduit metaphor: A case of frame conflict in our language about language. In A. Orotony (Ed.), *Metaphor and thought* (pp. 284–324). Cambridge, England: Cambridge University Press.

Roberts, C. (1997). Transcribing talk: Issues of representation. *TESOL Quarterly, 31*(1), 167–172.

Roberts, G., & Galantucci, B. (2016). Investigating meaning in experimental semiotics. *Psychology of Language and Communication, 20*, 130–153.

Rogoff, B. (1990). *Apprenticeship in thinking.* New York: Oxford University Press.

Rogoff, B. (2003). *The cultural nature of human development.* New York: Oxford University Press.

Rogoff, B., Mistry, J., Göncü, A., & Mosier, C. (1993). *Guided participation in cultural activity by toddlers and caregivers* (Vol. 58). Chicago: University of Chicago Press.

Rose, T. (2015). *The end of average: How we succeed in a world that values sameness.* New York: Harper Collins.

Rosin, H., & Spiegel. A. (2015). How to become a batman, No. 3. (January 23, 2015). C. Tallo (Producer). *Invisibilia*, NPR.org Podcast. Retrieved from www.npr.org/programs/invisibilia/378577902/how-to-become-batman]

Roth, W.-M. (2003). *Toward an anthropology of graphing: Semiotic and activity-theoretic approaches.* Dordrecht, The Netherlands: Kluwer.

Sacks, H., Schegloff, E. A., & Jefferson, G. (1974). A simplest systematics for the organization of turn-taking in conversation. *Language, 50,* 696–735.

Sacks, O. (1970). *The man who mistook his wife for a hat.* New York, NY: Harper & Row.

Sacks, O. (1984). *A leg to stand on.* New York, NY: Simon and Schuster.

Samuelsson, C., & Hydén, L.-C. (2017). Collaboration, trouble and repair in multiparty interactions involving couples with dementia or aphasia. *International Journal of Speech-Language Pathology, 19*(5), 454–464. doi:10.1080/17549507.2016.1221448

Scheflen, A. (1973). *Communicational structure: Analysis of a psychotherapy interaction.* Bloomington, IN: Indiana University Press.

Schegloff, E. A. (1996). Turn organization: One intersection of grammar and interaction. In E. Ochs, E. A. Schegloff, & S. A. Thompson (Eds.), *Interaction and grammar* (pp. 52–133). Cambridge, UK: Cambridge University Press.

Schieffelin, B. (1986). Teasing and shaming in Kaluli children's interactions. In B. Schieffelin & E. Ochs (Eds.), *Language socialization across cultures* (pp. 165–181). Cambridge, UK: Cambridge University Press.

Schön, D. A. (1983). *The reflective practitioner: How professionals think in action* (2013 Paperback ed.). Farnham, England: Ashgate.

Scollon, R. (2001). *Mediated discourse: The nexus of practice.* London: Routledge.

Scollon, R., & Scollon, S. W. (2003). *Discourses in place: Language in the material world.* New York: Routledge.

Sebeok, T. A. (2001). *Signs: An introduction to semiotics* (2nd ed.). Toronto, Canada: University of Toronto Press, Inc.

Selnes, O., & Hillis, A. (2001). Patient Tan revisited: A case of atypical global aphasia. *The Journal of the History of Neuroscience, 9,* 233–237.

Shapiro, J. P. (1993). *No pity: People with disabilities forging a new civil rights movement.* New York: Three Rivers Press.

Sherrill, M. H. (2018). *"When do I get to see the dog?": The communicative environment during animal assisted speech therapy sessions for adults with acquired cognitive-communication disorders* (PhD Dissertation). University of Illinois at Urbana-Champaign, Urbana, IL. IDEALS.

Sherzer, J. (2002). *Speech play and verbal art.* Austin, TX: University of Texas.

Silverstein, M., & Urban, G. (Eds.). (1996). *Natural histories of discourse.* Chicago: University of Chicago Press.

Simmons-Mackie, N., & Damico, J. S. (1999). Social role negotiation in aphasia therapy: Competence, incompetence, and conflict. In D. Kovarsky, J. F. Duchan, & M. Maxwell (Eds.), *Constructing (in)competence: Disabling evaluations in clinical and social interaction* (pp. 313–342). Mahwah, NJ: Lawrence Erlbaum Associates.

Simmons-Mackie, N., Damico, J. S., & Damico, H. L. (1999). A qualitative study of feedback in aphasia treatment. *American Journal of Speech-Language Pathology, 8*(3), 218–230.

Smith, F. (1986). *Insult to intelligence: The bureaucratic invasion of our classrooms.* New York: Arbor House.

Sohlberg, M., & Mateer, C. (1989). *Introduction to cognitive rehabilitation: Theory and practice.* New York: Guilford Press.

Solomon, O. (2015). "But-He'll Fall!": Children with autism, interspecies intersubjectivity, and the problem of "being social." *Culture, Medicine, and Psychiatry, 39*(2), 323–344.

Sperry, D., Sperry, L. L., & Miller, P. J. (2018). Reexamining the verbal environments of children from different socioeconomic backgrounds. *Child Development, (Pre-Publication)*, 1–16. doi:10.1111/cdev.13072

Spinuzzi, C. (2005). The methodology of participatory design. *Technical Communication, 52*(2), 163–174.

Sterponi, L., & Fasulo, A. (2010). "How to go on": Intersubjectivity and progressivity in the communication of a child with autism. *Ethos, 38*(1), 116–142.

St. Pierre, J., & St. Pierre, C. (2018). Governing the voice: A critical history of speech-language pathology. *Foucault Studies, 24*, 141–1894.

Straehle, C. A. (1993). "Samuel?" "Yes, dear?": Teasing and conversational rapport. In D. Tannen (Ed.), *Framing in discourse* (pp. 210–230). New York: Oxford University Press.

Streeck, J. (2008). Laborious intersubjectivity: Attentional struggle and embodied communication in an auto-shop. In I. Wachsmuth, M. Lenzen, & G. Knoblich (Eds.), *Embodied communication in humans and machines* (pp. 201–228). Oxford: Oxford University Press.

Sweatt, J. D. (2019). The epigenetic basis of individuality. *Current Opinion in Behavioral Sciences, 25*, 51–57.

Tannen, D. (2007). *Talking voices: Repetition, dialogue, and imagery in conversational discourse* (2nd ed.). Cambridge, UK: Cambridge University Press.

Tannen, D., & Wallat, C. (1987). Interactive frames and knowledge schemas in interaction: Examples from a medical examination/interview. *Social Psychology Quarterly, 50*(2), 205–216.

ten Have, P. (1991). Talk and institution: A reconsideration of the "asymmetry" of doctor-patient interaction. In D. Boden & D. H. Zimmerman (Eds.), *Talk and social structure: Studies in ethnomethodology and conversation analysis* (pp. 138–163). Cambridge, UK: Polity Press.

Theisen, C. A., Oberlander, J., & Kirby, S. (2010). Systematicity and arbitrariness in novel communication systems. *Interaction Studies, 11*, 14–32.

Thorne, S. L., Fischer, I., & Lu, X. (2012). The semiotic ecology and linguistic complexity of an online game world. *ReCALL, 24*, 279–301. doi:10.1017/S0958344012000158

Ukrainetz, T. A. (Ed.). (2006). *Contextualized language intervention: Scaffolding pre-K literacy achievement.* Greenville, SC: Thinking Publications, A Division of Super Duper, Inc.

Van Praag, H., Kempermann, G., & Gage, F. H. (2000). Neural consequences of environmental enrichment. *Nature Reviews Neuroscience, 1*(3), 191–198.

Van Riper, C. (1939). *Speech correction: Principles and methods* (1st ed.). New York: Prentice Hall.

Vidal, V., Robertson, S., & DeThorne, L. S. (2018). Illustrating a supports-based approach toward friendship with autistic students. *American Journal of Speech-Language Pathology, 27*, 592–601.

Vygotsky, L. S. (1978). *Mind in society: The development of higher psychological processes.* Cambridge, MA: Harvard University Press.

Vygotsky, L. S. (1987). Thinking and speech (N. Minick, Trans.). In R. W. Rieber & A. S. Carton (Eds), *The Collected Works of L. S. Vygotsky Vol. 1: Problems of General Psychology* (pp. 39–288). New York, NY: Plenum.

Wortham, S. (2006). *Learning identity: The joint emergence of social identification and academic learning.* Cambridge, UK: Cambridge University Press.

Ylvisaker, M., & Feeney, T. J. (2000). Reflections on Dobermanns, poodles, and social rehabilitation for difficult-to-serve individuals with traumatic brain injury. *Aphasiology, 14*(4), 407–431. doi:10.1080/026870300401432

Ylvisaker, M., Hanks, R., & Johnson-Greene, D. (2002). Perspectives on rehabilitation of individuals with cognitive impairment after brain injury: Rationale for reconsideration of theoretical paradigms. *Journal of Head Trauma Rehabilitation, 17*(3), 191–209.

Yule, G. (1997). *Referential communication tasks.* Mahwah, NJ: Lawrence Erlbaum Associates.

Index

Made in the USA
Columbia, SC
10 May 2021